RISKY BUSINESS

D1509261

Other books by Mark Litwak

Reel Power
Courtroom Crusaders
Contracts for the Film and Television Industry
Dealmaking in the Film and Television Industry
Litwak's Multimedia Producer's Handbook

RISKY BUSINESS

FINANCING & DISTRIBUTING INDEPENDENT FILMS

BY MARK LITWAK

SILMAN-JAMES PRESS
Los Angeles

Copyright © 2004 Hampstead Enterprises, Inc.

All rights reserved. No part of this book may be used or reproduced
in any manner whatsoever without written permission from the
publisher, except in the case of brief quotations
embodied in critical articles and reviews.

First Edition
10 9 8 7 6 5 4 3 2 1

Library of Congress Cataloging-in-Publication Data

Litwak, Mark.
Risky business : financing and distributing independent films /
by Mark Litwak. 1st ed.
p. cm.
Includes index.
1. Motion picture industry—United States—Finance
2. Motion pictures industry—Finance—Law and legislation—
United States.
3. Motion pictures—United States—Distribution.
4. Motion pictures—Distribution—Law and legislation—United States.
5. Motion picture industry—Law and legislation—United States.
6. Independent filmakers.
I. Title.
PN1993.5.U6L545 2004   343.83'0973—dc22   2004045287

ISBN: 1-879505-74-6

Cover design by Heidi Frieder

Printed and bound in the United States of America

SILMAN-JAMES PRESS
1181 Angelo Drive
Beverly Hills, CA 90210

For Michael, David, and Tiiu

DISCLAIMER

This book is designed to help readers understand legal issues frequently encountered in the entertainment industry. It will provide you with an understanding of basic legal principles, enabling you to better communicate with your attorney.

The information contained in this book is intended to provide general information and does not constitute legal advice. This book does not create an attorney-client relationship between the reader and the author or any of his associates, and you should not act nor rely on any information in this book without seeking the advice of an attorney and receiving counsel based on the relevant facts and circumstances. Many of the legal principles mentioned are subject to exceptions and qualifications, which may not be noted in the text. Furthermore, case law and statutes are subject to revision and may not apply in every state. Because of the quick pace of technological change, some of the information in this book may be outdated by the time you read it. Readers should be aware that business practices, distribution methods, and legislation continue to evolve in the rapidly changing entertainment industry.

THE INFORMATION IS PROVIDED "AS IS," AND THE AUTHOR MAKES NO EXPRESS OR IMPLIED REPRESENTATIONS OR WARRANTIES—INCLUDING WARRANTIES OF PERFORMANCE, MERCHANTABILITY, AND FITNESS FOR A PARTICULAR PUR-POSE—REGARDING THIS INFORMATION. THE AUTHOR DOES

NOT GUARANTEE THE COMPLETENESS, ACCURACY, OR TIMELINESS OF THIS INFORMATION. YOUR USE OF THIS INFORMATION IS AT YOUR OWN RISK. YOU ASSUME FULL RESPONSIBILITY AND RISK OF LOSS RESULTING FROM THE USE OF THIS INFORMATION. THE AUTHOR WILL NOT BE LIABLE FOR ANY DIRECT, SPECIAL, INDIRECT, INCIDENTAL, CONSEQUENTIAL, OR PUNITIVE DAMAGES OR ANY OTHER DAMAGES, WHETHER IN AN ACTION BASED UPON A STAT-UTE, CONTRACT, TORT (INCLUDING, WITHOUT LIMITATION, NEGLIGENCE), OR OTHERWISE, RELATING TO THE USE OF THIS INFORMATION.

The author can be contacted by email. However, if you communicate with him in connection with a matter for which he does not already represent you, your communication may not be treated as privileged or confidential. An attorney-client relationship can only be created with the author through a written retainer agreement signed by both parties.

ACKNOWLEDGEMENTS

I am grateful for the assistance of attorneys Shannon Hensley and Pete Wilke for their editorial comments and review, and to Jan Rofekamp for his review of certain portions of this book. I also want to thank my law clerks Cyndie Chang and Jessica Dubick and my assistant Emi Koda and paralegal Chrys Wu for fact-checking and research. Special thanks to AFMA and its director of legal affairs, Susan Cleary, for sharing information.

Finally, I am indebted to my publishers, Gwen Feldman and Jim Fox, for their helpful suggestions.

CONTENTS

CONTRACTS AND FORMS*

---

*All the contracts in this book are available on computer disk. See page 315 for information on how to order.

PREFACE

There is a venerable Latin saying: *caveat emptor*. It means *buyer beware*. This is good advice for anyone swimming in the shark-infested waters of the motion picture industry. Here, newcomers may not even be able to spot the sharks because they are charming, well-mannered, and highly educated. The sharks know many ways to defraud, cheat, and take advantage of novice filmmakers, and they can be ruthless. That is not to say that everyone in the industry is a scoundrel. Some make a point of keeping their word and possess great integrity. The difficulty is that one often doesn't fully know the character of the person or company you are dealing with when the contract is signed.

The manner in which independent films are financed and distributed has become increasingly complex. Most film schools focus on the creative aspects of filmmaking, often paying scant attention to the financial and legal issues that beginning film-makers face. This book was borne from the frustration of observing talented young writers and filmmakers being taken advantage of, or watching them make mistakes that could easily be avoided. I have seen filmmakers borrow large sums of money and work grueling hours to fulfill their dream of produc-ing a film, but they ultimately fail because they do not secure their legal rights or they neglect to arrange proper distribution for their picture. If the independent filmmaker does not repay his investors, he often doesn't get a second chance to make a film. The industry and the moviegoing public lose a lot of talented filmmakers as a result of unnecessary mistakes.

This book is designed to help level the playing field by informing the reader of potential pitfalls. Additional information is available on my website: *Entertainment Law Resources* at www.marklitwak.com. Readers can subscribe at the website to a free newsletter about entertainment law developments.

Much of the material in this book I developed for courses I have taught at UCLA Extension for the past 15 years. This work follows my previous books. *Reel Power, The Struggle for Influence and Success in the New Hollywood* (Morrow, 1986, NAL 1987) details the inner-workings of the movie business; *Dealmaking in the Film & Television Industry* (Silman-James Press, 2nd ed., 2002) and *Contracts for the Film & Television Industry* (Silman-James Press, 2nd ed., 1998) are entertainment law guides for non-lawyers. *Litwak's Multimedia Producer's Handbook* covers multimedia law and distribution. I have also created a software program entitled Automated Contracts for the Film & Television Industry.

I welcome comments and suggestions from readers. You can contact me at:

Law Offices of Mark Litwak & Associates
433 N. Camden Dr., Ste. 1010
Beverly Hills, CA 90210
Phone: (310) 859-9595
Fax: (310) 859-0806
Email: atty@marklitwak.com
Website: www.marklitwak.com

I hope this guide will prove useful to you.

Mark Litwak
February 2004

FILMMAKER SELF-DEFENSE CHECKLIST

Here is a summary of some of the most important ways film-makers can protect their interests:

1. OBTAIN ALL PROMISES IN WRITING. Don't accept oral assurances from a producer or studio executive. If they promise to spend $50,000 to promote your film, put that promise in writing. If there is not enough time to draft a long-form contract, insist on a letter agreement spelling out the essential terms.

2. REGISTER ALL WORKS WITH THE COPYRIGHT OFFICE OR THE WRITERS GUILD. Before you pitch a story, write it out and register it with the Writers Guild. Non-members may register manuscripts. Even better, register your work with the U.S. Copyright Office for maximum protection.

3. OBTAIN AN ARBITRATION CLAUSE: Make sure contractual disputes are subject to binding arbitration where the prevailing party is entitled to reimbursement of legal fees and costs. Arbitration is less costly than litigation, and going to court is not much of a remedy if you can't afford it.

4. WATER DOWN THE WARRANTIES: Warranties are promises. For example, when you sell a script, the buyer will want you to promise that you have not plagiarized another writer's work or defamed someone. If you make an absolute warranty, you will be liable, even if you made a good-faith mistake and honestly believed that you had secured all the rights. Therefore, it is best to make your warranties "to the best of your knowledge and belief," rather than making them absolute.

DEALMAKING
IN THE
FILM AND
TELEVISION
INDUSTRY—
2ND EDITION

XVIII

5. RETAIN POSSESSION OF YOUR NEGATIVE: Independent filmmakers should not relinquish possession of their master materials. Instead, give the distributor a lab access letter permitting it to order copies of your originals held in your lab under your name. This way, if the distributor ever breaches your contract or goes bankrupt, at least it will not possess your masters. You should also retain control of your original still photos and any artwork.

6. OBTAIN INSURANCE COVERAGE: Typically the producer purchases insurance, including Errors and Omissions (E&O) insurance, which protects the producer if he inadvertently infringes another's rights (*e.g.*, defames somebody, infringes their copyrighted material). It is best to purchase the E&O policy early so that coverage begins during preproduction. If you begin production and a claim is made, insurance companies may decline to issue a policy or insist that the policy exclude the pre-existing claim. E&O insurance will pay (minus a deductible) for your defense and any damages that may arise from liability for inadvertently defaming someone or infringing their rights.

7. CHECK REFERENCES: The most airtight contract in the world offers limited protection against a scoundrel who ignores its terms. Carefully investigate any party with whom you contemplate doing business. For distributors, confer with other filmmakers who have had dealings with a distributor over the course of several years. Check with the Filmmaker's Clearinghouse on my website (www.marklitwak.com) to see how indie filmmakers rate various distributors. Usually, people who have lousy reputations have earned them.

8. TERMINATION CLAUSE: If the other party defaults, it is best if you have the right to terminate the contract and regain all rights to your film in addition to monetary damages. Writers should insist on a reversion clause so that if a script is bought and not produced within a reasonable amount of time (*e.g.*, five years), all rights revert to the writer.

9. INVESTOR MONEY: Never make any "offers" to investors or accept any investor money without fully complying with all applicable state and federal securities laws. These laws apply when you offer investments to "passive" investors, which are

investors who provide financing but are not actively involved in making the movie. Have an entertainment attorney with experience in securities prepare appropriate disclosure documents (*e.g.*, a Private Placement Memorandum).

10. SAVE COPIES: Retain copies of all correspondence, contracts, and drafts of your screenplay. When you make a story suggestion or enter into an oral agreement, follow up with a letter documenting the extent of your contribution.

11. DEFINE ADVERTISING EXPENSES: Distribution contracts should specify in writing the minimum amount the distributor will spend to advertise and promote a film. It is wise to cap expenses as well. Obtain a detailed definition of which advertising, promotional, and marketing expenses are recoupable, thereby precluding the distributor from reimbursing itself for overhead and any inappropriate or undocumented expenses.

12. INDEMNITY: The filmmaker should be indemnified (reimbursed) for any losses incurred as a result of the distributor's breach of contract, and for any liability arising from material added to the script/film by the distributor.

13. RIGHT TO INSPECT BOOKS AND RECORDS: The distributor should be required to maintain complete books and records with regard to all sales and rentals of the motion picture. The filmmaker should receive quarterly producer reports with a detailed accounting statement along with any payment due. In the event the filmmaker wants to examine the distributor's books and records, he should be permitted to do so with reasonable notice. If an audit discloses a significant underpayment (*e.g.*, $5,000), the distributor should reimburse the filmmaker the cost of the audit.

14. LATE PAYMENTS/LIENS: All monies due and payable to the filmmaker should be held in trust by the distributor. In addition, the filmmaker should have a lien on the filmmaker's share of the gross receipts derived from the film. The distributor should be required to pay the filmmaker interest on any late payments.

15. REMEDIES: A filmmaker should be given at least three years from receipt of a financial statement, or from discovery of an accounting error, to object.

16. ASSIGNMENT: No assignment (transfer) of rights by the distributor should relieve it of its contractual obligations to the filmmaker unless the filmmaker consents to the assignment.

17. FILMMAKER DEFAULT: A distributor should give the filmmaker at least 10 days' written notice of any alleged filmmaker default (breach of agreement) before taking any action to enforce its rights.

CHAPTER 1

ORGANIZING YOUR COMPANY

CHOICE OF BUSINESS ENTITY

Filmmakers frequently establish a company to produce and own their movie. While not legally required, there may be some benefit to operating under the auspices of a company rather than making your film as an individual or as a partner. The most common business entities used by filmmakers are corporations (S or C type), limited liability companies (LLC), and limited partnerships (LP).

One reason to form a company is the desire to protect personal assets from potential liability. If a movie is produced by a company that is a separate legal entity from the filmmaker, then the filmmaker may not be liable for the debts and obligations of the company. However, for the filmmaker to avoid personal liability, he must sign all contracts in the name of the company and not give any personal guarantees.

Filmmakers and investors may be willing to accept the complete loss of their film investment but will hesitate to risk losing their homes and other assets. By establishing a separate business entity, investors can own the company that produces and owns the film without being personally liable for the actions of the company. With a corporation, investors become shareholders; with an LLC they become non-managing members; and with a limited partnership they become limited partners.

Conducting business through a company does not insulate an individual against all liability. If you are negligent and harm another, both you and your company may be liable. In other words, while establishing a company may protect you from liability for your company's breach of its contracts, it does not preclude other people from suing you for your own negligence. So, for example, if you carelessly run over someone with your car, you are liable even though no contract exists between you and the victim. It is irrelevant whether you even know the victim. Similarly, if you are negligent on a movie set and cause injuries to others, you may be liable even if you are operating under the auspices of a company.

Before forming a company, you should consider other ways to minimize liability. You could take extra care in conducting your affairs, and you could purchase insurance. Keep in perspective that every day as you engage in routine tasks, you are exposing yourself to liability if you act carelessly and injure others. The risk increases when you hire a cast and crew because, as their employer, you can be held liable for their negligence.

Another reason to establish a company is to reduce taxes. Corporations may be able to deduct certain expenses that would not be deductible, or only be partially deductible, by a sole proprietor. Some fringe benefits (*e.g.*, medical insurance, pension plans) that a company provides employees may be tax deductible for the company and not considered income to the employee. Therefore, by setting up a company, paying yourself a salary, and giving yourself generous fringe benefits, you may gain certain tax advantages. On the other hand, the tax benefits may not outweigh the cost of forming the company, which includes legal fees, filing fees, and the annual cost of preparing and filing a company tax return. Moreover, some states assess a minimum annual tax on companies even if they do not earn any income.

As you consider whether to set up a company, you should evaluate the relative advantages and disadvantages of different business vehicles.

Sole Proprietorship

A sole proprietor is nothing more than an individual engaged in a business. The business can operate under the individual's name or a fictitious business name. For example, Bob Jones could conduct his business under the name Serendipity Productions. In this case, Bob Jones is doing business as ("DBA") Serendipity Productions. While Bob may operate under the banner "Serendipity Productions," in the eyes of the law, Bob and Serendipity are one and the same.

If you choose to operate under an assumed name, you are required to file a Fictitious Business Name Statement with the local or state government. You should first check to make sure that no individuals or companies are using the same name you want to use or a similar name. An assumed name is any name other than your full legal name.

USEFUL WEBSITES:

CALIFORNIA BUSINESS PORTAL:
www.ss.ca.gov/business/tax.htm
INFORMATION OF HOW TO START A BUSINESS IN CALIFORNIA.

IRS:
www.irs.gov
ALLOWS USERS TO SEARCH THE DATABASE AND FIND INFORMATION TO A VARIETY OF TAX ISSUES.

EMPLOYMENT DEVELOPMENT DEPARTMENT (EDD):
www.edd.ca.gov
SITE THAT LINKS USERS TO JOB PLACEMENT AND REFERRALS, UNEMPLOYMENT INSURANCE, DISABILITY INSURANCE, EMPLOYMENT AND TRAINING, LABOR MARKET INFORMATION, AND PAYROLL TAXES.

NEW YORK STATE DEPARTMENT OF STATE:
www.dos.state.ny.us
INFORMATION ON HOW TO START A BUSINESS IN NEW YORK STATE.

The principal advantage of operating as a sole proprietor is that it is simple and inexpensive. No formalities are required, and no legal fees or expenses need be incurred (unless one operates under an assumed name, in which case there is the minor expense of filing and publishing a notice). If you are operating a business without co-owners or partners, and you do not form a separate legal entity to run the business, then by default you are functioning as a sole proprietor.

A sole proprietor does not file a separate tax return for his business, but he does need to attach Schedule C to his individual income tax return. This schedule discloses business revenues and expenses. In California, there is no minimum

FICTITIOUS BUSINESS NAMES (DBA)

IN CALIFORNIA YOU FILE A FICTITIOUS BUSINESS NAME STATEMENT WITH THE COUNTY CLERK'S OFFICE. FIRST CONDUCT A SEARCH TO ENSURE THAT THE NAME YOU WANT TO USE IS NOT ALREADY BEING USED BY ANOTHER PERSON OR ENTITY IN YOUR COUNTY. THIS SEARCH CAN BE DONE BY COMPUTER IN THE COUNTY CLERK'S OFFICE OR OVER THE INTERNET. VISIT THE COUNTY OF LOS ANGELES, REGISTRAR-RECORDER/COUNTY CLERK WEBSITE FOR AN APPLICATION AND TO CONDUCT AN INTERNET SEARCH FOR NAME CONFLICTS (http://regrec.co.la.ca.us/fbn/fbn.cfm).

CALIFORNIA CHARGES $10 TO REGISTER THE FIRST FICTITIOUS BUSINESS NAME AND $2 FOR EACH ADDITIONAL FICTITIOUS BUSINESS NAME FILED ON THE SAME STATEMENT AND CONDUCTING BUSINESS AT THE SAME SITE. CALIFORNIA REQUIRES PUBLICATION OF A STATEMENT WITHIN 30 DAYS OF YOUR USE OF A FICTITIOUS BUSINESS NAME. PUBLICATION MUST BE IN A NEWSPAPER OF GENERAL CIRCULATION IN THE COUNTY IN WHICH YOUR PRINCIPAL PLACE OF BUSINESS IS LOCATED. THE REGISTRAR-RECORDER/COUNTY CLERK WEBSITE LISTS NEWSPAPERS OF GENERAL CIRCULATION. IN CALIFORNIA, FICTITIOUS BUSINESS NAME STATEMENTS EXPIRE IN FIVE YEARS. A NEW STATEMENT NEEDS TO BE FILED BEFORE THE EXPIRATION DATE IF YOU WANT TO CONTINUE DOING BUSINESS UNDER THE ASSUMED NAME. A $10 FEE IS CHARGED TO RENEW, BUT THERE IS NO PUBLICATION REQUIREMENT FOR RENEWAL.

IN NEW YORK, THERE IS A $5 FEE FOR THE DEPARTMENT OF STATE TO SEARCH FOR NAME CONFLICTS. FOR INFORMATION ON HOW TO FILE A FICTITIOUS BUSINESS NAME IN NEW YORK STATE, VISIT THE NEW YORK STATE DEPARTMENT OF STATE WEBSITE: www.dos.state.ny.us. THIS SITE PROVIDES A STEP-BY-STEP GUIDE ON FILING A FICTITIOUS BUSINESS NAME. FOR ANSWERS TO A VARIETY OF QUESTIONS FILING A NAME, GO TO: www.dos.state.ny.us/corp/crpfaq.html.

(CONTINUED)

annual tax or use tax charged to sole proprietors. As with any business, the owner may need to obtain business licenses and permits, withhold taxes for salaries paid to employees, and acquire workers' compensation insurance.

The main drawback to operating as a sole proprietorship is the owner's liability for the obligations of the business. Because the owner has unlimited liability, it is wise to purchase insurance. General liability coverage is available to cover physical injuries to third parties such as bystanders injured during a movie shoot. An Errors and Omissions (E&O) policy insures a filmmaker if he inadvertently infringes the rights of third parties by defaming them, invading their privacy, or infringing their copyrights. Worker's compensation insurance covers injuries suffered by employees. Other policies can insure cameras, equipment, and film footage. For more information on insurance, conduct an Internet search using the keywords "entertainment" and "insurance," or visit my website (www.marklitwak.com) for a listing of insurance and completion bond companies.

FICTITIOUS BUSINESS NAMES (DBA)
(CONTINUED)

NEW YORK CHARGES A $20 FEE TO REGISTER A NAME FOR A BUSINESS ENTITY AND THE FILING CAN BE DONE BY MAIL, FAX, OVER THE PHONE USING A CREDIT CARD, AND IN PERSON AT THE ALBANY OFFICE. THE NECESSARY FORMS CAN BE DOWNLOADED FROM THE STATE DEPARTMENT'S WEBSITE. FOR MORE SPECIFIC INFORMATION ON THE FILING PROCESS, CALL THE NEW YORK STATE DIVISION OF CORPORATIONS AT (518) 473-2492. PARTNERSHIPS, CORPORATIONS, AND LLCS MAY OPERATE UNDER ASSUMED NAMES, BUT THEY MUST FILE FICTITIOUS BUSINESS NAME STATEMENTS. A PERSON OR COMPANY CAN OPERATE UNDER SEVERAL DBAS. NOTE THAT BANKS WILL NOT ALLOW YOU TO OPEN AN ACCOUNT UNDER A FICTITIOUS BUSINESS NAME UNTIL YOU HAVE FILED YOUR STATEMENT.

MERELY RECORDING A DBA STATEMENT DOES NOT PRECLUDE OTHERS FROM USING THE SAME OR A SIMILAR NAME. NOR DOES RECORDATION PREVENT OTHERS FROM CLAIMING THAT YOUR NAME INFRINGES THEIR RIGHTS. IF YOUR DBA IS SIMILAR TO ANOTHER'S NAME, THAT ENTITY MAY BRING AN ACTION AGAINST YOU FOR UNFAIR COMPETITION OR TRADEMARK INFRINGEMENT. IN ORDER TO MORE FULLY SECURE RIGHTS TO A NAME, YOU MAY WANT TO CONDUCT A TRADEMARK SEARCH TO SEE IF ANYONE IS USING THE NAME, AND IF THERE IS NO CONFLICT, REGISTER YOUR NAME AS EITHER A STATE OR FEDERAL TRADEMARK.

General Partnership

A general partnership is an association of two or more persons conducting a for-profit business as co-owners. Parties who operate as partners in running a business will be treated as partners under the law even if they don't specifically intend to be partners, and even if they don't formalize their relationship with an oral or written partnership agreement. It is always a good idea, however, for partners to enter into a written agreement to clarify the nature of their relationship.

It is often said that one should choose one's partners carefully. That is because each partner is liable for the acts of other partners in carrying on the partnership business. Although Partner A may not have the permission or consent of Partner B to take certain actions, Partner B may be liable for Partner A's conduct. For example, if partner A buys a photocopier for the partnership business without the agreement or knowledge of his partners, all the partners are responsible to pay for the equipment unless the vendor knew that Partner A did not have authority to make the purchase. Likewise, if Partner A crashes a car rented for the partnership business, Partner B may be liable for damage to the car and to any persons injured.

The rights and duties of partners are usually set forth in a written partnership agreement. If there is no agreement, the law will define the partner's relationship. For example, under California law (Cal. Corp. Code § 15018), absent an agreement otherwise, partners share management and control of a business equally, and share profits and losses equally. Furthermore, partners have the right to be repaid funds they contribute to the partnership, and a majority vote settles disagreements among the partners.

State law often requires that partners have certain rights that cannot be varied by agreement of the partners. For example, in California, partners have the right to inspect the partnership books, and have the right to a formal accounting. Each partner has an obligation to disclose to the other partners all information relating to the partnership business, and each partner has to account to the other partners for any benefits received by a partner from the partnership business.

For more information on general partnerships, see: www.ss.ca .gov/business/gp/gp.htm (California); www.dos.state.ny.us/corp/

crpfaq.html (New York); and www.irs.gov/businesses/partnerships (federal tax information for partnerships).

Limited Partnership

In a limited partnership there are two types of partners: general and limited. A general partner runs the business and essentially has the same rights and obligations of a partner in a general partnership. A limited partner is a passive investor who does not have any right to manage or control the business. A limited partner has limited control and limited liability.

If the partnership business incurs debts or liabilities, a general partner may be liable, while a limited partner is not. Thus, by establishing a limited partnership one can permit an investor to risk $50,000 of capital to produce a film, but the investor's house and other assets are not vulnerable. This is an important protection because investors with substantial assets are usually the ones who can afford to invest in a risky endeavor like filmmaking.

If a limited partner actively participates in the management and control of the partnership business, the limited partner can lose his limited liability status and become liable for the debts and obligations of the partnership. Sometimes investors get so caught up in the excitement of making a movie that they become actively involved in production. This may prove to be a mistake for both parties. When your dentist-investor comes down to the set and starts to tell you how to direct your picture, it may be time to point out that his participation may result in his loss of limited liability. Merely consulting with or advising a general partner, however, will not affect a limited partner's status.

In order for a filmmaker to insulate himself from liability as a general partner, the filmmaker could form a corporation and have the corporation serve as general partner. Thus the corporation, which is usually controlled by the filmmaker, is liable as the general partner, not the filmmaker. This structure was often used in the days before limited liability companies (LLCs) were permitted. With LLCs, both the managing members and non-managing members have limited liability, so there is no need to set up a corporation to shield the filmmaker.

Although limited partners cannot take an active role in producing a film, they are not entirely without rights. In California, for example, a limited partnership is required to maintain certain financial records and income tax returns, which the limited partners have the right to inspect and copy (Cal. Corp. Code § 15615, § 15634(b)). Limited partners representing more than 10% of the total interests of limited partners have the right to call a partnership meeting (Cal. Corp. Code § 15637(b)), and if the limited partnership has more than 35 limited partners, the partnership has to provide an annual report with financial statements (Cal. Corp. Code § 15634(c)(1)).

A limited partnership is formed in California by filing a Certificate of Limited Partnership (Form LP-1) with the Secretary of State's Limited Partnership Division. The filing fee is currently $70. A limited partnership does not have to pay an initial minimum franchise tax in order to be established. The minimum franchise tax is due when the partnership files its informational tax return. The Certificate of Limited Partnership needs to be filed before the partnership begins conducting business. Otherwise, the limited partners will not have limited liability. For more information on California limited partnerships, call the Secretary of State's Limited Partnership Unit at (916) 653-3365 or email them at partnerships@ss.ca.gov.

Partners in a limited partnership usually have a written agreement, although they can operate under an oral agreement (Cal. Corp. Code § 15611(y)). If the partnership agreement is

FEDERAL EMPLOYER IDENTIFICATION NUMBER

AN EIN CAN BE OBTAINED BY FILLING OUT A COPY OF FORM SS-4 (REPRINTED BELOW) AND APPLYING BY PHONE, FAX, OR MAIL. YOU SHOULD APPLY FOR AN EIN AS SOON AS YOU KNOW YOU WILL NEED ONE. INFORMATION ON EINS AND A DOWNLOADABLE FORM CAN BE OBTAINED FROM www.employers.gov OR FROM IRS AND SOCIAL SECURITY ADMINISTRATION OFFICES. TO APPLY BY MAIL OR FAX, SIGN AND DATE THE APPLICATION AND MAIL OR FAX IT TO THE IRS SERVICE CENTER FOR YOUR STATE. THE ADDRESSES AND FAX NUMBERS ARE AVAILABLE FROM THE SAME WEBSITE.

IF YOU FAX A COMPLETED FORM SS-4 TO THE SERVICE CENTER OF YOUR STATE, THEY WILL RESPOND WITH A RETURN FAX IN ABOUT ONE WEEK IF YOU INCLUDE A RETURN FAX NUMBER, OR TWO WEEKS FOR A REPLY BY MAIL. IF YOU SEND THE FORM BY MAIL, DO SO AT LEAST FOUR TO FIVE WEEKS BEFORE YOU WILL NEED YOUR EIN. YOU CAN ALSO APPLY FOR AN EIN BY TELEPHONE BY CALLING (866) 816-2065 FOR CALIFORNIA RESIDENTS.

oral, the burden of proving the terms of the agreement will be on the general partner.

No particular form of writing is required, but to the extent that the partners do not carefully define their relationship, state law will determine it for them. Thus, it is a good idea to have a written agreement so that disputes and misunderstandings can be avoided. A written agreement allows the partners to decide how they want to allocate income, gain, loss, deduction, and credit for tax purposes. The partners may want to modify various provisions of state law that would otherwise apply. However, some provisions of state law, such as those concerning the withdrawal or removal of a general partner, cannot be overridden by the partnership agreement.

Because a limited partnership is a separate legal entity for tax purposes, a federal employer identification number (EIN) needs to be obtained. This number will be required to open a bank account and to file tax returns. Likewise, other licenses and permits may be needed.

Since limited partners are passive investors, their interests are considered securities. Unless exempt, offers and sales of securities need to comply with federal and state security laws. See Chapter 3 for a discussion of these laws.

Corporation

A corporation is an entity created under the laws of a state. It is treated as a distinct legal entity from the individuals who own and manage it.

There are different types of corporations. This section will focus on for-profit corporations since they are typically used by filmmakers. However, non-profit corporations are sometimes formed, especially for documentaries or other projects funded by grants and donations. Donors who make a gift to a non-profit corporation with the proper tax status can deduct the amount of the gift in calculating their income taxes. Another type of corporation is known as a "close corporation" or "statutory close corporation." There may be advantages in setting up such a corporation if it is going to be owned by a single person or a closely knit group of shareholders.

There are two primary reasons to incorporate. First, incorporating establishes a separate legal entity from the filmmaker and therefore serves to protect the filmmaker from personal liability arising from corporate actions. Second, there may be tax benefits derived from incorporating: A corporation can deduct several expenses that individuals are not permitted to deduct.

While doing business as a corporation can insulate a filmmaker from personal liability, this shield will exist only if the corporation has been properly established and the required formalities have been complied with. If a court determines that a corporation is being used as an "alter-ego" of the principals, or if it is an undercapitalized "shell" company designed to

COMPANY FORMATION CHECKLIST

NAME CHOOSE A NAME FOR YOUR COMPANY THAT IS NOT THE SAME OR CONFUSINGLY SIMILAR TO ANOTHER BUSINESS NAME. (FOR L.A. COUNTY, CHECK DBAS AT regrec.co.la.ca.us/fbn/fbn.cfm; FOR CALIFORNIA CORPORATIONS, CHECK WITH THE SECRETARY OF STATE AT www.ss.ca.gov).

DOMAIN NAME CHECK IF YOUR DESIRED DOMAIN NAME IS AVAILABLE, AND IF THERE ARE ANY CONFLICTING STATE OR FEDERAL TRADEMARKS. FOR DOMAIN NAME SEARCHES AND REGISTRATIONS, www.domain.com AND www.1domain-name-registration.com ARE AMONG MANY SITES PROVIDING THIS SERVICE. FOR TRADEMARK SEARCHES, USE THE TRADEMARK OFFICE SEARCH ENGINE ("TESS") AT www.uspto.gov/main/trademarks.htm.

DBA FILE AND PUBLISH FICTITIOUS BUSINESS NAME STATEMENT, SUBMIT APPLICATIONS FOR STATE OR FEDERAL TRADEMARKS IF DESIRED.

ESTABLISH COMPANY FILE PARTNERSHIP, CORPORATE, OR LIMITED LIABILITY PAPERS WITH THE SECRETARY OF STATE'S OFFICE.

TAXES FILE STATE TAX FORMS WITH FRANCHISE TAX BOARD (www.ftb.ca.gov) OR STATE TAX AUTHORITY.

EMPLOYMENT OBTAIN STATE EMPLOYER ACCOUNT NUMBER FROM THE CALIFORNIA EMPLOYMENT DEVELOPMENT DEPARTMENT (EDD) (DOWNLOADABLE REGISTRATION FORM AT www.edd.ca.gov/taxrep/de1.pdf), OR CALL (916) 654-8706.

(CONTINUED)

unfairly insulate its owners from responsibility for their actions, the court may allow third parties to "pierce the corporate veil" and hold the principals liable. To ensure that shareholders, directors, and officers of the corporation are protected, the corporation should be adequately capitalized with a reasonable amount of money to function in view of its intended business. Moreover, the corporation's assets should not be commingled with those of its principals (*i.e.*, you should set up a separate bank account), and financial records, minutes of meetings, and other documentation should be maintained. Basically, if you don't treat your corporation as a separate legal entity, then you should not expect a court to view it any differently.

COMPANY FORMATION CHECKLIST
(CONTINUED)

EIN	APPLY FOR FEDERAL EMPLOYER IDENTIFICATION NUMBER (EIN) FROM THE IRS. COMPLETE FORM SS-4. A DOWNLOADABLE FORM CAN BE OBTAINED FROM www.irs.gov/pub/irs-pdf/iss4.pdf OR FROM IRS OR SOCIAL SECURITY ADMINISTRATION OFFICES.
LOCAL PERMITS	OBTAIN ANY REQUIRED LOCAL OR STATE PERMITS AND LICENSES. (CHECK WITH CITY HALL FOR THE CITY WHERE YOU WILL BE LOCATED, OR FOR UNINCORPORATED AREAS IN LOS ANGELES COUNTY, CONTACT THE COUNTY TREASURER-TAX COLLECTOR AT (213) 974-2011).
INSURANCE	OBTAIN ANY REQUIRED INSURANCE (*E.G.*, WORKERS' COMPENSATION) AND ANY DESIRED INSURANCE (*E.G.*, GENERAL LIABILITY). WORKERS' COMPENSATION INSURANCE IS NORMALLY OBTAINED THROUGH AN INSURANCE AGENT OR BROKER. CONTACT YOUR LOCAL CHAMBER OF COMMERCE FOR INFORMATION, OR IN CALIFORNIA, GO TO THE DIVISION OF WORKERS' COMPENSATION WEBSITE AT www.dir.ca.gov.
SALES TAX	IF YOU INTEND TO SELL MERCHANDISE, APPLY FOR A PERMIT FROM THE BOARD OF EQUALIZATION IN CALIFORNIA (www.boe.ca.gov) OR APPROPRIATE STATE AGENCY IN OTHER STATES.
BANK ACCOUNT	OPEN COMPANY BANK ACCOUNT.

A corporation is formed by filing articles of incorporation with the Secretary of State (Cal. Corp. Code § 200) along with a filing fee. In addition, in California, a minimum annual tax must be paid.

After formation, the shareholders or incorporator must designate the members of a board of directors, and the directors in turn can appoint officers such as a President, Vice President, and Treasurer. Bylaws need to be adopted and shares of stock issued. All of these actions should be documented in the corporation's minutes. Minutes should also be taken at board of directors' and shareholder meetings. California requires that there be an annual election of at least a portion of the board of directors (Cal. Corp. Code §§ 301, 301.5).

Stock is considered a security, and its sale is subject to state and federal securities laws. Generally, unless there is an applicable statutory exemption, stock cannot be sold or offered for sale without compliance with state and federal securities laws. In addition, full disclosure to potential investors is usually required before offering to sell stock. The sanctions for securities-law violations can be severe, including criminal penalties. Stock should not be sold or transferred without consulting an attorney.

Corporations formed under California law are considered "domestic" corporations in California. Corporations formed in other states or countries are called "foreign" corporations. Foreign corporations can conduct business in California, and set up offices in the state, if they qualify (register) to do so.

Corporations are subject to state and federal income taxes. Thus, the corporation has to pay a tax on its income, and amounts it pays out to shareholders as dividends are taxable to the shareholders. This potential double-taxation is the major drawback of the corporate form of business.

One way to minimize the tax bite is to have the corporation pay out its accumulated net income to its officers or directors in the form of salaries, or to the shareholders in the form of dividends. If the corporation has no net income at the end of the tax year, there is no tax due other than any minimum tax. This method of minimizing taxes is legal provided that the salaries are not excessive.

Another way to avoid double-taxation is to elect to become an S corporation. An S corporation can avoid most federal and state taxes on income by passing through profits and losses to the shareholders. In other words, the S corporation is treated for tax purposes like a partnership, with profits and losses passed through to the partners and not taxed at the company (partnership or corporate) level.

Not all corporations can elect S status. An S corporation cannot have more than 75 shareholders. It can only have one class of stock, and shareholders cannot be nonresident aliens. The decision whether to request that the IRS treat a corporation as a C or an S corporation is made after you set up the corporation. The corporation can change its status from C to S and back again by filing the appropriate forms with the IRS.

California law allows a great deal of discretion in selecting a corporate name. Generally, the words "corporation" or "incorporated" need not be included. Corporate names can be reserved with the Secretary of State before incorporating.

Limited Liability Company (LLC)

The limited liability company (LLC) is a relatively new form of business entity that combines some of the best aspects of partnership and corporate forms of business while avoiding some of the drawbacks of each. Members of an LLC have the same limited liability protection granted limited partners and corporate shareholders. Unlike a corporation, however, an LLC has more flexibility as to how to pay taxes, and can largely avoid the problem of double-taxation.

An LLC has two classes of members: managing members and non-managing members. Like general partners, the managing members run the business. Like limited partners, the non-managing members are investors who do not operate the business. Both managing and non-managing members have limited liability.

An LLC can elect to be treated like a partnership for federal income tax purposes, and thereby avoid federal tax at the company level. LLC members report their respective shares of LLC income or losses on their individual tax returns. Although the LLC is not a tax-paying entity, the LLC must report its taxable income and file an informational return with the IRS.

In California, LLCs are subject to state income tax, but the amount of tax is modest, and no tax is assessed until there is total income of $250,000 or more per year. However, like corporations and limited partnerships, LLCs are subject to an annual tax of $800 for the privilege of doing business in California.

An LLC is established by filing Articles of Organization with the Secretary of State (Form LLC-1). The filing fee currently is $70. As of January 1, 2000, an LLC can be established with a single member.

An LLC can be managed by one or more managers (a "manager-managed" LLC) or by all the members (a "member-managed" LLC). A manager-managed LLC is like a limited partnership with two classes of members: managers who actively

CALIFORNIA TAX INFORMATION:

FRANCHISE TAX BOARD: THE TAXING ENTITY FOR PERSONAL, CORPORATE, AND FRANCHISE TAXES FOR THE STATE.
(800) 852-5711
www.ftb.ca.gov
www.taxes.ca.gov/index2.html (FOR BUSINESSES)

INTERNAL REVENUE SERVICES: ADMINISTERS THE FEDERAL PERSONAL, BUSINESS, AND PAYROLL TAXES (SOCIAL SECURITY, MEDICARE, FEDERAL UNEMPLOYMENT, FEDERAL INCOME TAX WITHHOLDING).
(800) 829-1040
www.irs.gov

BOARD OF EQUALIZATION: HANDLES SALES-TAX SELLER PERMITS FOR BUSINESSES AND COLLECTS SALES TAXES.
(800) 400-7115
www.boe.ca.gov
www.boe.ca.gov/sutax/faqseller.htm (FOR SELLER'S PERMIT APPLICATIONS AND SALES TAX INFO)

EMPLOYMENT DEVELOPMENT DEPARTMENT: ISSUES STATE EMPLOYER IDENTIFICATION NUMBERS FOR BUSINESSES WITH EMPLOYEES AND ADMINISTERS STATE PAYROLL TAXES (INCLUDING UNEMPLOYMENT AND DISABILITY INSURANCE, PERSONAL INCOME TAX WITHHOLDING, ETC.).
(888) 745-3886
www.edd.ca.gov
www.edd.ca.gov/employer.htm (FOR EMPLOYERS)

supervise the enterprise and non-managers who do not. Similarly, a member-managed LLC is like a general partnership where all the partners are involved in running the business.

In a manager-managed LLC, a manager need not be a member, but can be an outsider hired to manage the enterprise. Managers are considered agents of the LLC and they can bind the LLC to contracts with third parties. In a manager-managed LLC, the non-managing members are not considered agents of the LLC.

The interest of a non-managing member is a security, and securities laws apply. If all the members are active in the management of the LLC (*i.e.*, all members are managers), there are no passive investors and the members' interests are not considered securities.

The LLC's name must end with the words "limited liability company" or the abbreviations "LLC" or "L.L.C." The name cannot include such words as "Trust," "Inc.," or "Corporation." The name cannot be one that is likely to mislead the public and cannot be confusingly similar to the name of another LLC. To determine if a name is available, contact the Secretary of State's office.

As with other business entities, if the LLC operates under a fictitious business name, the company will need to file a DBA. Since the LLC is a separate legal entity, it will need to apply for an EIN, obtain any applicable state and local business licenses, and file state and federal tax returns.

COMPARISON OF ENTITY CHOICES

	SOLE PROPRIE-TORSHIP	S CORPORA-TION	C CORPORA-TION	LIMITED PARTNER-SHIP	GENERAL PARTNER-SHIP	LIMITED LIABILITY COMPANY
LIMITED LIABILITY FOR OWNER(S)	No	Yes	Yes	Yes	No	Yes
COMPOSITION OF OWNERSHIP	One person.	Limited to 75 shareholders and one class of stock. Shareholders cannot be foreign individuals, corporations, or trusts (except certain qualified trusts).	Generally no restrictions.	Need 1 limited partner and 1 general partner.	Need 2 partners.	Some states require 2 or more. In CA, as of 1/1/2000, only 1 member is required.
CONTINUITY OF LIFE	No	Perpetual	Perpetual	Partnership agreement determines term.	Partnership agreement determines term.	Articles of organization determine term.
ADMINISTRATIVE COMPLEXITY	Simple	Complex	Complex	Varies	Varies	Complex
DISSOLUTION OF ENTITY ON DEATH, BANKRUPTCY, RESIGNATION, EXPULSION, OR DISSOLUTION OF PARTICIPANT	Yes	No	No	Yes, unless Partnership Agreement provides otherwise by vote of majority in interest of remaining partners.	Yes, unless Partnership Agreement provides otherwise by vote of majority in interest of remaining partners.	Yes, unless Operating Agreement provides otherwise by vote of majority in interest of remaining members.
DOUBLE-TAXATION OF INCOME	No	No	Yes	No	No	No. (LLC can be treated as partnership for tax purposes.)
IS ENTITY TAXED?	Yes. Company and individual are one and the same.	No. Income passes through to shareholders.	Yes	No. Income passes through to partners.	No. Income passes through to partners.	Entity can elect to have income pass through to members.

CHAPTER 2

COLLABORATIONS AND CO-PRODUCTIONS

A co-production can be as simple as a director and producer collaborating on a project, or as complex as two multi-national corporations sharing risk and revenue on a movie. In independent film, it is maybe two producers deciding to pool their resources to make a film. If the producers are from different countries, you have an international co-production.

A co-production should be distinguished from an employer/employee relationship. If a producer hires a director to work on the producer's project, and the producer owns and controls the distribution of the completed picture, then the director may be an employee, even if the director has certain creative rights (*e.g.*, final cut) or is entitled to share in profits.

The fact that a person receives a "producer" or "co-producer" credit does not necessarily define the nature of the relationship. Some films list five or more producers. These "producers" may garner a credit because they were the manager of a star who agreed to accept a role in the picture. Or the credit could be given to a dentist who is one of the principal financiers of the movie. An "assistant producer" or "associate producer" credit might be a perk given to compensate someone who agreed to accept a reduced wage. Since the Producers Guild is a professional association and not a union, it is not party to a collective bargaining agreement that restricts the granting of producing credits. Therefore, unlike director and writer credits, producer credits can be freely granted—even to people who don't deserve them.

Co-productions are often based on each party bringing something valuable to the project that the other collaborators lack. For instance, one producer might contribute a script and have the ability to attract a star, while another producer might be able to raise financing and recruit a talented director. For the relationship to work, the parties need to realistically value their contributions. If parties make unequal contributions, their control, fees, and ownership of the project can be adjusted to reflect that so the deal is fair for all parties.

It is not unusual for collaborations to fail. After spending a lot of time developing a project, the parties may come to a creative impasse, or there may be so much interpersonal conflict that they can't continue to work together. If there is no agreement providing for resolution of disputes, and how to divide material developed together, the project may die. Once a relationship has deteriorated and become antagonistic, it may be difficult for the parties to agree on anything.

One should get to know a potential collaborator before rushing forward and encumbering a project. The parties should discuss their expectations of one another and determine whether those expectations are realistic. If one party, for example, is expected to raise production financing, there might be a deadline for the funds to be delivered, and the terms of the deal might be modified if that deadline is not met.

It is not a good idea to take on a collaborator simply because you are lonely. When you collaborate with another, that person may make creative contributions and submit the project to third parties. If the collaboration dissolves, the law may imply that your former collaborator has rights to jointly developed material. Under copyright law, when two writers collaborate on a work, it is presumed they will own the copyright equally unless there is an agreement that provides otherwise.

In negotiating a collaboration or co-production agreement, it is important to understand the difference between sharing ownership of the property and sharing revenue derived from it. The copyright owner of a motion picture determines how the work may be distributed and exploited, and whether to allow any derivative works to be adapted from it. On the other hand, a party that "owns" 50% of the net profits from a picture has an interest in the revenue stream derived from the movie. Such a profit participant does not necessarily have any control over how the property is exploited.

Frequently, collaborators who desire to make an independent film will set up and co-own a new legal entity (*e.g.*, corporation, LLC, limited partnership) that will hold the copyright to the picture. Collaborators may share the management and control of this entity, or management may be delegated to one collaborator or to an outside manager. Samples of collaboration agreements can be found in my book *Contracts for the Film and Television Industry, 2nd. Edition,* by Silman-James Press.

INTERNATIONAL CO-PRODUCTIONS

Unlike other nations, the United States government does not provide any special tax benefits or incentives to encourage filmmaking. Perhaps because U.S. films are widely exported and generate more revenue than pictures from other countries, our government may not feel there is a need to encourage filmmaking. Many other countries, however, believe that American product dominates their marketplace so much that it is difficult for indigenous movies to compete against Hollywood fare.

Foreign governments consider movies to be more than just another product. Movies may be an important part of a nation's culture and heritage. They can promote a country's language, customs, and attractions to audiences worldwide. Consequently, many governments try to encourage their citizens to create films, especially those with local content.

The domestic and export market for many films may be limited, and therefore it may make sense for governments to encourage their filmmakers to collaborate with foreign nationals. International co-production treaties can permit filmmakers from different countries to work together and receive government incentives from several countries.

Government incentives are offered in a variety of forms. Some countries provide tax benefits to investors in order to encourage production by its nationals. Sometimes these benefits are so generous that investors are more motivated by the tax savings than the quality of the films to be made. This can lead to a glut of bad movies.

Grants can also be used to encourage filmmaking. When governments provide grants or loans, they tend to be conservative in selecting the pictures they support. They often prefer to fund projects by directors with proven track records, and they may avoid controversial topics that might subject officials to public criticism.

U.S. filmmakers can enter into co-production agreements, although their films may not benefit from an official treaty. The American partner may supply financing, a script, and some stars while the foreign partner provides goods, services, and local production expertise. Moreover, some incentives are given for merely shooting or performing postproduction in a community because these activities employ local residents and generate economic benefits from goods and services purchased. For example, there are local and regional incentives to encourage American producers to shoot in Canada. A purely American movie may be eligible to receive a rebate on money spent in Canada, and benefit from a favorable currency exchange rate achieved when American dollars are converted into Canadian dollars. For movies that qualify as Canadian Content, additional incentives are available.

When contemplating an international co-production, the parties need to consider the nature of the relationship. What is each company contributing to the endeavor? An American company planning to shoot one of its projects abroad may want to employ a local company to provide services and expertise. In such a relationship, the American company controls the project and pays the local company for its services. The local company might not have any ownership interest or control over how the movie is produced and distributed.

At other times, the parties may be operating as partners, sharing creative control and financial risk. When crafting an agreement, the parties need to consider the consequences if one party is unable to contribute that which it has promised. How long will each party have to fulfill its commitments? What conditions need to be fulfilled before a party can make its contribution? Sometimes a foreign co-production partner is looking for the American partner to secure a U.S. theatrical release for the picture. What type of distribution commitment will fulfill this requirement? Does the film have to be shown on a minimum number of screens? Does a minimum amount of marketing dollars need to be spent?

If one of the parties is planning to arrange a government subsidy or tax benefit, the parties need to closely review the rules for eligibility to make sure they qualify. Even if qualified, a government entity may have discretion whether to provide financing.

Choosing where the production will occur will impact the cost of making the movie, including any sales or income taxes that may be assessed. A number of American producers have been

CO-PRODUCTION WEBSITES

CANADIAN GUIDE:
www.telefilm.gc.ca/04/41.asp

A GUIDE TO CANADA'S FILM OR VIDEO PRODUCTION SERVICES TAX CREDIT (PSTC):
www.pch.gc.ca/progs/ac-ca/progs/bcpac-cavco/progs/cisp-pstc/index_e.cfm

SOME PRACTICAL TIPS FOR INTERNATIONAL CO-PRODUCTION/ DISTRIBUTION:
www.usindependents.com/forproducers/content/4.html

INTERNATIONAL JOINT VENTURES IN THE PRODUCTION OF AUSTRA-LIAN FEATURE FILMS AND TELEVISION PROGRAMS:
www.wlu.ca/~wwwpress/jrls/cjc/BackIssues/24.1/hoskins.pap.html

"PLUS ÇA CHANGE, PLUS C'EST LA MÊME CHOSE": EUROPEAN CO-PRODUCTION REMAINS VIABLE, FOR NOW:
www.phillaw.com/html/co-productions.html

UNITED KINGDOM'S CREATIVE MEDIA AND ARTS: CO-PRODUCTION AGREEMENTS:
www.culture.gov.uk/creative-industries/film/Co-productionagreements.html

BRITISH FILM COMMISSION:
www.bfc.co.uk

AUSTRALIAN CO-PRODUCTION GUIDE:
www.afc.gov.au/services/funding/guides/co-prod/icpg1.html

bringing productions to South Africa or Eastern Europe because the costs of goods and wages is so much lower than in the U.S. or Western Europe.

Once the parties have determined what each will contribute, they need to decide how they will share any returns. Often investors recoup their capital contribution from the first proceeds. Ownership of the copyright to the film may be shared by the parties, or it may need to reside with a company set up

FILM COMMISSIONS

FILM COMMISSIONS CAN PROVIDE DETAILED INFORMATION ABOUT TERMS AND CONDITIONS TO APPLY FOR CO-PRODUCTION INCENTIVES.

UNITED STATES
CALIFORNIA FILM COMMISSION/FILM LIAISONS IN CALIFORNIA, STATEWIDE (FLICS)
www.film.ca.gov
E-MAIL: filmca@commerce.ca.gov

FLORIDA FILM COMMISSION
www.filminflorida.com
E-MAIL: mattingr@eog.state.fl.us

NEW YORK STATE GOVERNOR'S OFFICE FOR MOTION PICTURE & TV DEVELOPMENT
www.nylovesfilm.com
E-MAIL: nyfilm@empire.state.ny.us

AUSTRALIA
NEW SOUTH: NEW SOUTH WALES FILM & TELEVISION OFFICE
www.fto.nsw.gov.au
E-MAIL: fto@fto.nsw.gov.au

QUEENSLAND: PACIFIC FILM & TELEVISION COMMISSION
www.pftc.com.au
E-MAIL: pftc@pftc.com.au

VICTORIA: MELBOURNE FILM OFFICE
www.film.vic.gov.au/MFO/
E-MAIL: mfo@cinemedia.net

CANADA
YUKON: YUKON FILM COMMISSION
www.reelyukon.com
E-MAIL: info@reelyukon.com

(CONTINUED)

under the laws of a country that is providing a financial incentive. Distribution rights may be divided among the parties. One party may want the right to distribute the film in certain territories, or the parties may share revenue from all territories.

The selection of principal cast can be an important decision. To be eligible for some incentives, the film may need to employ cast members from certain countries. It is not unusual for an American producer to shoot abroad and bring along one or two

NUNAVUT TERRITORY/CANADA'S EASTERN ARCTIC: NUNAVUT FILM COMMISSION
E-MAIL: dmonteith@gov.nu.ca

NORTHWEST TERRITORIES (YELLOWKNIFE/ARCTIC CANADA): NORTHWEST TERRITORIES FILM COMMISSION
www.gov.nt.ca/RWED/nwtfilm
E-MAIL: garry_singer@gov.nt.ca

BRITISH COLUMBIA: BRITISH COLUMBIA FILM COMMISSION
www.bcfilmcommission.com
E-MAIL: shootbc@bcfilm.gov.bc.ca

COLUMBIA SHUSWAP: COLUMBIA SHUSWAP FILM COMMISSION
www.filmcolumbiashuswap.com
E-MAIL: elverhoy@csrd.bc.ca

OKANAGAN-SIMILKAMEEN: OKANAGAN FILM COMMISSION
www.okfilm.bc.ca
E-MAIL: inquiries@okfilm.bc.ca

THOMPSON-NICOLA: THOMPSON-NICOLA FILM COMMISSION
www.tnrd.bc.ca/tnfc/abouttnfc2.htm
E-MAIL: admin@tnrdlib.bc.ca

VICTORIA/VANCOUVER ISLAND: GREATER VICTORIA FILM COMMISSION
www.filmvictoria.com
E-MAIL: islandfilm@home.com

ALBERTA: ALBERTA FILM COMMISSION
www.albertafilm.com
E-MAIL: tblake@telusplanet.net

CALGARY: CALGARY FILM OFFICE
E-MAIL: bbasham@ceda.calgary.ab.ca

EDMONTON: EDMONTON FILM OFFICE
www.filminedmonton.com
E-MAIL: kfiske@ede.org

(CONTINUED)

American stars to enhance the value of the film. These American stars are almost always members of SAG while the locally employed actors are not, although the local actors may be members of a local union. SAG's Rule One does not allow SAG members to work for producers who are not SAG signatories. In the past, however, SAG didn't enforce this rule when a SAG actor worked abroad. As of May 1, 2002, SAG announced that it intends to strictly enforce Rule One, threatening disciplinary

FILM COMMISSIONS
(CONTINUED)

SASKATCHEWAN: SaskFILM/Locations Saskatchewan
   E-Mail: saskfilm@sk.sympatico.ca

SASKATOON: Saskatoon Regional Economic Development
   Authority
   www.buysaskatoon.com
   E-Mail: info@sreda.com

MANITOBA: Manitoba Film & Sound
   www.mbfilmsound.mb.ca
   E-Mail: explore@mbfilmsound.mb.ca

WINNEPEG: City of Winnepeg Film Commission
   510 Main St., 3rd Floor, Mayor's Office
   Winnepeg, Manitoba, MB R3B 1B9 CANADA
   (204) 986-3058
   Cellular: (204) 955-9659
   Fax: (204) 986-3350
   www.city.winnipeg.ca/filmandculture/film_office
   Visitors may email directly from the website.

ONTARIO: Ontario Film Development Corporation
   www.to-ontfilm.com
   E-Mail: gthomson@ofdc.on.ca

HAMILTON: Economic Development Department - City of
   Hamilton
   www.city.hamilton.on.ca
   E-Mail: scoverda@city.hamilton.on.ca

TORONTO: Toronto Film and Television Office
   www.to-ontfilm.com
   E-Mail: rsilvers@city.toronto.on.ca

(CONTINUED)

action against any SAG actors who work for non-signatory companies. This will force producers who are shooting abroad to either employ only non-SAG actors or become a SAG signatory with its accompanying obligations, including rules on working conditions and contributing pension and health insurance payments.

When contemplating an international co-production, it is important to consider the expectations of the parties. Are these

QUEBEC:
  ARGENTEUIL FILM AND TV COMMISSION
  www.argenteuil.qc.ca
  E-MAIL: ceeargen@citenet.net

MONTREAL FILM & TELEVISION COMMISSION
  E-MAIL: film_tv@ville.montreal.qc.ca

QUEBEC CITY FILM BUREAU & TELEVISION COMMISSION
  www.filmquebec.com
  E-MAIL: bfq@clic.net

NEW BRUNSWICK: NEW BRUNSWICK FILM
  www.nbfilm.com
  E-MAIL: nbfilm@gnb.ca

NOVA SCOTIA: NOVA SCOTIA FILM DEVELOPMENT CORPORATION
  www.film.ns.ca
  E-MAIL: novascotia.film@ns.sympatico.ca

SOUTH WEST SHORE: SOUTH WEST SHORE FILM COMMISSION
  www.yarmouth.org/swsfc
  E-MAIL: swsday@auracom.com

PRINCE EDWARD ISLAND: PRINCE EDWARD ISLAND FILM
  OFFICE
  www.gov.pe.ca
  E-MAIL: mbwood@gov.pe.ca

NEWFOUNDLAND: NEWFOUNDLAND & LABRADOR FILM
  DEVELOPMENT CORPORATION
  E-MAIL: newfilm@thezone.net

IRELAND
SCREEN COMMISSION OF IRELAND
  www.filmboard.ie
  E-MAIL: screencommirl@tinet.ie

(CONTINUED)

expectations realistic? Cultural differences can make it difficult to assess a potential partner's suitability. Parties may vary greatly in their expertise, sophistication, and experience in the movie business. Production methods may differ. The more details the parties discuss, the less room there is for misunderstandings.

The parties should discuss which partner would have the primary responsibility for producing the film. What approvals will the other party have? How will disagreements be re-

FILM COMMISSIONS
(CONTINUED)

NORTHERN IRELAND
NORTHERN IRELAND FILM COMMISSION
   www.nifc.co.uk
   E-MAIL: info@nifc.co.uk

UNITED KINGDOM
WALES:
   MID WALES FILM COMMISSION
   www.midwalesfilm.com
   E-MAIL: info@midwalesfilm.com

NORTH WALES FILM COMMISSION
   www.gwynedd.gov.uk/adrannau/economaidd/
   Uned_Ffilm/English/default.html
   E-MAIL: film@gwynedd.gov.uk

SOUTH WALES FILM COMMISSION
   E-MAIL: 106276.223@compuserve.com

ENGLAND:
   BRITISH FILM COMMISSION
   www.britfilmcom.co.uk
   E-MAIL: info@britfilmcom.co.uk

ISLE OF MAN FILM COMMISSION
   E-MAIL: filmcom@dti.gov.im

BATH FILM OFFICE
   E-MAIL: bath_filmoffice@bathnes.gov.uk

EAST MIDLANDS SCREEN COMMISSION
   www.emsc.org.uk
   E-MAIL: emsc@emsc.org.uk

LIVERPOOL FILM OFFICE
   E-MAIL: lfo@dial.pipex.com

NORTHERN SCREEN COMMISSION (NORTH ENGLAND)
   www.nsc.org.uk
   E-MAIL: nsc@nfmo.co.uk

(CONTINUED)

solved, and in which country—and under which country's laws—will they be resolved? Who will disburse production funds? Who will sign checks? What if the production goes over budget? Will there be a completion bond? Who will pay for any over-budget items? What if the currency of one partner is devalued? If a co-production is dependent on government approval and receipt of benefits, what are the precise requirements for eligibility? Are they met? If certain

SOUTH WEST SCREEN
   www.swscreen.co.uk
   E-MAIL: infosouth@swfilm.co.uk

YORKSHIRE SCREEN COMMISSION
   www.ysc.co.uk
   E-MAIL: ysc@workstation.org.uk

SCOTLAND:
   SCOTTISH SCREEN
   www.scottishscreen.com
   E-MAIL: info@scottishscreen.demon.co.uk

EDINBURGH FILM FOCUS (EDINBURGH/THE LOTHIANS/THE
   SCOTTISH BORDERS)
   www.edinfilm.com
   E-MAIL: elsio@edinfilm.co.uk

SCOTTISH HIGHLANDS AND ISLANDS FILM COMMISSION
   www.scotfilm.org
   E-MAIL: info@scotfilm.org

GERMANY
BERLIN-BRANDENBURG FILM COMMISSION
   E-MAIL: location@filmboard.de
   FFF FILMFERNSEHFONDS BAYERN GMBH (MUNICH)
   www.fff-bayern.de
   E-MAIL: Location@fff-bayern.de

FILMSTIFTUNG NORDRHEIN-WESTFALEN GMBH (NORTH RHINE -
   WESTPHALIA)
   www.filmstiftung.de
   E-MAIL: info@filmstiftung.de

FILM COMMISSION REGION STUTTGART
   www.film.region-stuttgart.de
   E-MAIL: info@film.region-stuttgart.de

FOR A MORE EXTENSIVE LIST OF FILM COMMISSIONS, GO TO THE
ASSOCIATION OF FILM COMMISSIONERS INTERNATIONAL'S WEBSITE,
www.afci.org, OR VISIT www.marklitwak.com

elements must meet nationality or residence requirements, what are those requirements? Is local content required? How is it defined? Who decides and when?

When parties from different nations co-produce a film, they need to carefully consider the tax consequences of their collaboration. Careful structuring of the collaboration may significantly reduce the tax burden on the parties. For example, a co-production between two parties may be consid-

CO-PRODUCTION CHECKLIST— ESTABLISHING A PARTNERSHIP OR LLC TO PRODUCE ONE FILM

DATE OF AGREEMENT:

PARTIES, ADDRESSES, AND PHONE NUMBERS AND THEIR ATTORNEYS OR AGENTS (SPECIFY TYPE OF ENTITY, CORP., LLC, ETC.):

CURRENT OWNER OF SCRIPT:

HAS SCRIPT BEEN OPTIONED? IF SO, FROM WHOM TO WHOM?

AUTHOR OF SCRIPT:

SCRIPT CREDIT:

PRODUCTION FINANCING (LIST CONTRIBUTIONS OF EACH INVESTING PARTY):

PARTY   AMOUNT INVESTED

DOES ANY PARTY OBTAIN DISTRIBUTION RIGHTS? LIST WITH TERRITORY:

NATURE OF PRODUCTION ENTITY:

LLC   C CORP.   S CORP.   GENERAL PARTNERSHIP
LIMITED PARTNERSHIP

ARE THERE ANY PASSIVE INVESTORS?

NAME OF DIRECTOR:

DIRECTOR'S DEAL:

—DIRECTOR'S RIGHT TO DIRECT SEQUELS OR REMAKES?

NAME(S) OF PRODUCERS AND THEIR CREDIT(S):

PRESENTATION CREDITS:

OTHER CREDITS:

BUDGET FOR PRODUCTION:

COMPLETION BOND?

WILL ESCROW ACCOUNT BE ESTABLISHED?

CONDITIONS FOR BREAKING ESCROW (APPROVALS):

DEADLINE FOR DEPOSITING FUNDS:

APPROVALS. PARTIES THAT HAVE APPROVAL OVER:

SCRIPT:

DIRECTOR:

BUDGET:

LEAD ACTORS:

CASH FLOW SCHEDULE:

SELECTION OF DISTRIBUTOR:

LINE PRODUCER:

DP:

PRODUCTION ACCOUNTANT:

(CONTINUED)

ered a partnership for tax purposes. As a partner engaged in a trade or business in the United States, a foreign national may be subject to U.S. income tax, and the partnership may be required to pay withholding tax on the foreign national's share of income. Since the U.S. tax rate may exceed what the foreign national is taxed in his country, this may be an undesirable consequence. If the deal is fashioned so that the foreign investor retains non-U.S. distribution rights, and has no U.S.

WHO ARE SIGNATORIES ON PRODUCTION ACCOUNT?

WHO SELECTS PRODUCTION ACCOUNTANT?

DIVISION OF VOTING INTERESTS:

NAME	% OF VOTING INTEREST

TOTAL: 100%

DIVISION OF NET PROFITS:

NAME	NET PROFIT %

TOTAL: 100%

WHO IS RESPONSIBLE FOR CASTING AND OTHER PREPRODUCTION EXPENSES?

NAMED INSURED(S) ON E&O POLICY:

LENGTH OF SHOOT:

DATES OF SHOOT:

WHO WILL PREPARE BUDGET?

FOREIGN SALES COMPANY:

   TERM:

   COMMISSION:

DOMESTIC DISTRIBUTOR:

TERM:

COMMISSION:

IF DISTRIBUTION NOT SET, WHO SELECTS DISTRIBUTOR(S)?

OWNERSHIP OF PICTURE:

ANY RIGHTS RESERVED:

AMOUNT OF DEFERMENTS:

DEFINITION OF DEFERMENTS:

WHO DETERMINES HOW MUCH WILL BE GRANTED IN DEFERMENTS:

RECOUPMENT OF OVERHEAD EXPENSES BY ANY PARTY?

WHO PAYS LEGAL EXPENSES? CASTING EXPENSES? OTHER PREPRODUCTION EXPENSES?

APPROVALS OVER ARTWORK AND MARKETING?

trade or business, he may avoid paying U.S. tax from income derived from the film outside the U.S.

Likewise, an American individual or company may become liable for foreign taxes. Many foreign countries withhold tax on income paid from sources in those countries to residents of other countries. The United States, however, has tax treaties with many countries that may reduce or eliminate such taxes. U.S. entities generally need to prove that they are U.S. residents to receive the treaty-reduced tax rate. The IRS will certify U.S. residency using Form 6166, which is a computer-generated letter on Treasury Department letterhead. This document, and any application forms required by a foreign country, will need to be sent to the appropriate agency in the foreign country in order to claim the benefit of a tax treaty. (See IRS Publication 686 for details at www.irs.gov).

A sample agreement between a producer and a foreign sales company to co-finance and co-produce a film is included at the end of this chapter.

PRODUCTION INCENTIVES

There are a wide variety of production incentives offered in many countries. Among the most popular are programs offered in Germany, Ireland, Luxembourg, United Kingdom, Australia, Canada, Thailand, Belgium, and the Netherlands. There are regional organizations such as MEDIA Programme of the European Union that supports the European film industry, and Eurimages, founded by the Council of Europe, which provides financing for European co-productions. The rules for participation in these programs are subject to change, and producers should regularly check with the appropriate authority for any changes in guidelines before applying.

In addition to whatever formal incentives may be offered by governments wanting to encourage production, producers should always consider the cost to shoot in a foreign country. A producer can achieve substantial savings, for instance, by shooting a film in Eastern Europe, where the cost of wages is dramatically less than Western Europe or the United States. If a producer can hire crew members or book a hotel for 20% of what those items would cost in the U.S., then the producer is receiving a benefit equivalent to an 80% subsidy. Moreover, the film-maker will avoid having to fill out complicated paperwork and pay substantial legal and accounting fees.

A listing of production incentives is included in Appendix B. An updated list is available at Entertainment Law Resources (www.marklitwak.com). Contact the appropriate agency to obtain detailed requirements before relying on this information as the rules and regulations governing incentives and subsidies are often quite complex and subject to frequent change.

The following agreement is between a foreign sales company and a producer. Both will contribute production funds. As part of the deal, the foreign sales company obtains the right to distribute the film in foreign territories.

CO-PRODUCTION AGREEMENT

Agreement dated_____, 20__, between _____ ("DISTRIBUTOR") at _____ [Distributor Address]; _____ ("PRODUCER") at _____ [Producer Address]; _____ ("INVESTOR 1") at _____ [Address]; and _____ ("INVESTOR 2") at _____ [Address].

WHEREAS, PRODUCER has the exclusive option to purchase motion picture and other rights to the original screenplay currently entitled "_____" (the "Screenplay"), which was written by _____ ("WRITER") and which will be directed by _____ ("DIRECTOR"); and

WHEREAS, PRODUCER, and DISTRIBUTOR desire to produce the Screenplay as a motion picture (the "Picture") for exploitation throughout the world; and

WHEREAS, PRODUCER desires that DISTRIBUTOR: (1) provide $_____ in production financing, and up to $_____ additional funding for cast breakage, if needed; (2) act as sales agent for the Picture and all Ancillary Productions throughout the world, except for the United States and English-speaking Canada; and (3) present and co-produce the Picture; and

WHEREAS, PRODUCER desires to establish a California limited liability company, tentatively named _____ (the "LLC"), to produce the Picture; and

WHEREAS, INVESTOR 1 desires to provide $_____ in production financing for the Picture, and up to $_____ additional for cast breakage if needed; and

WHEREAS, INVESTOR 2 desires to provide $_____ in production financing for the Picture; and

WHEREAS, DIRECTOR desires to direct the Picture; and

WHEREAS, the estimated Budget for the Picture is $_____ million cash plus another possible $_____ for cast breakage and any deferments. The cast breakage amounts and any deferments (above the $_____ budget) granted in excess of a total budget of $_____ shall be mutually approved by DISTRIBUTOR and PRODUCER.

NOW, THEREFORE, the parties hereby agree as follows:

1. FINANCING

(a)　　DISTRIBUTOR will contribute $_____ toward the production of the Picture, provided that INVESTOR 1 and INVESTOR 2 contribute a total of at least $_____ toward the production of the Picture, for a cash Budget of _____ dollars ($_____) plus cast breakage of up to _____ dollars ($_____) to be contributed by DISTRIBUTOR, and _____ ($_____) to be contributed by INVESTOR 1 for a total budget of up to _____ dollars ($_____). DISTRIBUTOR will provide its share of financing, provided that INVESTOR 1 and INVESTOR 2 secure their respective shares up to a total of $_____ or more of matching funds no later than one (1) week after the last to occur of the following: this Agreement has been signed by all parties; the parties have formed the LLC; the LLC has acquired an Option to the Screenplay from PRODUCER; DISTRIBUTOR has approved the chain of title for the Picture, and received copies of all applicable documents establishing chain of title; DISTRIBUTOR has approved the final top-sheet for the budget of the Picture (the "Budget") and accompanying cash-flow schedule referred to at Section 1(b); DISTRIBUTOR has approved the final shooting script of the Picture; and bank accounts for the production of the Picture have been opened with reputable banks. In that connection, the LLC will open two (2) bank accounts in its name at a reasonably rated bank. The first account will be a "holding" account into which the funds identified in this section will be deposited. The signatures of two (2) persons will be required in order to withdraw funds from this account. Those persons will be _____ and _____. The LLC will also establish a second account, which will be a "production" account. Funds periodically will be transferred from the "holding" account into the "production" account as required in order to fund production. All disbursements related to the production of the Picture will be made from the "production" account. The signatures of two (2) persons will be required in order to withdraw funds from this account. Those persons will be any two (2) of the following: _____, _____, _____, and the production accountant. The term "secured" shall mean that the committed funds actually have been deposited into the "holding" account.

(b)   DISTRIBUTOR, INVESTOR 1, and INVESTOR 2 will deposit their respective share of the financing into the Production Account no later than one (1) week after fulfillment of the contingencies set forth at Section 1(a). In the event that any investor fails to contribute its share of financing after fulfillment of the contingencies set forth at Section 1(a), then this Agreement shall terminate; and all funds shall be returned to each respective investor. PRODUCER shall prepare a detailed operating Budget and accompanying cashflow analysis, which shall be submitted to DISTRIBUTOR, INVESTOR 1, and INVESTOR 2. While the allocation of individual cost items within the Budget will be within PRODUCER'S discretion, DISTRIBUTOR will have approval of the overall allocation of the Budget into general cost categories (the socalled Budget "top sheet"), the cash-flow analysis, and the final shooting script, as a condition precedent to DISTRIBUTOR'S financing commitment. In connection with the Picture and/or any Ancillary Productions, as applicable, all financial and creative decisions in connection therewith shall be made by PRODUCER; provided, however, that PRODUCER and DISTRIBUTOR shall have mutual approval of the following: the final shooting script (the Picture must be shot substantially in accordance with such approved script), the selection of the domestic distributor(s), the principal cast, the director of photography, the line producer, casting director, editor, composer, and department heads. PRODUCER shall consult and obtain the approval of INVESTOR 1 and INVESTOR 2 in regard to the final shooting script and the Budget top sheet.

(c)   Voting Interests in the LLC shall be as follows:

PRODUCER: __%
DISTRIBUTOR: __%
INVESTOR 1:   __%
INVESTOR 2:   __%

The Members of the LLC shall not vote in such a manner to cause the LLC to act inconsistently with this Agreement or to breach any of its contractual obligations.

(d)   For the purposes of allocating Net Profits [defined at Section 3(c)], the "PRODUCER'S Share" of Net Profits shall be defined as 50% of 100% of all Net Profits (each percentage point of 100% of all Net Profits may be referred to as "1 point"). The "INVESTORS' Share" of Net Profits shall be defined as 50% of 100% (*i.e.*, 50 points) of Net Profits to be shared among the investors *pari passu*. PRODUCER and DISTRIBUTOR shall share the PRODUCER'S Share of Net Profits (*i.e.*, 50% of 100%, or 50 points) in equal shares, after payment to all third-party profit participants (*i.e.*, any actor or crew profit participants); and after DIRECTOR (who shall receive 5 points or 5% of 100% of Net Profits) and after WRITER (who shall receive 2.5 points or 2.5% of 100% of Net Profits). The amount of Net Profits remaining with Producers after deduction of the aforesaid participations is the "Residual Producer Net Profits"; provided, however, that in no case shall either DISTRIBUTOR or PRODUCER each receive less than 10 of the 50 PRODUCER points (*i.e.*, each shall receive not less than 10% of 100% of the Net Profits). To illustrate, if DISTRIBUTOR contributes $500,000 of a one million dollar Budget, DISTRIBUTOR would have contributed 50% of the Budget, and would thus be entitled to 50% of the Investor's Share of Net Profits (50% of 50 points = 25 points) as an investor. In addition, DISTRIBUTOR is guaranteed a minimum of 10 PRODUCER points from the PRODUCER'S 50 points. Thus, DISTRIBUTOR would receive a total minimum of 35 points, which is 35% of 100% of the Net Profits, if any. If DISTRIBUTOR contributes more production financing, then DISTRIBUTOR's share of the INVESTORS' Share of Net Profits would increase commensurately (but in any event DISTRIBUTOR'S share will not be less than the percentages set forth). To illustrate the calculation of Residual Producer Net Profits, if from the 50 points that comprise the PRODUCER'S Share of Net Profits, DIRECTOR received her 5 points for directing and WRITER received his

2.5 points for writing, and another 12.5 points were granted to the actors and crew (for a total 20 points given to these profit participants), then DISTRIBUTOR and PRODUCER would share the remaining 30 points, with each receiving 15 points.

(e)   PRODUCER and DISTRIBUTOR shall have the discretion to determine, after reasonable consultation with each other, how to allocate Net Profits to talent within the limits set forth at Section 1(d). As mentioned above, in addition to its share of Residual Producer Net Profits, DISTRIBUTOR shall share in the INVESTORS' portion of Net Profits *pari passu* with the other investors in accordance with the terms of this Agreement, after investor recoupment as set forth at Section 3(c).

(f)   In the event that DISTRIBUTOR fails to provide its portion of the financing, then PRODUCER shall have no obligation to DISTRIBUTOR for any expenses incurred by DISTRIBUTOR in its attempt to arrange financing for the Picture, and DISTRIBUTOR shall have no rights whatsoever in the Project. In the event that any of the other parties fail to provide their respective portion of the financing, then DISTRIBUTOR shall have no obligation to any of such other parties for any expenses incurred by them or any one of them in their attempts to arrange financing for the Picture.

(g)   The Budget shall include funds for a production photographer, and funds to produce as part of the delivery items both an M&E track and a D-1 master (in both NTSC and PAL formats), all music clearances, and all other items necessary to deliver the Picture to foreign licensees of rights. $_____ shall be budgeted for E&O insurance. There will be no completion bond, but the customary insurance taken by independent producers shall be secured, including (but not limited to) comprehensive general liability coverage and worker's compensation coverage. The Picture will be produced subject to _____ [applicable union] agreements, but not _____ [inapplicable unions] agreements. The Budget will include funds for an IP and an IN but not for advertising and promotion of the Picture. If DISTRIBUTOR advances any postproduction costs in DISTRIBUTOR'S sole discretion, then DISTRIBUTOR in its capacity as the Picture's foreign sales agent may recoup same from the gross proceeds (as well as any other recoupable expenses) before remitting funds to the LLC. If any party purchases E&O insurance for the Picture, all other parties (including DIRECTOR and _____) shall be added as an additional named insureds. The parties shall use DISTRIBUTOR'S E&O insurance carrier if a policy can be purchased at a reasonable price.

(h)   As set forth at Section 1(b), a Budget top sheet shall be prepared by PRODUCER and approved by DIS-TRIBUTOR. DIRECTOR shall be consulted in the preparation of the budget and it shall be subject to her approval, in accordance with the terms of her employment agreement, provided that in the event the parties cannot agree on any budget item after good-faith negotiation, DISTRIBUTOR and PRODUCER shall have the final decision on all budgetary matters. On a weekly basis during preproduction, production, and postproduction, PRODUCER, or the production accountant, shall report to DISTRIBUTOR on the previous week's expenditures and the projected expenditures for the next week. The production accountant shall be selected by DIS-TRIBUTOR and approved by PRODUCER. For the period during which the accountant is employed (estimated at 11 weeks of preproduction, production, and postproduction), all checks shall be co-signed by the production accountant (or another DISTRIBUTOR representative) and a representative of PRODUCER. The Production Account shall be located in Los Angeles. After completion of the Picture, the LLC shall establish a bank account for receipt of revenues and disbursement of funds. All checks shall be co-signed by a representative of DISTRIBUTOR and a representative of PRODUCER. The LLC shall retain an independent CPA to administer the funds and make disbursements. The cost of the CPA shall be an operating expense of the LLC.

2.   REPRESENTATION RIGHTS

(a)   In the event that DISTRIBUTOR provides all of its firmly committed share of the financing (*i.e.*, $_____ plus up to $_____ in cast breakage), then DISTRIBUTOR shall have the exclusive right in perpetuity to act as sales agent for the commercial exploitation of the Picture and all Ancillary Productions throughout the world (except for the domestic market, which is the United States and English-speaking Canada) for a sales agency fee equal to twenty percent (20%) of all gross proceeds collected by or on behalf of DISTRIBUTOR. In the event that the LLC does not license English-speaking Canada to the Picture's domestic distributor, and DISTRIBUTOR arranges for the sale of rights for English-speaking Canada, then DISTRIBUTOR shall be entitled to receive a twenty percent (20%) sales agency fee for licensing English-speaking Canada. The LLC and DISTRIBUTOR shall enter into a Sales Agency Agreement in substantially the form attached hereto as Exhibit A. DISTRIBUTOR'S marketing expenses for marketing the Picture and each Ancillary Production throughout the world excluding the United States shall be defined and limited as set forth in Exhibit A. DISTRIBUTOR may screen a trailer for the Picture beginning at the _____ [name and year of festival or market] for potential buyers of the Picture (at which time DISTRIBUTOR may start selling the Picture), and the LLC will deliver slides and elements to make a flyer and trailer for such purpose, and grant DISTRIBUTOR access thereto. The LLC will endeavor to complete the Picture no later than _____, 20__.

(b)   PRODUCER and DISTRIBUTOR shall jointly select a domestic distributor for the Picture. A domestic sales agency fee of 10% of domestic Gross Revenues may be deducted from domestic gross revenues before same are remitted to the LLC. This fee shall be divided as follows: ___ % to DISTRIBUTOR; ___% to PRODUCER; and ___% to _____ [attorney/producer rep]. The LLC shall collect all domestic revenues for disbursement as set forth herein and at Section 1(h).

3.   OWNERSHIP RIGHTS

In the event that all parties to this Agreement provide their respective share of financing, and the Picture is actually produced, then:

(a)   The LLC shall then own, exclusively and forever, throughout the Universe, all rights in and to the Screenplay (except those rights reserved to the Screenplay's author) ("Reserved Rights"), including (without limitation) all motion picture rights, all ancillary and all incidental rights, including (but not limited to) all serialization, spin-off, remake, and sequel rights to the extent heretofore or hereafter owned by PRODUCER (the "Exclusive Screenplay Rights"). The Picture, the Exclusive Screenplay Rights, and all products produced and/or derived from the Exclusive Screenplay Rights (*e.g.*, merchandising and music publishing) may hereinafter be referred to as the "Project." Products produced and/or derived from the Exclusive Screenplay Rights other than the Picture may hereinafter be referred to as "Ancillary Productions."

The following rights are reserved to the Screenplay's WRITER: radio, publication, stage rights, author-written sequel rights, and the limited right to use the characters in an author-written sequel.

(b)   In accordance with the terms of her employment agreement, DIRECTOR shall have the right of first negotiation to write and direct any sequel, remake, or ancillary productions (including TV movies and series, subject to network approval), taking into consideration normal industry standards for a director of the stature of DIRECTOR (such stature to take into account any success that may result from the Picture). DIRECTOR shall receive reasonable and customary compensation, including passive royalties (which compensation shall be at least what was paid for the original picture),on any sequels, remakes, and television spin-offs, for the writing and directing services performed on the Picture.

(c)   As used in this Agreement, the term "Net Profits" means the gross proceeds actually paid to and received by the LLC in connection with the Picture and the Project (i) after the deduction of DISTRIBUTOR'S twenty percent (20%) sales agency fee, and advertising and marketing expenses and any postproduction expense recoupment (subject to a $_____ overall cap for marketing, advertising, and other expenses, of which DISTRIBUTOR'S costs to attend film markets shall not exceed one-eighth (1/8) of all of its costs to attend film markets for all pictures represented by DISTRIBUTOR then in their first (1st) year market cycle, as set forth at Exhibit A, but there is no cap on reimbursement to DISTRIBUTOR of any reasonable direct, out-of-pocket, third-party costs incurred to manufacture and deliver elements to foreign buyers), and any domestic sales agency fee as provided for at Section 2(b), off the top; (ii) after investor recoupment of one hundred ten percent (110%) of their investment; (iii) after recoupment or payment of any other outstanding reasonable and verifiable production costs (mutually approved by DISTRIBUTOR and PRODUCER), financing costs, if any, and such other reasonable and customary costs chargeable in connection with the production and financing of the Picture (all substantial expenses to be approved by DISTRIBUTOR and PRODUCER), and Ancillary Productions (in the case of ancillary productions, pre-approved by DISTRIBUTOR and PRODUCER), as applicable; and (iv) after the deduction of such sums (if any) that are payable to any third persons (*e.g.*, deferments, residuals, and marketing expenses). PRODUCER and DISTRIBUTOR shall determine in their discretion the amount of any deferments granted (other than those deferments set forth in this Agreement, which are pre-approved).

(d)   No recoupment shall be allowed DISTRIBUTOR or PRODUCER for any general staff, overhead, or legal expenses.

(e)   DISTRIBUTOR and PRODUCER shall have mutual approval, not to be unreasonably withheld or delayed, over the marketing materials and artwork for the domestic and foreign release. DIRECTOR shall be meaningfully consulted in regard to the marketing plan and materials, including artwork, in accordance with the terms of her employment agreement.

4.   PRODUCTION

In the event that DISTRIBUTOR contributes the DISTRIBUTOR Financing, then DISTRIBUTOR shall:

(a)   In connection with the Picture and/or the Ancillary Productions, as applicable, DISTRIBUTOR shall receive the sole "presented by" credit on a single card in the opening credit scroll, the wording of which shall be determined by DISTRIBUTOR. The opening credits shall be as follows: first "_____ [name of Distributor] Presents," a single card, followed by "A _____ [name of Producer] Production," on a single card, followed by "A _____ [name of Director] Film," on a single card. PRODUCER may modify the PRODUCER card to add a credit for another entity (*e.g.*, "In Association with ABC Corporation"). The DISTRIBUTOR presentation card shall be first in order.

(b)   DISTRIBUTOR will also receive a "Produced by" credit for _____ name(s) of Distributor personnel receiving individual producer credit _____ on a single card following the presentation cards in the opening scroll, and immediately preceding either the Director credit or the "Produced by" credit to be given _____ [name(s) of Producer personnel receiving individual producer credit] on another single card. PRODUCER shall have the discretion to determine all other credits, subject to any union and guild rules, and subject to consultation with DISTRIBUTOR. While no other "Producer" credits may be given, PRODUCER and DISTRIBUTOR may grant "Executive Producer," "Co-Producer," "Associate Producer," and other similar production credits to others, all of which (if granted), shall follow DISTRIBUTOR'S producer credit in the ending scroll and precede it in the opening scroll. _____ [name of co-producer] shall receive either a sole or shared "Co-Producer" credit. _____ [name of executive producer] shall receive a shared "Executive Producer" credit. _____ [name of executive producer] shall receive a shared "Executive Producer" credit.

    (c)   Except where such matters are subject to consultation with DISTRIBUTOR or DISTRIBUTOR'S prior approval as set forth elsewhere herein, PRODUCER and DIRECTOR shall have mutual approval over the selection of all of the cast and crew (in the case of DIRECTOR, subject to the terms and conditions of DIRECTOR'S employment agreement). DIRECTOR shall be consulted in the preparation of the schedule and selection of the composer, provided that in the event that the parties cannot agree after good-faith negotiation, DISTRIBUTOR and PRODUCER shall have the final decision on such matters.

    PRODUCER shall receive a $_____ fee, $_____ up front from the production Budget, and $_____ deferred until after the investors recoup. Producer _____ [name of individual Producer] shall receive a $_____ producer fee, all of which shall be paid up front as part of the production Budget. All fees payable to co-producer _____ [name of co-producer] shall come out of the compensation otherwise payable to either PRODUCER or _____ [name of individual Producer], and shall not be separately budgeted. DIRECTOR shall receive a $_____ director fee, $_____ up front from the production Budget, and $_____ deferred until after the investors recoup. For writing the script, DIRECTOR shall receive the compensation set forth in the Option/Purchase Agreement with PRODUCER. If, and only if, the Picture is unable to be completed on Budget (*i.e.*, for $_____ cash or less unless the parties mutually agree to increase the Budget), DIRECTOR shall convert some of her aforementioned up-front fee into additional deferments on a dollar-for-dollar basis. In the aforesaid over-Budget condition, DIRECTOR shall defer up to $_____ of her up-front fee, in order to bring the production in on Budget. DIRECTOR shall only be required to defer as much of her up-front fee as needed to bring the production in on Budget. For the purpose of illustration and clarity, if part of the aforementioned up-front fee is converted into an additional deferment, DIRECTOR would receive a $_____ deferment (in addition to her pre-existing $_____ deferment), for a total deferment of $_____.

DISTRIBUTOR shall receive a $_____ producer fee, $_____ of which shall be deferred until after the investors recoup. The production legal counsel shall be _____ [name of attorney], and he shall receive a $_____ flat fee from the Budget for production legal and producing services ($_____ shall be paid up front from the production Budget and $_____ shall be deferred until after the investors recoup). _____ [name of co-producer] shall receive a co-producer fee of $_____ from the Budget.

DISTRIBUTOR shall have the right to approve all the material terms of the LLC Agreement. PRODUCER shall select the sound lab and the postproduction supervisor in consultation with DISTRIBUTOR; PRODUCER shall select the locations (the Picture will be shot almost exclusively on location rather than in a studio). The LLC shall pay for phone, fax, and other production-related expenses.

The following table summarizes compensation from the Budget, deferred compensation, and maximum possible over-Budget conversion of budgeted compensation to deferred compensation (which will reduce the "budgeted compensation" column and increase the "deferred compensation" column in the dollar amount set forth), for all parties:

Party	Budgeted Compensation	Deferred Compensation	Over-Budget Conversion
PRODUCER			
PRODUCER			
DIRECTOR			
WRITER			
DISTRIBUTOR			
CO-PRODUCER			
PRODUCTION LEGAL ATTY.			

(d)   With regard to final cut, PRODUCER and DISTRIBUTOR shall have mutual final cut. In accordance with the terms of DIRECTOR'S employment agreement, DIRECTOR shall have the creative rights guaranteed by the DGA (if applicable).

5.   TERMINATION

In the event that any party is unable to provide its share of financing in a timely fashion, the other parties shall each have the right any time thereafter before preproduction commences to terminate this Agreement on ten (10) days' prior written notice to all parties.

6. ACCOUNTINGS

(a)   Once foreign exploitation of the Picture has commenced, for the first two (2) years of exploitation, DISTRIBUTOR shall orally report sales to the LLC within thirty (30) days of the close of each film or television market at which the Picture is sold. DISTRIBUTOR shall account to the LLC for the LLC's share of revenues (pursuant to the sales agency agreement) within thirty (30) days following the close of each calendar quarter, and any monies shown to be owing the LLC shall accompany each such statement.

(b)   All monies due and payable to the LLC ("LLC Monies") paid to DISTRIBUTOR shall be deemed to be held in trust by DISTRIBUTOR. DISTRIBUTOR may deduct any funds owing to it in its capacity as sales agent prior to remitting the balance to the LLC or to the persons otherwise entitled thereto. The procedure for disbursing LLC monies is set forth at Section 1(h).

(c)   All statements and accounts rendered by DISTRIBUTOR shall be binding upon PRODUCER and not be subject to any objection unless such objection is made in writing, stating the basis thereof, within two (2) years from the date of such statement or account, and after such notice of objection, unless Demand for Arbitration is instituted within one (1) year after the date upon which DISTRIBUTOR notifies PRODUCER in writing that it denies the validity of the objection. PRODUCER shall have the right, upon giving DISTRIBUTOR thirty (30) days' prior written notice, by independent accountants, to audit DISTRIBUTOR'S books and records insofar as they relate to this Agreement, at DISTRIBUTOR'S office in _____ and during DISTRIBUTOR'S regular working hours. Such audit shall be conducted at PRODUCER'S sole cost and expense. In addition, such audit shall be conducted no more frequently than once per year, no statement may be audited more than once, and no such audit shall be conducted in a manner that will unreasonably interfere with the normal operations of DISTRIBUTOR'S business.

7. APPLICABLE LAW AND ARBITRATION

(a)   This Agreement shall be interpreted in accordance with the laws of the State of California, applicable to agreements executed and to be wholly performed therein.

(b)   Any controversy or claim arising out of or in relation to this Agreement or the validity, construction, or performance of this Agreement, or the breach thereof, shall be resolved by arbitration in accordance with the rules and procedures of the American Film Marketing Association, as said rules may be amended from time to time with rights of discovery if requested from the arbitrator. Such rules and procedures are incorporated and made a part of this Agreement by reference. If the American Film Marketing Association shall refuse to accept jurisdiction of such dispute, then the parties shall arbitrate such matter before and in accordance with the rules of the American Arbitration Association under its jurisdiction in Los Angeles before a single arbitrator familiar with entertainment law. The parties shall have the right to engage in pre-hearing discovery in connection with such arbitration proceedings if approved by the arbitrator. The parties hereto will abide by and perform any award rendered in any arbitration conducted pursuant hereto, that any court having jurisdiction thereof may issue a judgment based upon such award and that the prevailing party in such arbitration and/or confirmation proceeding shall be entitled to recover its reasonable attorneys' fees and expenses. The arbitration award shall be final, binding, and non-appealable.

8.   CURE RIGHTS

No failure by any party hereto to perform any of its obligations under this Agreement shall be deemed to be a breach of this Agreement until the non-breaching party has given the breaching party written notice of its failure to perform and such failure has not been corrected within thirty (30) days (fifteen (15) days for any non-payment of money) from and after the giving of such notice.

9.   REPRESENTATIONS AND WARRANTIES

(a)   PRODUCER hereby represents and warrants as follows:

(1)   PRODUCER has the full right and power to enter into this Agreement and to grant to DISTRIBUTOR the rights herein granted by PRODUCER to DISTRIBUTOR. Further, PRODUCER is not subject to any obligation or disability that will or might prevent or interfere with the performance and observance by PRODUCER of all of the covenants, conditions, and agreements to be performed and observed by PRODUCER hereunder. PRODUCER has not made, nor will hereafter make, any grant or assignment that will or might conflict with or impair the complete enjoyment of the rights and privileges granted to DISTRIBUTOR hereunder.

(2)   All material of any kind whatsoever included in the Screenplay shall be wholly original with PRODUCER and/or DIRECTOR, and DISTRIBUTOR'S exercise or use of any and all rights, licenses, privileges, and Screenplay material conveyed herein will not in any way infringe upon or violate the rights of privacy or publicity or constitute a libel or slander against any person, nor infringe upon the copyright, trademark, trade name, literary, dramatic, photoplay, common law rights, or other rights, whether now or hereafter recognized, of any person. Notwithstanding anything to the contrary set forth herein, PRODUCER'S representation and warranty does not extend to any material in the Screenplay that may be contributed by DISTRIBUTOR or DIRECTOR, or any changes made in the Picture by any subdistributor. Furthermore, DIRECTOR'S representation and warranty does not extend to any material in the Screenplay that may be contributed by DISTRIBUTOR or PRODUCER, or any changes made in the Picture by any subdistributor.

(3)   PRODUCER will not undertake any action that might impair PRODUCER'S and/or DISTRIBUTOR'S rights in and to the Picture and/or any Ancillary Production.

(4)   There are no claims, liens, or litigation, pending or threatened, against or relating to the Screenplay Rights or the Screenplay or any material contained therein.

(b)   DISTRIBUTOR represents and warrants that DISTRIBUTOR has the right and capacity to enter into this Agreement, that DISTRIBUTOR is not currently insolvent.

(c)   Each party hereto (the "indemnitor") shall defend and indemnify and hold the other parties ("indemnitees") free and harmless from and against any claim inconsistent with any agreement, material representation, and/or warranty made by the indemnitor in this Agreement and shall promptly reimburse the indemnitees for any sums, including (but not limited to) reasonable attorneys' fees and expenses expended by the indemnitees in defending any such claims.

10. NOTICES

(a)   All notices, documents, or payments that PRODUCER may be required or desire to serve upon DISTRIBUTOR may be served by depositing same, postage prepaid, in any mail box, chute or other receptacle authorized by the United States Postal Service for mail addressed to DISTRIBUTOR at the address set forth on page 1 hereof, or at such other address as

DISTRIBUTOR may from time to time designate by written notice to PRODUCER, or, alternately, such notices or documents may be transmitted by facsimile to _____ or to such other number (if operable) as DISTRIBUTOR may from time to time designate by written notice to PRODUCER with a copy to be sent by mail. The date of service of any notice or document deposited in the mail shall be deemed to be the date of deposit. A courtesy copy of all notices to DISTRIBUTOR shall be sent to _____ [name of Distributor's attorney], _____ [attorney's address and fax number].

(b)   All notices, documents, or payments that DISTRIBUTOR may be required or desire to serve upon PRODUCER may be served by depositing same, postage prepaid, in any mail box, chute, or other receptacle authorized by the United States Postal Service for mail addressed to PRODUCER at the address set forth on page 1 hereof, or at such other address as PRODUCER may from time to time designate by written notice to DISTRIBUTOR, or, alternately, such notices or documents may be transmitted by facsimile to _____ (if operable) or to such other number (if operable) as PRODUCER may from time to time designate by written notice to DISTRIBUTOR with a copy to be sent by mail. The date of service of any notice or document deposited in the mail shall be deemed to be the date of deposit. A courtesy copy of all notices to PRODUCER shall be sent to _____ [name of producer's attorney/production legal counsel], at _____ [attorney's address and fax number].

11. MISCELLANEOUS

(a)   This Agreement supersedes all prior negotiations, understandings, and agreements between the parties hereto, and both parties acknowledge that neither party shall rely on any representations or promises in connection with this Agreement or the subject matter hereof not contained herein, except that the terms of the attached Exhibits and all other agreements referred to herein shall not be negated by the terms of this paragraph. This Agreement may not be modified or waived except by a writing signed on behalf of the party to be charged.

(b)   All signatories to this Agreement hereby acknowledge that they have read this Agreement, fully understand the terms and conditions contained herein, and have been given the opportunity to consult legal representation prior to execution of same.

(c)   Should any paragraph or provision of this Agreement be held to be void, invalid, or inoperative, such decision shall not affect any other paragraph or provision hereof, and the remainder of this Agreement shall be effective as though such void, invalid, or inoperative provision had not been contained herein.

(d)   This Agreement may be executed contemporaneously in counterparts and transmitted by facsimile, each copy of which shall be deemed an original, but all of which together shall constitute one and the same instrument.

DISTRIBUTOR:

_____

By: _____
Its: _____

PRODUCER:

_____

By: _____
Its: _____

INVESTOR 1:

_____

By: _____
Its: _____

INVESTOR 2:

_____

By: _____
Its: _____

EXHIBIT A1

Distributor Sales Agency Agreement[1]

> *An example of this type of contract may be found in Chapter 6, page 184 (Distribution Agreement).*

---

[1] Since the foreign sales company is obtaining the right to distribute the picture in certain territories, that distribution agreement is attached as an exhibit to principal agreement.

CHAPTER 3

FINANCING INDEPENDENT FILMS

Independent films can be financed in a variety of ways. In addition to a filmmaker using his own funds to make a movie, the most common methods are 1) loans; 2) borrowing against pre-sales (a loan against distribution contracts); 3) investor financing; and 4) distributor-supplied financing.

LOANS

Loans can be secured or unsecured. A secured loan is supported or backed by security or collateral. When one takes out a car or home loan, the loan is secured by that property. If the person who borrows money fails to repay the loan, the creditor may take legal action to have the collateral sold and the proceeds applied to pay off the debt.

An unsecured loan has no particular property backing it. Credit card debt and loans from family or friends may be unsecured. If a debtor defaults on an unsecured loan, the creditor can sue for repayment and force the sale of the debtor's assets to repay the loan. If the debtor has many debts, however, the sale of his property may not be sufficient to satisfy all creditors. In such a case, creditors may end up receiving only a small portion of the money owed them.

A secured creditor is in a stronger position to receive repayment. In the event of a default, designated property (the secured property) will be sold and all the proceeds will be applied first to repay the secured creditor's debt. Unsecured creditors will share in whatever is left, if anything.

The advantage of a loan, from a legal point of view, is that the transaction can often be structured in a fairly simple and inexpensive manner. A short promissory note can be used, and the transaction often is not subject to the complex security laws that govern many investments. Thus, there is usually no need to prepare a private placement memorandum (PPM). Keep in mind that if the agreement between the parties is labeled a "loan" but in reality is an investment, the courts will likely view the transaction as an investment. Giving a creditor a "piece of the back-end," or otherwise giving the creditor equity in the project, makes the transaction look like an investment.

The difference between a loan and an investment has to do with risk. With a loan, the entity that borrows funds, the debtor, is obligated to repay the loan and whatever interest is charged, regardless of whether the film is a flop or a hit. The creditor earns interest but does not share in the upside potential (*i.e.,* profits) of a hit. Since the creditor is entitled to be repaid even if the film is a flop, the creditor does not share in the risk of the endeavor. Of course, there is some risk with a loan because loans are not always repaid, especially unsecured loans that don't have any collateral backing them. That risk is minimal, however, compared to the risk of an equity investment.

PROMISSORY NOTE

Date: _____. $_____ (Loan Amount)

    FOR GOOD AND VALUABLE CONSIDERATION, receipt of which is hereby acknowledged, I _____ (Payor Name) ("Payor"), for myself individually, promise to pay to _____ (Payee Name) ("Payee"), at _____ (Payee Address), or at such other place as Payee may designate, the sum of _____ dollars ($_____) plus interest at the rate of ____ percent (____%) per annum payable at a minimum of _____ dollars ($_____) per year. In any given month, a minimum of _____ dollars ($_____) shall be paid in payments of no more than two payments per month in the amount of no less than _____ dollars ($_____) per payment. Once _____ dollars ($_____) has been paid in any given year, no additional payments need be paid during the course of that calendar year. There is no penalty for making additional payments.

If the Payor fails to make payments as provided, then Payee shall provide written notice to Payor, who shall have ten (10) days from the date of such notice to cure the default.

Payments hereunder shall continue until the total principal amount and any interest due is paid.

The obligation to pay money hereunder shall be secured by all of my right, title, and interest in _____, in which I have an interest.

This promissory note is executed in connection with an agreement dated _____.

This promissory note is payable in lawful money of the United States of America. Should any action be commenced to enforce the terms hereof, such shall be by arbitration before a single arbitrator in _____ (city and state) pursuant to the rules of the American Arbitration Association. The prevailing party shall be entitled to recover all reasonable attorneys' fees and costs incurred. Service on Payor can be by any method approved by the Code of Civil Procedure of the State of _____ and by mailing any Demand for Arbitration to Payor at _____ (Payor Address) or any update of those addresses supplied to Payee by Payor. Payor will not defend such arbitration on any grounds other than whether Payor has been fully credited for the payments that Payor has made to Payee.

_____ (Payor Name)

_____
Signature

PROMISSORY NOTE WITH GUARANTEE

Repayment of this promissory note is guaranteed by another person or company. If the borrower fails to repay the loan, the lender can proceed against the guarantor for repayment.

PROMISSORY NOTE WITH GUARANTEE

_____ (City), _____ (State)

For value received, _____ (Name of Maker/Borrower) of _____ (Maker Address), herein referred to as Maker, promises to pay to the order of _____ (Name of Lender) of _____ (Lender Address), his/her successors and assigns, herein referred to as Holder, the sum of _____ dollars ($_____) in installments as follows: _____ dollars ($_____) (First Installment Amount) by _____ (due date for first installment), _____ dollars ($_____) per month to be applied against the remaining balance of _____ dollars ($_____) (Balance after first installment) commencing with the second payment of _____ dollars ($_____) (Second Installment Amount) on _____ (Second Installment due date), the third payment of _____ dollars ($_____) (Third Installment Amount) on _____ (Third Installment due date), the fourth payment of _____ dollars ($_____) (Fourth Installment Amount) on _____ (Fourth Installment due date), and a fifth payment of _____ dollars ($_____) (Fifth Installment Amount) on _____ (Fifth Installment due date), together with a delinquency charge on each installment in default for ten (10) days in an amount equal to ten percent (10%) of such installment but not less than ten dollars ($10.00). The obligation to make these payments shall be discharged when they are received by Holder or his attorney.

1. Acceleration of Maturity: In the event of default in the payment of any of the installments or interest when due as herein provided, time being of the essence hereof, Holder may without notice or demand declare the entire principal sum then unpaid immediately due and payable. Further, if Maker should at any time fail in business or become insolvent, or commit an act of bankruptcy, or if any writ of execution, garnishment,

attachment, or other legal process is issued against any deposit account or other property of Maker, or if any assessment for taxes against Maker, other than taxes on real property, is made by the federal or state government, or any department thereof, or if Maker fails to notify Holder of any material change in his financial condition, all of the obligations of Maker shall, at the option of Holder, become due and payable immediately without demand or notice.

2.   Any controversy or claim arising out of or relating to this agreement or any breach thereof shall be settled by arbitration in accordance with the Rules of the American Arbitration Association for expedited arbitration before an arbitrator; and judgment upon the award rendered by the arbitrators may be entered in any court having jurisdiction thereof. The prevailing party shall be entitled to reimbursement for costs and reasonable attorneys' fees. The determination of the arbitrator in such proceeding shall be final, binding, and non-appealable. This agreement is entered into and shall be construed and interpreted in accordance with the laws of the State of

_____.

3.   Collection Costs: Maker shall pay a reasonable collection charge should this note be referred to a collection agency.

4.   Waiver of Rights by Maker: Maker hereby waives presentment, demand, protest, notice of dishonor, and/or protest and notice of non-payment.

5.   Interest on Unpaid Amounts: All sums remaining unpaid on the agreed or accelerated date of maturity of the last installment shall thereafter bear interest at the rate of ten percent (10%) per year.

In Witness whereof, this note and agreement has been executed at _____ (City), _____ (State), on _____ (Date of execution).

_____ (Maker Name)

_____
Signature

GUARANTEE

_____ (Guarantor Name) ("Guarantor") hereby guarantees payment of the above. Guarantor agrees that the Holder may proceed against Guarantor directly and independently of the Maker, and that the cessation of the liability of the Maker for any reason other than full payment, or any extension, renewal, forbearance, change of rate of interest, or acceptance, release, or substitution of security, or any impairment or suspension of the Holder's remedies or rights against the Maker, shall not in any way affect the liability of Guarantor.

Dated: _____ (Date of execution)

_____ (Guarantor Name)

_____
Signature

STATE OF   )
) ss.:
COUNTY OF   )

On the _____ day of _____, 20__, before me personally came _____ to me known and known to be the individual described in and who executed the foregoing instrument, and he/she did duly acknowledge to me that he/she executed the same.

_____
Notary Public

BORROWING AGAINST PRE-SALE AGREEMENTS

In a pre-sale agreement, a buyer licenses or pre-buys movie distribution rights for a territory before the film has been produced. The deal works something like this: Filmmaker Henry, or his sales agent, approaches Distributor Juan to sign a contract to buy the right to distribute Henry's next film. Henry gives Juan a copy of the script and tells him the names of the principal cast members.

Juan has distributed several of Henry's films in the past. He paid $50,000 for the right to distribute Henry's last film in Spain. The film did reasonably well and Juan feels confident, based on Henry's track record, the script, and the proposed cast, that his next film should also do well in Spain. Juan is willing to license Henry's next film sight-unseen before it has been produced. By buying distribution rights to the film now, Juan is obtaining an advantage over competitors who might bid for it. Moreover, Juan may be able to negotiate a lower license fee than what he would pay if the film were sold on the open market. So Juan signs a contract agreeing to buy Spanish distribution rights to the film. Juan does not have to pay (except if a deposit is required) until completion and delivery of the film to him.

Henry now takes this contract, and a dozen similar contracts with buyers, to the bank. Henry asks the bank to lend him money to make the movie with the distribution contracts as collateral. Henry is "banking the paper." The bank will not lend Henry the full face value of the contracts, but instead will discount the paper and lend a smaller sum. So if the contracts provide for a cumulative total of $1,000,000 in license fees, the bank might lend Henry $800,000.

Henry uses the loan from the bank to produce his film. When the movie is completed, he delivers it to the companies that have already licensed it. They in turn pay their license fees to Henry's bank to retire Henry's loan. The bank receives repayment of its loan plus interest. The buyers receive the right to distribute the film in their territory. Henry can now license the film in territories that remain unsold. From these revenues Henry makes his profit.

Juan's commitment to purchase the film must be unequivocal, and his company financially secure, so that a bank is willing to lend Henry money on the strength of Juan's promise and ability to pay. If the contract merely states that the buyer will review and consider purchasing the film, this commitment is not strong enough to borrow against. Banks want to be assured that the buyer will accept delivery of the film as long as it meets certain technical standards, even if artistically the film is a disappointment. The bank will also want to know that Juan's company is fiscally solid and likely to be in business when it comes time for it to pay the license fee. If Juan's company has been in business for many years, and if the company has substantial assets on its balance sheet, the bank will usually lend against the contract.

In some circumstances, banks are willing to lend more than the face value of the contracts. This is called gap financing, and since the bank is assuming a greater risk of not being repaid its loan, higher fees are charged. Gap financing is helpful if the filmmaker is unable to secure enough pre-sales

---

ENTERTAINMENT FINANCE COMPANIES

BANK OF AMERICA NT COMMERCIAL BANKING
ENTERTAINMENT OFFICE
CONTACT: KAPIL SHARMA
2049 CENTURY PARK EAST, SUITE 200
LOS ANGELES, CA 90067
TEL (310) 785-6015 FAX (310) 785-6100
(FOR PRODUCTIONS OF $5,000,000 OR MORE)

UNION BANK OF CALIFORNIA
CONTACT: CHRISTINE BALL
495 S. FIGUEROA, 16TH FLOOR
LOS ANGELES, CA 90071
TEL (213) 236-5828 FAX (213) 236-5852

J.P. MORGAN ENTERTAINMENT IND. GROUP
CONTACT: JOHN W. MILLER, MANAGING DIRECTOR;
P. CLARK HALLREN, CHRISTA THOMAS, KENNETH R.
WILSON, VPS; ELIZABETH FJELSTUL, ASSOCIATE;
DAVID SHAHEEN, ANALYST
1800 CENTURY PARK EAST, SUITE 400
LOS ANGELES, CA 90067
TEL (310) 788-5600 FAX (310) 788-5629

CITY NATIONAL BANK ENTERTAINMENT DIVISION
CONTACT: DANIEL ZBOJNIEWICZ, SR. VP
400 N. ROXBURY DR., 4TH FLOOR
BEVERLY HILLS, CA 90210
TEL (310) 888-6183 FAX (310) 888-6159

(CONTINUED)

to cover the loan. The bank lends more than the amount of pre-sales based on its belief that the gap will be covered when unsold territories are licensed. Before agreeing to supply gap financing, the bank will carefully review the existing pre-sales and extrapolate from those sales an estimate as to what other territories might fetch. The estimate might be based on the bank's experience that a film licensed to Italy for $150,000 usually fetches $100,000 in Spain. Of course, there is no guarantee that when the film is completed that a Spanish buyer will license the film, so the bank wants to see projected revenue that is at least twice the amount of any gap. This ensures that even if some territories remain unsold, the gap is likely to be covered. Moreover, the bank will rely on the reputation and track record of the sales agent and/or producer in judging whether these estimates are realistic. Banks may decline to lend funds based on projections from a sales agent with a history of overly optimistic projections.

The bank often insists on a completion bond to ensure that the filmmaker has sufficient funds to

ENTERTAINMENT FINANCE COMPANIES
(CONTINUED)

MERCANTILE NATIONAL BANK ENTERTAINMENT
   INDUSTRIES DIVISION
   CONTACT: MELANIE KRINSKY, EXEC. VP
   1840 CENTURY PARK EAST
   LOS ANGELES, CA 90067
   TEL (310) 282-6708 FAX (310) 788-0669

LEWIS HOROWITZ ORGANIZATION
   CONTACT: LEW HOROWITZ, PRES.; ARTHUR STRIBLEY,
   SR. VP; BRENDA DOLBY, VP
   1840 CENTURY PARK EAST, 2ND FLOOR
   LOS ANGELES, CA 90067
   TEL (310) 275-7171 FAX (310) 275-8055

COMERICA ENTERTAINMENT GROUP
   CONTACT: MORGAN RECTOR, PRES.
   9777 WILSHIRE BLVD., 4TH FLOOR
   BEVERLY HILLS, CA 90212
   TEL (310) 281-2400 FAX (310) 281-2476

NEWMARKET CAPITAL GROUP LP
   CONTACT: CHRIS BALL, WILL TYRER, CO-FOUNDERS
   202 N. CANON DR.
   BEVERLY HILLS, CA 90210
   TEL (310) 858-7472 FAX (310) 858-7473

HSBC BANK USA
   CONTACT: DAVID C. WALKER
   16311 VENTURA BLVD., SUITE 120
   ENCINO, CA 91436
   TEL (818) 386-1715 FAX (818) 386-1556

finish the film. Banks are not willing to take much risk. They know that Juan's commitment to buy Henry's film is contingent on delivery of a completed film. But what if Henry goes over budget and cannot finish the film? If Henry doesn't deliver the film, Juan is not obligated to pay for it, and the bank is not repaid its loan.

To avoid this risk, the bank wants a completion guarantor, a type of insurance company, to agree to put up any money needed to complete the film should it go over budget. Before issuing a bond, a completion guarantor will carefully review the proposed budget and the track record of key production personnel. Unless the completion guarantor is confident that the film can be brought in on budget, no completion bond will be issued.

First-time filmmakers may find it difficult to finance their films based on pre-sales. With no track record of successful films to their credit, they may not be able to persuade a distributor to pre-buy their work. How does the distributor know that the filmmaker can produce something their audiences will want to see? Of course, if the other elements are strong, the distributor may be persuaded to take that risk. For example, even though the filmmaker may be a first-timer, if the script is from an acclaimed writer, and several big-name actors will participate, the overall package may be attractive.

INVESTOR FINANCING

An equity investment can be structured in a number of ways. For example, an investor could be a stockholder in a corporation, a non-managing member of a Limited Liability Company (LLC), or a limited partner in a partnership.

An investor shares in potential rewards as well as the risks of failure. If a movie is a hit, the investor is entitled to receive his investment back and share in proceeds as well. Of course, if the movie is a flop, the investor may lose his entire investment. The producer is not obligated to repay an investor his loss.

Securities are the interests of those who do not manage the enterprise they invest in. These investors may be described using a variety of terms, including silent partners, limited partners, passive investors, and stockholders. They are putting money into a business that they are not managing (*i.e.*, not running). State and federal securities laws are designed to protect such investors by ensuring that the people managing the business (*e.g.*, the general partners in a partnership or the officers and directors of a corporation) do not defraud investors by giving them false or misleading information, or by failing to disclose information that a reasonably prudent investor would want to know.

In a limited partnership agreement, for example, investors (limited partners) put up the money needed to produce a film.

Because limited partnership interests are considered securities, they are subject to state and federal securities laws. These laws are complex and have strict requirements. A single technical violation can subject general partners to liability. Therefore, it is important that filmmakers retain an attorney with experience in securities work and familiarity with the entertainment industry. This is one area where filmmakers should not attempt to do it themselves.

Registration and Exemptions

The federal agency charged with protecting investors is the U.S. Securities and Exchange Commission (SEC). Various state and federal laws require that most securities be registered with state and/or federal governments. Registration for a public offering is time-consuming and expensive, and not a realistic alternative for most low-budget filmmakers. Filmmakers can avoid the expense of registration if they qualify for one or more statutory exemptions. These exemptions are generally restricted to private placements, which entail approaching people one already knows (*i.e.*, the parties have a pre-existing relationship). Compare a private placement with a public offering where offers can be made to strangers, such as soliciting the public at large through advertising. Generally, a public offering can only be made after the U.S. Securities and Exchange Commission (SEC) has reviewed and approved it.

There are a variety of exemptions to federal registration. For example, there is an exemption for intrastate offerings that are limited to investors who all reside within one state. To qualify for the intrastate offering exemption, a company must: be incorporated in the state where it is offering the securities, and it must carry out a significant amount of its business in that state. There is no fixed limit on the size of the offering or the number of purchasers. Relying solely on this exemption can be risky, however, because if an offer is made to a single non-resident, the exemption could be lost.

Under SEC Regulation D (Reg. D) there are three exemptions from federal registration. These can permit filmmakers to offer and sell their securities without having to register the securities with the SEC. These exemptions are under Rules 504, 505, and 506 of Regulation D. While companies relying on a Reg. D exemption do not have to register their securities and usually do not have to file reports with the SEC, they must file a document known as Form D when they first sell their securities. This document gives notice of the names and addresses of the company's owners and promoters. State laws also apply, and the offeror will likely need to file a document with the appropriate state agency for every state in which an investor resides.

Investors considering an investment in an offering under Reg. D can contact the SEC's Public Reference Branch at (202) 942-8090 or send an email to publicinfo@sec.gov to determine whether a company has filed Form D, and to obtain a copy. A potential investor may also want to check with his/her state regulator to see if the offering has complied with state regulations. State regulators can be contacted through the North American Securities Administrators Association at (202) 737-0900 or by visiting its website at www.nasaa.org/nassa/abtnasaa/find_regulator.asp. Information about the SEC's registration requirements and exemptions is available at www.sec.gov/info/smallbus/qasbsec.htm.

An "offering" is usually comprised of several documents including a private placement memorandum (PPM), a proposed limited partnership agreement (or operating agreement for an LLC, or bylaws for a corporation), and an investor questionnaire used to determine if the investor is qualified to invest. A PPM contains the type of information usually found in a business plan, and a whole lot more. It is used to disclose the essential facts that a reasonable investor would want to know before making an investment. The offeror may be liable if there are any misrepresentations in the PPM, or any omissions of material facts.

State registration can be avoided by complying with the requirements for limited offering exemptions under state law. These laws are often referred to as "Blue Sky" laws. They were enacted after the stock market crash that occurred during the Great Depression. They are designed to protect investors from being duped into buying securities that are worthless—backed by nothing more than the blue sky.

The above-mentioned federal and state exemptions may restrict offerors in several ways. Sales are typically limited to 35 non-accredited investors, and the investors may need to have a pre-existing relationship with the issuer (or investment sophistication adequate to understand the transaction), the purchasers cannot purchase for resale, and advertising or general solicitation is generally not permitted. There is usually no numerical limit on the number of accredited investors.

A "pre-existing relationship" is defined as any relationship consisting of personal or business contacts of a nature and duration such as would enable a reasonably prudent purchaser to be aware of the character, business acumen, and general business and financial circumstances of the person with whom the relationship exists.

Other documents may need to be filed with federal and state governments. For example, a Certificate of Limited Partnership may need to be filed with the Secretary of State to establish a partnership. In California, a notice of the transaction and consent to service of process is filed with the Department of Corporations. If the transaction is subject to federal law, Form D will need to be filed with the Securities and Exchange Commission (SEC) soon after the first and last sales. Similar forms may need to be filed in every state in which any investor resides.

In the independent film business, PPMs are usually: a Rule 504 offering to raise up to $1,000,000; or a Rule 505 offering, which allows the filmmaker to raise up to $5,000,000; or a Rule 506 offering, which doesn't have a monetary cap on the amount of funds to be raised. A 506 offering also offers the advantage of preempting state laws under the provisions of the National Securities Markets Improvement Act of 1996 ("NSMIA").

504 Offering

Under Rule 504, offerings may be exempt from registration for companies when they offer and sell up to $1,000,000 of their securities in a 12-month period.

A company can use this exemption so long as it is not a so-called "blank check" company, which is one that has no specific business plan or purpose. The exemption generally does not allow companies to solicit or advertise to the public, and purchasers receive restricted securities, which they cannot sell to others without registration or an applicable exemption.

Under certain limited circumstances, Rule 504 does permit companies to make a public offering of tradable securities: for example, if a company registers the offering exclusively in states that require a publicly filed registration statement and delivery of a substantive disclosure document to investors; or if the company sells exclusively according to state law exemptions that permit general solicitation, provided the company sells only to accredited investors.

505 Offering

Under a Rule 505 exemption, a company can offer and sell up to $5,000,000 of its securities in any 12-month period. It may sell to an unlimited number of "accredited investors" and up to 35 non-accredited investors who do not need to satisfy the sophistication or wealth standards associated with other exemptions. The company must inform investors that they are receiving restricted securities that cannot be sold for at least a year without registering them. General solicitation and advertising is prohibited.

Rule 505 allows companies to decide what information to give to accredited investors, so long as it does not violate the anti-fraud prohibitions of federal securities laws. But companies must give non-accredited investors disclosure documents that are comparable to those used in registered offerings. If a company provides information to accredited investors, it must provide the same information to non-accredited investors. The offeror must also be available to answer questions from pro-spective investors.

506 Offering

Under Rule 506, one can raise an unlimited amount of capital. However, the offeror cannot engage in any public solicitation or advertising. The number of accredited investors who can participate is unlimited. However, only 35 non-accredited investors can participate.

Accredited investors include (among others) the following:

a. any natural persons whose individual net worth, or joint net worth with that person's spouse, at the time of the purchase exceeds $1,000,000;

b. any natural person with an individual income in the two prior years and an estimated income in the current year in excess of $200,000 or joint income with spouse of $300,000;

c. any director, executive officer, or general partner of the issuer of the securities being offered or sold, or any director, executive officer, or partner of a general partner of the issuer.

Under Rule 506, each purchaser of units must be "sophisticated," as that term is defined under federal law. Note that an "accredited investor" is not the same as a "sophisticated" investor. The term "accredited investor" is specifically defined by the federal securities laws, while the term "sophisticated investor" has no precise legal definition. Both terms generally refer to an investor who has a sufficiently high degree of financial knowledge and expertise such that he/she does not need the protections afforded by the SEC. An investor who is considered "sophisticated" might not meet the precise definition of an accredited investor.

As with Rule 505 offerings, it is up to the offeror to decide what information is given to accredited investors, provided there is no violation of the anti-fraud provisions. Non-accredited investors must be given disclosure documents similar to those used in registered offerings. If the offeror provides information to accredited investors, the same information must be given to non-accredited investors. The offeror must be available to answer questions by prospective purchasers.

Under Rule 506, each purchaser must represent that he or she is purchasing the units for his or her own investment only and not with plans to sell or otherwise distribute the units. The units purchased are "restricted" and may not be resold by the investor except in certain circumstances.

Intrastate Offering Exemption

Section 3(a)(11) of the Securities Act provides for an intrastate offering exemption. This exemption is designed for the financing of local businesses. To qualify for the intrastate offering exemption, a company needs to be incorporated in the state where it is offering the securities, carry out a significant amount of its business in that state, and make offers and sales only to residents of that state.

There is no fixed limit on the size of the offering or the number of purchasers. The company needs to carefully determine the residence of each purchaser. If any of the securities are offered or sold to even one out-of-state person, the exemption may be lost. Moreover, if an investor resells any of the securities to a person who resides out of state within a short period of time after the company's offering is complete (the usual test is nine months), the entire transaction, including the original sales, might violate the Securities Act.

Accredited Investor Exemption

Section 4(6) of the Securities Act exempts from registration offers and sales of securities to accredited investors when the total offering price is less than $5,000,000.

The definition of accredited investors is the same as that used under Regulation D. Like the exemptions in Rule 505 and 506, this exemption does not permit any public solicitation. There are no document delivery requirements but the anti-fraud provisions mentioned below do apply.

California Limited Offering Exemption

SEC Rule 1001 exempts from registration offers and sales of securities, in amounts of up to $5,000,000, which satisfies the conditions of Section 25102(n) of the California Corporations Code. This California law exempts from California state law registration offerings made by California companies to "qualified purchasers" whose characteristics are similar to, but not the same as, accredited investors under Regulation D. This exemption allows some methods of general solicitation prior to sales.

Anti-Fraud Provisions

All security offerings, even those exempt from registration under Reg. D, are subject to the anti-fraud provisions of the federal securities laws and any applicable state anti-fraud provisions. Consequently, the offeror will be responsible for any false or misleading statements, whether oral or written. Those who violate the law can be pursued criminally and civilly. Moreover, an investor who has purchased a security on the basis of misleading information, or the omission of relevant information, can rescind the investment agreement and obtain a refund of his/her investment.

DISTRIBUTOR SUPPLIED FINANCING

Established filmmakers with a successful track record may not need to seek financing from private investors. Many major and mini-major studios are willing to supply all the production funds needed in return for ownership of the picture. Of course, there are strings attached. The distributor will often insist on having the right to modify the script and the right to determine the final cut of the motion picture based on it.

In seeking financing from studios, a filmmaker usually needs to assemble a package with impressive elements attached that can be produced on a reasonable budget. The elements that matter most are name actors, a director with a track record, and a solid script.

When a distributor finances production, the filmmaker typically receives a fee for his services (*i.e.*, writing, directing, producing), and may also receive additional payments such as deferments, box office bonuses, and net profit participation. The amount of compensation the filmmaker can obtain depends on the filmmaker's stature in the industry and the desirability of the project.

FINDERS

Producers sometimes use intermediaries, or finders, to help them raise funds. Finders are subject to the same state and federal restrictions as the offeror. Finders can introduce the offeror to a potential investor, but cannot negotiate for the offeror. Finders often receive 5% or less of the financing they find. When large sums are secured, the finder's fee may be determined according to a sliding scale. For example, the finder might receive 5% of the funds raised for the first one million, four percent for the second million, and so forth.

Here is a sample finder agreement:

FINDER AGREEMENT

THIS AGREEMENT, made and entered into as of _____
(Date), by and between _____
("Finder") and _____ ("Producer"),
with respect to the following facts:

Producer owns, controls, or otherwise has the right to produce a screenplay tentatively entitled _____
(title of screenplay) written by _____ (screenplay author).

Finder is a company engaged in financing and distribution activities in the motion picture business.

The parties want to enter an agreement whereby Finder would be encouraged to introduce Producer to third parties (herein collectively referred to as the "Financier" or "Financiers") who may be interested in lending for, investing in, or in any other way financing all or a portion of development, production, and/or distribution of a Picture ("Picture") based on the Screenplay.

WHEREFORE, for good and valuable consideration, the parties agree as follows:

1. SERVICES, TERM: Commencing on the date hereof, and continuing until the earlier of: (a) termination by either party of this Agreement; or (b) the execution of an agreement between Producer (or any designee, assignee, transferee, or other successor-in-interest of Producer in or to the Screenplay and/or Picture, collectively referred to hereinafter as "Producer")

and a Financier, Finder shall use its best efforts to introduce Producer to parties who may be interested in financing, investing, or lending money with respect to the production of the Picture or in otherwise becoming a Financier. The foregoing period of time is hereinafter referred to as the "Term."

2. COMPENSATION: If at any time during the Term or any time thereafter Producer enters into any agreement with any Financier to invest in, lend for, or finance production and/or distribution of the Picture, then Finder shall receive an amount equal to _____ percent (___%) of the amount of any funds, credits, or other consideration paid or lent by Financiers to Producer and used by Producer in the development and Production of the Picture, provided that the amounts paid to Finder shall not exceed a total of _____ dollars ($_____). Finder shall receive his/her Commission when Producer has the right to use the amounts provided by financier(s).

3. NO OBLIGATION: Nothing in this agreement shall obligate Producer to enter into an agreement with any Financiers.

4. NO SALE OF SECURITIES: Finder agrees not to sell or offer to sell securities related to investing in the development and/or production of the Picture. Finder agrees to indemnify and hold Producer harmless from all damage and expense (including reasonable attorneys' fees) upon a breach or claim of breach of this provision.

5. RELATIONSHIP OF THE PARTIES: Finder is an independent contractor and shall not act as an employee, agent, or broker of Producer.

6. FINDER'S REPRESENTATIONS AND WARRANTIES:

Finder represents and warrants to Producer that the following statements are true and correct in all respects:

(a) Finder is in the business of arranging financing of motion pictures, has substantial experience in said business, is not insolvent or in any danger of insolvency or bankruptcy, and is not in dissolution proceedings.

(b) Finder represents and warrants to Producer that finder has the full and complete authority to enter into this agreement, and that there is no outstanding claim or litigation pending against Finder.

If Finder breaches any of its warranties and representations, or otherwise breaches this agreement, Producer, in addition to its other equitable and legal remedies, may rescind this agreement and recover any reasonable amounts expended by Producer in developing or exploiting this property with Finder, and reasonable attorneys' fees. Finder shall at all times indemnify and hold Producer, its licensees, assignees, officers, employees, and agents harmless against and from any and all claims, damages, liabilities, costs, and expenses, including reasonable attorneys' fees arising out of any breach or alleged breach by Finder of any representation, warranty, or other provision hereof.

7. ADDITIONAL DOCUMENTS: Finder agrees to execute, acknowledge, and deliver to Producer and to procure the execution, acknowledgment, and delivery to Producer of any additional documents or instruments that Producer may reasonably require to fully effectuate and carry out the intent and purposes of this agreement.

8. ARBITRATION: Any controversy or claim arising out of or relating to this Agreement or the validity, construction, or performance of this Agreement or the breach thereof, shall be resolved by arbitration according to the rules and procedures of the American Arbitration Association, as they may be amended. Such rules and procedures are incorporated herein and made a part of this Agreement by reference. The parties agree that they will abide by and perform any award rendered in any such arbitration, and that any court having jurisdiction may issue a judgment based upon the award. Moreover, the prevailing party shall be entitled to reimbursement of reasonable attorneys' fees and costs.

9. ASSIGNMENT: Finder shall not have the right to assign this agreement or any part hereof.

10. SECTION HEADINGS: The headings of paragraphs, sections and other subdivisions of this agreement are for convenient reference only. They shall not be used in any way to govern, limit, modify, or construe this agreement or any part or provision thereof or otherwise be given any legal effect.

11. ENTIRE AGREEMENT: This agreement contains the full and complete understanding and agreement between the parties with respect to the within subject matter, and supersedes all other agreements between the parties whether

written or oral relating thereto, and may not be modified or amended except by written instrument executed by both of the parties hereto. This agreement shall in all respects be subject to the laws of the State of _____ applicable to agreements executed and wholly performed within such State.

AGREED TO AND ACCEPTED:

_____ (Name of Finder)

_____
Signature
"Finder"

_____ (Name of Producer)

_____
Signature
"Producer"
By: _____
       (Name of and title of signatory)

INTERNATIONAL DISTRIBUTION

The terms of an agreement between the territory buyer (licensee or distributor) and the international distributor (a.k.a. sales agent or licensor) can be quite complex. Often the parties will sign a short-form deal memo at a market and follow up with a long-form agreement. Here is a sample long-form agreement.

INTERNATIONAL DISTRIBUTION LICENSE AGREEMENT

This International Multiple Rights Distribution License Agreement is made as of this _____ day of _____, 20__, by and between _____ ("Licensor"), whose address is _____ [tel: _____/fax: _____] and _____ ("Distributor"), whose address is _____ [tel: _____/fax: _____], with respect to the Picture and Territory briefly described for reference purposes only as follows:

Picture: _____

Territory: _____

Subject to timely payment of all monies due Licensor and Distributor's due performance of all other terms of this Agreement, Licensor licenses exclusively to Distributor, and Distributor accepts from Licensor, the above Picture in the above Territory on all the terms and conditions of this Agreement.

This Agreement consists of the following parts: Deal Terms, being the Basic License Deal Terms; Financial Deal Terms and Delivery Deal Terms; Standard Terms and Conditions; and the Schedule of Definitions.

All parts of this Agreement will be interpreted together to form one Agreement. Where not defined where they first appear, words used in this Agreement are otherwise defined in the Standard Terms and Conditions and the Schedule of Definitions.

Where either party is an agent acting for a principal, that party represents and warrants to the other that it has full authority to execute this Agreement on behalf of its principal and that its principal will be bound by its terms.

IN WITNESS WHEREOF, Licensor and Distributor have executed this Agreement as of the date first written to constitute a binding contract between them.

LICENSOR   **DISTRIBUTOR**

By: _____   By: _____
An Authorized Signatory   An Authorized Signatory

DEAL TERMS

BASIC LICENSE DEAL TERMS

Picture: _____

Authorized Languages: _____
Authorized Number of Television Runs: _____
Authorized Video Format(s): _____

Territory: _____

Term: Starting on execution and ending _____ (__) years from Licensor's notice to Distributor that Licensor is ready to deliver the Initial Materials.

Licensed Rights, Reserved Rights, and Holdbacks:

	Licensed Rights*	Reserved Rights	Holdbacks (on Distributor)
Theatrical	X	_____	_____
Non-Theatrical	X	_____	_____
Public Video	X	_____	_____
Home Video	X	_____	_____
Commercial Video	X	_____	_____
Pay-Per-View	X	_____	_____
Demand View	X	_____	_____
Pay TV			
Terrestrial	X	_____	_____
Cable	X	_____	_____
Satellite	X	_____	_____
Free TV			
Terrestrial	X	_____	_____
Cable	X	_____	_____
Satellite	X	_____	_____

*Licensed Rights exclude airlines, ships, and hotel/motel, unless specified above.

Delivery Date: Distributor hereby guarantees payment in full and acceptance of Delivery of the Initial Materials no later than ___ (__) months from the date of Licensor's notice that it is ready to deliver the Initial Materials.

FINANCIAL DEAL TERMS

A. Guarantee: NET US $_____ payable:

20% (US $_____) shall be immediately payable by wire transfer immediately upon execution of this Agreement; and

80% (US $_____) shall be payable by wire transfer upon Notice of Delivery of the initial materials.

The Guarantee is a minimum net sum and no taxes or other charges may be deducted from it. If Theatrical Rights are granted, one hundred percent (100%) of the Guarantee is allocated to the Theatrical Rights.

Unless otherwise specified above, unless the first installment of the Guarantee is received by Licensor within _____ (__) days of execution of this Agreement, Licensor, in its sole discretion, may: (i) commence arbitration proceedings to collect the first installment of the Guarantee; (ii) terminate this Agreement upon written notice to Distributor; or (iii) attempt to re-sell the rights licensed herein, provided that if Licensor cannot re-sell the rights or if Licensor re-sells the rights for less than the full amount of the Guarantee, Licensor may commence arbitration against Distributor for the full amount of the Guarantee or the difference between the full amount of the Guarantee specified above and the amount which Licensor receives from any re-sale of the rights, without prejudice. If any subsequent installment of the Guarantee is not paid within _____ (__) days of its due date, Licensor, in its sole discretion, may (i) commence arbitration proceedings to collect the balance of the Guarantee; (ii) terminate this Agreement upon written notice to Distributor, in which event any and all payments theretofore received by Licensor will be retained by Licensor as partial liquidated damages; or (iii) attempt to re-sell the rights licensed herein, provided that if Licensor cannot re-sell the rights or if Licensor re-sells the rights for less than the amount specified above, Licensor may commence arbitration against Distributor for the outstanding balance of the Guarantee or the difference between the outstanding amount of the Guarantee specified above and the amount which Licensor receives from any re-sale of the rights, without prejudice.

B. Cross-Collateralization: It is agreed that cross-collateralization shall be allowed in the Territory and between and amongst the rights licensed pursuant to this Agreement. Notwithstanding

the foregoing, there shall be no cross-collateralization between the Picture covered by this Agreement and any other
picture covered by any other agreement.

C. Payment Requirements: Timely payment of all amounts
due Licensor is of the essence of this Agreement and an
express condition precedent to Distributor's right to exercise
any of the Licensed Rights. Distributor will make payments of
the installments of the Guarantee indicated in this Agreement
and all other payments due Licensor (*e.g.,* Material Costs) at
Licensor's sole election either by check drawn on a United
States bank or by wire transfer, and all such wire transfers
shall be of unencumbered and unconditional funds, free of
any transmission charges. Notwithstanding the foregoing, the
Guarantee as set forth hereinabove shall be paid to Licensor
by wire transfer. All wire transfers shall be made to the
following account or to such other account as Licensor may
hereafter advise Distributor:

Bank: _____
Address: _____
Acct. Name: _____
Account #: _____
Bank ABA Routing #: _____

D. Disposition of Gross Receipts:

1. Video: From Home Video Receipts and Commercial
Video Receipts, as applicable (for ease of drafting only, the
"Video Gross Receipts"), Distributor will make continuing
payments as follows:

Basic Royalty Amounts:

	Royalty Percent At "Wholesale Level"	Royalty Percent At "Direct Consumer Level"
Home Video	50%	50%
Comm. Video	50%	50%

Distributor will pay to Licensor the indicated Royalty percentages of the Video Gross Receipts from exploitation of Videocassettes of the Picture at the "Wholesale Level" and "Direct
Consumer Level."

2. Pay-Per-View: From the Pay-Per-View Gross Receipts,
Distributor will make the continuing payments as follows:

50% of the Gross Receipts shall be paid to Licensor; and

100% of the remaining Gross Receipts shall be retained by Distributor.

3. Pay Television: From the Pay Television Gross Receipts, Distributor will make the continuing payments as follows:

50% of the Gross Receipts shall be paid to Licensor; and

100% of the remaining Gross Receipts shall be retained by Distributor.

4. Free Television: From the Free Television Gross Receipts, Distributor will make the continuing payments as follows:

50% of the Gross Receipts shall be paid to Licensor; and

100% of the remaining Gross Receipts shall be retained by Distributor.

5. Theatrical and Non-Theatrical: If Theatrical rights are exercised, from the Theatrical and Non-Theatrical Gross Receipts, Distributor will make continuing payments and recoupments in the following order of priority:

After Recoupable Distribution Costs have been recouped in accordance with the terms of this Agreement including the Guarantee, Theatrical and Non-Theatrical Gross Receipts will be shared as follows:

40% of Gross Receipts shall be paid to Licensor;

100% of the remaining Gross Receipts shall be retained by Distributor.

E. Recoupment of Guarantee: In accordance with Paragraph B hereinabove, Distributor shall have the right to recoup the Guarantee paid to Licensor from all sums due Licensor under Paragraph D above.

F. Subtitles/Dub: It is understood and agreed that Distributor shall be responsible for and prepare the Subtitled and/or Dubbed versions in the _____ languages at

Distributor's sole cost and expense. It is further understood and agreed that Licensor shall have free access to the _____ Subtitled and/or Dubbed versions of the Picture at no charge to Licensor if requested.

DELIVERY DEAL TERMS

A. Method of Delivery:

By Physical Delivery, Lab Access, Loan of Materials, Satellite Delivery, or otherwise as Licensor may designate for each item.

B. Materials Payment Instructions:

All Material costs shall be the sole responsibility of Distributor and shall be made at the same time as the second installment of the Guarantee is paid to Licensor.

C. Materials Shipping Instructions:

Distributor shall bear all shipping charges and shall timely notify Licensor of shipping destinations.

MULTIPLE RIGHTS

1. RIGHTS LICENSED

a. General Grant: Subject to the terms of this Agreement, Licensor exclusively licenses to Distributor only the specific Licensed Rights in the Picture(s) during the Term throughout the Territory as set forth in the Basic License Deal Terms. In exercising these Licensed Rights, Distributor may only exploit the Picture(s) in the Authorized Language(s) listed in the Basic License Deal Terms. All rights not expressly licensed to Distributor are Reserved Rights, even if not expressly checked in the Basic License Deal Terms. The extent of each of the Licensed Rights and Reserved Rights is defined in the attached Schedule of Definitions.

b. Terminology: The inclusion of provisions in this Agreement for any rights not specifically licensed to Distributor in the Basic Licensed Deal Terms is for ease of drafting only. Their inclusion does not grant to Distributor explicitly or by implication any rights not specifically licensed in the Basic License Deal Terms.

c. Reservation: Licensor reserves all the specific Reserved Rights listed in the Basic License Deal Terms and all other rights in each Picture not licensed to Distributor. Licensor may exploit them as Licensor sees fit without restriction, except as otherwise expressly provided in this Agreement.

2. ADVERTISING AND BILLING

a. Licensor's Requirements: Licensor will timely provide Distributor with a list of all required screen credits (if not already contained in the Picture), paid advertising, publicity and promotional requirements, and Videocassette packaging credit requirements (if needed). Distributor will comply with all of these requirements at all times.

b. Distributor's Rights: Subject to Licensor's requirements and the provisions of this Agreement, Distributor will have the non-exclusive right at its sole expense to: (i) advertise, publicize, and promote each Picture; (ii) include in all such advertising, promotion, or publicity for the Picture the name, voice, and likeness of any person who has rendered services on the Picture but not as an endorsement for any product or service other than the Picture; and (iii) include in the beginning or at the end of each Picture the credit or logo of Distributor.

c. Limitations: In exercising these rights Distributor may not: (i) change the title of any Picture without Licensor's prior written approval; (ii) alter or delete any credit, logo, copyright notice, or trademark notice appearing on any Picture; (iii) include any advertisements or other material in any Picture other than the credit or logo of Distributor as described in Subparagraph 2(b) or an approved anti-piracy warning as provided in Paragraph 17 or commercials for a Picture exploited on Free TV as provided in Paragraph 13(c).

d. Liability: Failure to comply with the provisions of this Paragraph 2 may subject Distributor to liability to third parties or to Licensor due to agreements concerning credits between Licensor and such third parties.

3. DUBBING AND EDITING

a. Licensor's Requirements: Licensor will timely provide Distributor with any dubbing and editing requirements applicable to the Picture and its trailers. Distributor will comply with all these requirements in creating any allowed dubbed or edited version of the Picture or its trailers. Except as expressly provided in this Agreement, each Picture and its trailers as supplied by Licensor will be exhibited in their original continuity, without alteration, interpolation, cut, or elimination.

b. Distributor's Rights: Subject to Licensor's requirements and the provisions of this Agreement, Distributor will have the non-exclusive right at its sole expense and after consultation with Licensor to: (i) dub or subtitle the Picture, but only in the Authorized Language(s) listed in the Basic License Deal Terms; and (ii) edit the Picture to meet any censorship requirements.

c. Limitations: In exercising these rights Distributor may not: (i) alter or delete any credit, logo, copyright notice or trademark notice appearing on the Picture, (ii) include any advertisements or other materials in any Picture other than the credit or logo of Distributor as described in Subparagraph 2(b) or an approved anti-piracy warning as provided in Paragraph 17 or commercials for a Picture exploited on Free TV as provided in Paragraph 13(c).

d. Liability: Failure to comply with the provisions of this Paragraph 3 may subject Distributor to liability to third parties or to Licensor due to agreements concerning dubbing and editing between Licensor and such third parties.

4.   TERRITORY

a. General: The Territory means only the countries listed in the Basic License Deal Terms, but only as their political borders exist on the date of this Agreement. The Territory excludes foreign countries, embassies, military and governmental installations, oil rigs and marine installations, airlines-in-flight, and ships-at-sea located within the Territory.

b. Exclusion: In exploiting the Theatrical, Home Video, Free TV, or Pay TV Licensed Rights, the Territory also excludes the countries' non-contiguous territories and possessions as well as embassies, military and governmental installations, oil rigs and other marine installations, airlines-in-flight, and ships-at-sea flying the flag of any country in the Territory.

c. Inclusion: In exploiting only the Non-Theatrical or Commercial Video Licensed Rights, the Territory includes the countries' embassies, military and governmental installations, oil rigs and marine installations wherever located, but only to the extent that they may be exploited in accordance with the Non-Theatrical or the Commercial Video Licensed Rights.

5. EXPLOITATION PERIODS

a. Term: The "Term" for each Picture will start and end on the dates set forth in the Basic License Deal Terms, subject to extension per Paragraph 15. Distributor will not allow or authorize any exploitation of any Picture after the Term.

b. Distributor "Holdbacks": Where the Deal Terms indicate a "Holdback" on any Licensed Right granted to Distributor, then during that Holdback period Distributor may not exercise or authorize the exercise in the Territory of that Licensed Right.

c. Licensor "Holdbacks": Where the Deal Terms indicate a "Holdback" on any of Licensor's Reserved Rights, then during that Holdback period Licensor may not exercise or authorize the exercise in the Territory of that Reserved Right. However, Licensor may enter into agreements at any time authorizing the exercise of such Reserved Right after the expiration of the Holdback period.

d. Release Date(s): The "Release Date(s)" are the earliest dates on which Distributor may begin exploiting the Picture in the indicated medium in the Territory. Where the Deal Terms state that the Picture may not be exploited until after a certain date, then Distributor may not authorize or allow distribution, exhibition, or other exploitation of the Picture until after that date. Where the Deal Terms indicate a "not later than" date, then Distributor must make the Picture available to the paying public throughout the Territory in the indicated medium, by no later than such date.

e. First Theatrical Release: The "First Theatrical Release" of a Picture means the earlier of: (i) the date on which the Picture is first exhibited in theaters within the Territory to the paying public, including screenings to qualify for awards presentations; or (ii) six (6) months after Licensor's Notice that Licensor can Deliver the Initial Materials.

f. First Video Release: The date of the "First Video Release" of the Picture will mean the earlier of: (i) the date on which the Picture is first made available for sale or rental to the paying public in retail outlets in the Territory; or (ii) six (6) months after Licensor's notice that Licensor can make Delivery of the Initial Materials.

6. FINANCIAL TERMS

a. General: Distributor will make payments to Licensor and retain recoupments from the Gross Receipts derived from the exploitation of the Licensed Rights in each Picture only in the manner and sequence specified in the Financial Deal Terms. For purposes of such payments and recoupments, the terms used in the Financial Deal Terms will have the meanings given in this Paragraph 6 and in Paragraph 7.

b. Guarantee: The "Guarantee" is the sum payable to Licensor against Licensor's share of Gross Receipts as indicated in the Financial Deal Terms. The Guarantee is non-returnable but recoupable in strict conformity with the Terms of this Agreement. The Guarantee stated in the Financial Deal Terms is a minimum net sum and no taxes or charges of any sort may be deducted from it, except the non-resident withholding tax, if applicable.

c. Gross Receipts: "Gross Receipts" means the sum on a continuous basis of the "Theatrical or Non-Theatrical Gross Receipts" as defined in Paragraph 7(a), the "Home Video or Commercial Video Gross Receipts" as defined in Paragraph 7(d), and the "Free TV or Pay TV Gross Receipts" as defined in Paragraph 7(g).

d. No Fees to Others: Distributor's subsidiaries, parent or affiliated company, and approved subdistributors or agents may not deduct or charge any fee against Gross Receipts in calculating all amounts due Licensor. It is the intent of this provision that, for the purpose of determining Licensor's share of Gross Receipts, all Gross Receipts be calculated at "source." By way of clarification, Theatrical or Non-Theatrical Gross Receipts will be calculated at the level at which payments are remitted by local exhibitors of the Picture to the public, Home Video or Commercial Video Gross Receipts will be calculated at the Wholesale Level or Direct Consumer Level, as appropriate, and Free TV or Pay TV Gross Receipts will be calculated at the level at which payments are remitted by local telecasters of the Picture.

e. Recoupable Distribution Costs: The "Recoupable Distribution Costs" are those costs defined in Paragraph 7(b). Recoupable Distribution Costs apply only to exploitation of the Theatrical, Non-Theatrical Licensed Rights and Television Rights. No costs incurred by Distributor in exploiting the Home Video or Commercial Video Licensed Rights, may be deducted from any monies due Licensor. All costs incurred in exploiting these Licensed Rights are to be borne solely by Distributor.

f. Royalty Income: All amounts collected by an authors' rights organization, performing rights society, or governmental agency that are payable to authors, producers, or distributors and which arise from royalties, compulsory licenses, cable retransmission income, tax rebates, exhibition surcharges, or the like, will as between Licensor and Distributor be the sole property of Licensor. By way of illustration but not limitation, this will apply to such amounts arising from theatrical exhibition of any Picture, from any tax or royalty payable with regard to blank audio or videocassettes or discs, or the sale or rental of VCRs or other hardware, from royalties collected by AGICOA or similar organizations from cable retransmissions of television programs and from collections by music performing or mechanical rights societies. Licensor has the sole right to apply for and collect all these amounts. If any of them are paid to Distributor, then Distributor will immediately remit them to Licensor with an appropriate statement identifying the payment.

g. Documentation: Where, under the laws or rules of any country in the Territory, Distributor is required to make any registration or filing or to obtain any permits or clearances with respect to the exploitation of any Licensed Rights in the Picture, then Distributor will do so promptly at Distributor's expense and provide Licensor with copies of all documents indicating full compliance with such requirements. For the sake of clarity, such requirements may include obtaining certificates of local dubbing or copyright registration, acquiring quota permits or censorship clearances, or filing author certificates, certificates of origin, or music cue sheets with appropriate authorities or societies, or registering the Picture to obtain royalties, rebates, or other allowances.

7. GROSS RECEIPTS AND RECOUPMENT PROVISIONS

a. Theatrical and Non-Theatrical Gross Receipts - Defined: "Theatrical or Non-Theatrical Gross Receipts" means for each Picture the sum on a continuous basis of:

(1)   All monies or other consideration of any kind (including all amounts from advances, guarantees, security deposits, awards, subsidies, and other allowances) received by, used by, or credited to Distributor or subdistributors or agents (collectively referred to in subparagraph 7(a) of this Agreement as "Distributor and Affiliated Parties") from the lease, license, rental, diffusion, exhibition, performance, or other exercise of the Theatrical or Non-Theatrical Rights Licensed in the Picture, all without any deductions; and

(2)   All monies or other consideration of any kind received by, used by, or credited to Distributor and Affiliated Parties as recoveries for the infringement by third parties of any of the Theatrical or Non-Theatrical Licensed Rights in the Picture; and

(3)   All monies and other consideration of any kind received by, used by, or credited to Distributor and Affiliated Parties from any authorized dealing in trailers, prints, posters, or advertising accessories supporting the Theatrical release of the Picture in the Territory.

b. Theatrical and Non-Theatrical Recoupable Distribution Costs - Defined: Theatrical or Non-Theatrical "Recoupable Distribution Costs" mean for each Picture all direct, auditable, out-of-pocket, reasonable, and necessary costs, exclusive of salaries and overhead, and less any discounts, credits, rebates, or similar allowances, actually paid by Distributor for exploiting the Picture in arms-length transactions with third parties, all of which will be advanced by Distributor and recouped under this Agreement, for:

(1)   Customs duties, import taxes, and permit charges necessary to secure entry of the Picture into the Territory;

(2)   Sales, use, VAT, admission, and turnover taxes and related charges assessable against any Gross Receipts realized from the exploitation of the Rights Licensed in the Picture, but not including corporate income, franchise, or windfall profits taxes, and not including any such amounts assessable against any sums payable to Licensor;

(3)   Remittance taxes on sums payable to Licensor, but only to the extent allowed by Paragraph 8(b);

(4)   Shipping and insurance charges for Delivery of the Materials to Distributor, but not including any amounts for shipping within the Territory;

(5)   Positive prints and trailers of the Picture in an amount pre-approved by Licensor;

(6)   Costs of allowed subtitling and dubbing, but only in the Authorized Language(s);

(7)   Costs of allowed advertising, promotion, and publicity in the amount pre-approved by Licensor;

(8)   Legal costs and charges paid to third parties to obtain recoveries for infringement by third parties of any of the Licensed Rights in the Picture, but only to the extent reasonably pre-approved by Licensor;

(9)   Actual and normal expenses incurred in recovering debts from defaulting licensees; and

(10)   Censorship fees and costs of editing to meet censorship requirements as allowed pursuant to this Agreement.

In no case may any item be deducted more than once. All costs not expressly covered by the above will be Distributor's sole responsibility.

c. Third-Party Costs: Where any of Distributor's subsidiaries, parent or affiliated companies, or approved subdistributors or agents incur any expense that would be a Recoupable Distribution Cost if incurred by Distributor, then such expense may be treated as a Recoupable Distribution Cost. Otherwise, no costs of any third party may be recouped from any monies owing to Licensor.

d. Home Video or Commercial Video Gross Receipts - Defined: "Home Video or Commercial Video Gross Receipts" means for each Picture the sum on a continuous basis of:

(1)   With regard to the Home Video Licensed Rights, all gross income of any kind received by, used by, or credited to Distributor or distributor's subsidiaries, parent or affiliated companies, or approved subdistributor or agents (collectively referred to in subparagraph 7(d) of this Agreement as "Distributor and Affiliated Parties") from the sale,

rental, license, or other disposition of Videocassettes embodying the Picture by Distributor for Home Video use at the "Wholesale Level" or "Direct Consumer Level," all without any deductions; and

(2)   With regard to the Commercial Video Licensed Rights, all gross income of any kind received by, used by, or credited to Distributor and Affiliated Parties from the sale, rental, license, or other disposition, or the authorized public performance, exhibition, or diffusion of, Videocassettes embodying the Picture by Distributor for Commercial Video use, at the "Wholesale Level" or "Direct Consumer Level," all without any deductions; and

(3)   All gross income of any kind received by, used by, or credited to Distributor and Affiliated Parties as recoveries for the infringement by third parties of any of the Home Video or Commercial Video Licensed Rights in the Picture, less only the reasonable costs approved by Licensor actually paid by Distributor in obtaining such recoveries; and

(4)   All gross income or other consideration received by, used by, or credited to Distributor and Affiliated Parties from any authorized dealing in trailers, prints, posters, or advertising accessories supporting the Home Video release of the Picture.

e. Wholesale Level - Defined: The "Wholesale Level" means the level of Videocassette distribution from which Videocassettes are shipped directly to retailers for ultimate sale or rental to the paying public. The "Wholesale Level" may include intermediate distribution levels between the manufacturer and the retailer, such as rack jobbers and the like if such distribution is performed by a parent, subsidiary, or affiliated company of Distributor, or unless Distributor participates in the profits from such intermediate distribution, but then only to the extent of such participation.

f. Direct Consumer Level - Defined: The "Direct Consumer Level" means the level of Videocassette distribution at which Videocassettes are sold or rented directly to the paying public. The "Direct Consumer Level" includes the sale or rental of Videocassettes by means of retail outlets, mail order, video clubs, and similar methods. Where Commercial Video rights are licensed, the "Direct Consumer Level" also includes the authorized public performance, exhibition, or diffusion of Videocassettes in accordance with the Commercial Video

Licensed Right. Distributor will not be deemed to be engaged in distribution at the Direct Consumer Level unless such distribution is performed by a parent, subsidiary, or affiliated company of Distributor or unless Distributor participates in the profits from such distribution, and then only to the extent of such participation.

g. Free TV or Pay TV Gross Receipts - Defined: "Free TV or Pay TV Gross Receipts" will mean for each Picture the sum on a continuous basis of:

(1) All gross income or other consideration of any kind received by, used by, or credited to Distributor or by Distributor's subsidiaries, parent or affiliated companies, or authorized subdistributors or agents (collectively referred to in subparagraph 7(g) of this Agreement as "Distributor and Affiliated Parties") from the exercise of the Free TV or Pay TV Licensed Rights in the Picture, all without any deductions; and

(2) All gross income or other consideration of any kind received by, used by, or credited to Distributor and Affiliated Parties as recoveries for the infringement by third parties with any of the Free TV or Pay TV Licensed Rights in the Picture, less only the reasonable costs approved by Licensor and actually paid by Distributor in obtaining such recoveries.

8. PAYMENT REQUIREMENTS

a. Timely Payment: Timely payment is the essence this Agreement, and is an express condition precedent to distributor's exercise of any rights in the Picture. Payment will only be considered made when Licensor has immediate and unencumbered use of funds in the required currency in the full amount due. Distributor will timely obtain all governmental permits necessary to make all payments to Licensor.

b. Limitation on Deductions: There will be no deductions from any payments due Licensor because of any bank charges, withholding taxes, conversion costs, sales, use, or VAT taxes, "Kontingents," quotas, or any other taxes, levies, or charges unless separately agreed to in writing by Licensor. No remittance taxes of any sort may be deducted from the Guarantee, but any remittance taxes paid by Distributor on the Guarantee may be recouped as a Recoupable Distribution Cost after Distributor provides Licensor with appropriate documentation.

If Distributor is legally required to pay any remittance taxes on any amounts due Licensor other than the Guarantee, then Distributor will provide Licensor with all necessary documentation indicating Distributor's payment of the agreed amount on Licensor's behalf before deducting Distributor's payment from any sums due Licensor.

c. Blocked Funds: If it is legally impossible to transmit any monies due to Licensor, then Distributor will immediately so notify Licensor. Distributor will then deposit such monies in Licensor's name, but at Distributor's expense, in a suitable depository designated by Licensor.

d. Finance Charge on Late Payments: If Licensor does not receive any payment within _____ (_) days of its due date, then, in addition to any other right or remedy, Licensor may assess a finance charge on such payment at the lesser of two (2) percentage points over the then-current advertised prime rate on the date payment was due at Licensor's lead bank or the highest applicable legal contract rate. A finance charge, if made, will be retroactive to the date payment was due and will continue until payment in full.

e. Exchange Provisions, Payment: All payments to Licensor will be in United States dollars or such other freely transmittable currency as Licensor may designate. Where applicable, all payments due Licensor will be computed at the prevailing exchange rate on the date due at a bank designated by Licensor promptly after execution of this Agreement, or, if no bank is designated, the official government rate in the country of the currency. For a late payment, Licensor will be entitled to the most favorable exchange rate between the due date and the payment date.

f. Exchange Provisions, Recoupment: Distributor will calculate and recoup the Guarantee and all Recoupable Distribution Costs solely in the currency of the Territory. Where any such payments are not made in the currency of the Territory, they will be converted to the currency of the Territory for recoupment purposes using the exchange rate applicable on the date the Guarantee was received by Licensor or the Recoupable Distribution Cost was paid.

9. ACCOUNTINGS

a. Limits on Cross-Collateralization: Each Picture will be treated separate and apart from any other picture licensed to

Distributor, whether in this Agreement or otherwise, and the payments applicable to each Picture will be treated as separate and independent accounting units and not cross-collateralized or set-off. Amounts due for any Picture or other picture(s) may not be used to recoup amounts unrecouped for any other Picture or picture(s), or vice versa. Gross Receipts and Recoupable Distribution Costs may only be cross-collateralized among the Licensed Rights in a Picture to the extent specifically authorized in the Financial Deal Terms.

b. <u>Segregation of Gross Receipts:</u> All Gross Receipts, on receipt by Distributor or Distributor's subsidiaries, parent or affiliated companies, or approved subdistributors or agents, will be the exclusive property of Licensor, who authorizes Distributor to retain its share of Gross Receipts as provided in the Financial Deal Terms. Distributor will deposit all Gross Receipts in a special bank account opened by Distributor, which may not be used for any other funds or purpose. The bank account and all Gross Receipts in it will be deemed held by Distributor in trust for Licensor and Distributor, and those Gross Receipts may not be commingled with Distributor's other monies.

c. <u>Limits of Allocations:</u> If any Picture is exploited in connection with other pictures, then Distributor will only allocate receipts and expenses among such pictures in the manner approved by Licensor in its sole discretion in advance.

d. <u>Financial Records:</u> Distributor will maintain complete and accurate records in the currency of the Territory of all financial transactions regarding each Picture in accordance with generally accepted accounting principles in the theatrical, video, and television distribution business on a consistent, uniform, and non-discriminatory basis throughout the Term. The records will include without limitation all Gross Receipts derived, all Recoupable Distribution Costs paid, all allowed adjustments or rebates made, and all cash collected or credits received. Where Home Video or Commercial Video rights are licensed, such records will also include all Videocassettes manufactured, sold, rented, and returned. Unless Licensor pre-approves otherwise in writing, all such financial records will be maintained on a cash basis, except where Distributor permits any off-set, refund, rebate, or other reduction in sums due Distributor, then the amount will nonetheless be included in Gross Receipts. Distributor will also keep complete and accurate copies of every statements from third parties and contracts, vouchers, receipts, computer records, audit reports, correspondence, and other writings from authorized subdistributors and agents and all other parties pertaining to the Picture.

e. <u>Statements:</u> In addition to any other reporting requirements in this Agreement, starting after Delivery of the Initial Materials, Distributor will furnish Licensor a statement in English setting forth from the time of the immediately prior statement, if any, with respect to each Picture all Gross Receipts derived, all Recoupable Distribution Costs paid, identifying to whom, and all exchange rates used, all on a country-by-country basis. Where Home Video or Commercial Video rights are licensed, the statements will also include: (i) all Videocassettes manufactured, sold, rented, and returned; (ii) the wholesale and retail prices of all Videocassettes; and (iii) all allowable deductions taken. Such information will be provided in reasonable details on a current and cumulative basis. Each statement will be accompanied by payment of any monies then due Licensor. Distributor will render such statements within ___ (__) days after the end of each of Distributor's fiscal quarters for the first _____ (__) years and semi-annually thereafter.

f. <u>Audit Rights:</u> Continuing until _____ (__) years after the Term, Licensor may examine and copy on its own or through its auditors Distributor's financial records (and, to the extent applicable, the financial records of Distributor's subsidiaries, parent or affiliated companies, and approved subdistributors or agents) regarding the Picture(s) on ___ (__) days' notice. The examination will be at Licensor's expense unless an underpayment of more than five percent (5%) is discovered, in which case Distributor will pay the costs of the examination on demand.

10. <u>DELIVERY AND RETURN</u>

a. <u>Delivery:</u> "Delivery" of a Picture means delivery to Distributor of the Initial Materials, and, at a later time if and when mutually agreed, any additional materials, all as further described below.

b. <u>Delivery of Initial Materials:</u> The Initial Materials are the Initial Physical Materials and the Initial Advertising & Promotional Materials specified in the Delivery Deal Terms or, if not so specified, such Initial Physical materials and

Initial Advertising and Promotional Materials as Licensor deems customary for the Licensed Rights granted Distributor in this Agreement. Licensor will give Distributor written notice that it can Deliver the Initial Materials. Within fifteen (15) days of this notice, Distributor will notify Licensor of the number of prints, advertising, and promotional materials and accessories, and required trailers relating to the Picture, all of which will be subject to Licensor's reasonable approval. Licensor will then send Distributor a pro forma invoice setting forth the cost F.O.B. place of shipment for delivery of the approved Initial Materials. Distributor will immediately pay for such Initial Materials, and Licensor will then deliver such Initial Materials to Distributor as specified below. In any case, Distributor must take delivery of all approved Initial Materials within sixty (60) days of Licensor's notice that Licensor can deliver them.

c. Delivery of Physical Materials: Delivery of the Initial Physical Materials, and, if mutually agreed, any additional physical materials (which shall collectively be referred to in this Paragraph 10 of this Agreement as "Physical Materials"), will be accomplished by one of the methods listed below selected by Licensor for each item:

(1)   Where Physical Delivery is selected, for each Picture Licensor will deliver to the delivery location specified by Distributor the Physical Materials suitable for the manufacture of necessary exploitation materials. Unless otherwise specified in the Delivery Deal Terms, the Physical Materials will be shipped to Distributor by air transport.

(2)   Where Laboratory Access is selected, for each Picture Licensor will provide Distributor with laboratory access to the Physical Materials suitable for the manufacture of necessary exploitation materials. Access will be on the terms of the standard AFMA Laboratory Access Letter, or other mutually approved Access Letter, which will be provided to Distributor upon payment to Licensor of the appropriate portion of the License Fee specified in the Financial Deal Terms. The Physical Materials will always be held in a recognized laboratory or facility of Licensor's choosing, in Licensor's name and subject to Licensor's reasonable requirements. Distributor may order prints and other exploitation materials for the Picture to be manufactured from the accessible Physical Materials at Distributor's sole expense.

(3)   Where Loan of Physical Materials is selected, for each Picture Licensor will deliver on loan to the
delivery location specified by Distributor the Physical Materials suitable for the manufacture of necessary preprint materials. Unless otherwise specified in the Delivery Deal Terms,
the Physical Materials will be shipped to Distributor by air
transport. These Physical Materials will only be used to make
new preprint materials at Distributor's sole expense from
which necessary exploitation materials can be made. These
Physical Materials will always be held in a laboratory or
facility subject to Licensor's reasonable approval, and will be
returned to Licensor within a reasonable time designated by
Licensor.

(4)   Where Satellite Delivery is selected, Licensor may deliver the Physical Materials to Distributor by
satellite transmission commensurate with available materials
and Distributor's equipment. Licensor will be responsible for
all "uplinking" transmission costs, and Distributor will be
responsible for reception costs. Distributor's failure to make
suitable "downlinking" receiving arrangements, or failure to
receive any Picture due to technical "downlink" or reception
failure, will not affect Distributor's obligations under this
Agreement. If Distributor experiences a technical failure of
transmission or reception, Licensor upon receipt of timely
notice will attempt to assist Distributor to receive the transmission. Distributor will pay for each missed satellite feed a
charge of the greater of US$25 or the amount specified in the
Delivery Deal Terms.

d. Evaluation of Physical Materials: All Physical Materials
will be considered technically satisfactory for the manufacture
of first-class preprint and exploitation materials if Distributor
does not notify Licensor otherwise within twenty (20) days
after their Delivery. If Distributor so notifies Licensor and
Distributor's notice is accurate, then Licensor will, at its
election, either: (i) timely correct any defects or deliver new
Physical Materials; or (ii) exercise its rights of suspension and
withdrawal pursuant to Paragraph 15.

e. Delivery of Initial Advertising & Promotional Materials: Licensor will also provide, at Distributor's request and
expense, available stills, advertising materials, and other
Initial Advertising & Promotional Materials for each Picture
as specified in the Delivery Deal Terms, or, if not so
specified, such materials as Licensor deems customary for

the Licensed Rights granted Distributor in this Agreement. If Distributor does not use these Initial Advertising and Promotional Materials, then Distributor will obtain Licensor's prior written consent before using any other advertising or promotional materials.

f. <u>Holding of Materials:</u> Title to all Physical Materials and Initial Advertising and Promotional Materials delivered to Distributor under this Agreement (which shall collectively be referred to in this Paragraph 10 of this Agreement as "Materials") will remain with Licensor, subject to the rights of Distributor. Distributor will exercise due care in safeguarding all Materials and will assume all risk for theft or damage while they are in Distributor's possession.

g. <u>Materials Payment Instructions:</u> Distributor will pay for all Materials Delivered as indicated in the Delivery Deal Terms or in Licensor's notice. All costs of Delivery and Return (including shipping charges, import fees, duties, brokerage fees, storage charges, and related charges) will be Distributor's sole responsibility.

h. <u>Distributor-Created Materials:</u> Licensor will at all times have unimpeded and free access to all foreign-language tracks and dubbed versions, masters, advertising and promotional materials, artwork, and all other materials created by Distributor pursuant to this Agreement.

i. <u>Return of Materials:</u> Upon termination of this Agreement for each Picture, Distributor will at Licensor's election either: (i) return all Materials to Licensor at Licensor's expense; or (ii) destroy all Materials and provide Licensor with a customary certificate of destruction under penalty of perjury.

11. <u>THEATRICAL EXPLOITATION OBLIGATIONS</u>

a. <u>General:</u> In exploiting the Theatrical & Non-Theatrical Licensed Rights, Distributor will abide by the following exploitation requirements in addition to any other exploitation requirements in this Agreement.

b. <u>Approval Obligations:</u> Licensor will have prior approval on an ongoing basis of all significant aspects of the distribution of each Picture in the Territory, including the initial release campaign, distribution policy, exhibition contract terms, minimum and maximum print order, the total amount and specific items of the advertising and publicity budget, the advertising and marketing campaign, the release dates, the release pattern, the theaters in key cities, marketing strategy, short-subject allocations, and any modifications or amendments to them. Distributor will timely submit each item to Licensor for Licensor's prior approval.

c. <u>Release Obligations:</u> In releasing each Picture Distributor will:

(1)   Not begin distributing or exhibiting the Picture before the Release Date, if any, specified in the Basic License Deal Terms;

(2)   Place the Picture in general theatrical release throughout the Territory in no less than the number of cities and theaters reasonably required by Licensor and no later than the date specified in the Deal Terms;

(3)   Order and pay for no less than the minimum number of prints reasonably required by Licensor;

(4)   Expend monies pursuant to the approved advertising budget and otherwise conform with the pre-approved advertising and marketing campaign for the Picture;

(5)   Give Licensor reasonable advance notice of all premieres of the Picture in the Territory;

(6)   Not discriminate against the Picture or use the Picture to secure more advantageous terms for any other picture, product, or service;

(7)   Not enter the Picture in any festivals, charitable screenings, or the like without Licensor's prior approval in its sole discretion;

d. <u>Release Notices:</u> Promptly after Delivery, Licensor will provide Distributor with its release information requirements. Distributor will comply with such requirements. To the extent not covered by such requirements, during the period between the First Theatrical Release of the Picture in the Territory and the rendition of the first accounting statement due from Distributor, Distributor will furnish weekly reports to Licensor by telex or telegram setting forth all information available to Distributor regarding the results of such release, including exhibition terms, box office receipts as received, and expenses as incurred, on a weekly and cumulative basis.

e. <u>Exhibition Obligations:</u> In arranging for the exhibition of each Picture, Distributor will conform with all of the following:

(1)   All exhibition agreements for the Picture will be made separate and independent from exhibition agreements for any other picture, product, or service;

(2)   Distributor will audit all exhibition engagements for the Picture consistent with the practices of first-class distributors in the Territory and will promptly supply Licensor with the results of such audits;

(3)   Distributor will do all things necessary to maximize collections from exhibitors as quickly as is reasonably possible;

(4)   Distributor will not authorize or allow the Picture during its first run to be exhibited on a flat license or four-wall basis, or as part of a multiple feature engagement, unless all relevant terms of such proposed exhibition, including the proposed allocation to the Picture of box office receipts, permitted advertising costs, license fees, and film rentals has been approved by Licensor in writing;

(5)   Distributor will not authorize or allow the Picture during its first run to be exhibited with any other feature or short subject, provided that, if required to do so by law, then Distributor will only allocate to such feature or short subject for that exhibition run the least of: (i) one percent (1%) of total exhibition receipts per theater; (ii) the equivalent of US$500 in the currency of the Territory per theater for each continuous playdate; or (iii) the equivalent of US$2,500 for the entire exhibition run in all theaters; and

(6)   Distributor will not cancel, nullify, or amend any exhibition agreement once made without Licensor's prior written approval.

f. <u>Controlled Theaters:</u> A "controlled theater" is one in which Distributor, any of Distributor's subsidiary or affiliated companies, or any officer, director, partner, owner, or shareholder owning more than one percent (1%) of the outstanding evidence of equity ownership of any of them, has any interest, direct or indirect, in the ownership or operation of such theater. Distributor will not license any Picture to a controlled theater except on terms and conditions consistent with arms-length transactions between such controlled theater and third-party distributors for the exhibition of comparable motion pictures. Distributor will promptly provide Licensor with copies, certified to be accurate, or all agreements with controlled theaters for exhibition of any Picture.

g. Continuing Obligations: Throughout the Term, Distributor will use its best efforts and skill in the distribution and exhibition of each Picture so as to maximize its Gross Receipts and minimize its Recoupable Distribution Costs. Each Picture will be distributed and exploited consistent with the quality standards of first-class motion picture distributors in the Territory. Distributor will maintain each Picture in continuous distribution throughout the Territory for a period consistent with reasonable business judgment.

12. VIDEO EXPLOITATION OBLIGATIONS

a. General: In exploiting the Home Video & Commercial Video Licensed Rights, Distributor will abide by the following exploitation requirements in addition to any other exploitation requirements in this Agreement.

b. Best Efforts, Quality: Distributor will use distributor's best efforts and skill in the manufacture, distribution, and exploitation of the Videocassettes. The Videocassettes manufactured by Distributor will meet quality standards at least comparable to other Videocassettes commercially available through legitimate outlets in the Territory.

c. Limits on Early Exploitation: Distributor may not begin distributing Videocassettes of any Picture until the end of the applicable Holdback period of such Picture. Distributor may not authorize or begin advertising the availability of Videocassettes of any Picture to the public until two (2) months before the end of the applicable Holdback period for such Picture.

d. Catalog Availability: From the end of the applicable Holdback period until the end of the Term, Distributor will make Videocassettes embodying the Picture available in the Territory through its catalog, and will not allow them to leave normal channels of distribution for an unreasonable period of time.

e. Licensor's Ad Campaign Approval Rights: Intentionally deleted.

f. Licensor's Packaging Approval Rights: Intentionally deleted.

g. Limits on Included Material: Distributor will not authorize or allow any other picture, advertising, or other material to be included on any Videocassette for any Picture without Licensor's prior written approval.

h. Minimum Retail Price: Where a Minimum Retail Price is contained in the Financial Deal Terms, Distributor, if not prohibited by applicable laws, will not exploit or authorize the sale of Videocassettes to the consumer at a price less than such Minimum Retail Price. In any case, for purposes of calculating all amounts due Licensor, all Videocassettes will be deemed sold at retail for not less than the Minimum Retail Price set forth in the Deal Terms.

i. Minimum Wholesale Price: Where a Minimum Wholesale Price is contained in the Deal Terms, Distributor, if not prohibited by applicable laws, will not exploit or authorize the sale of Videocassettes at the Wholesale Level at a price less than such Minimum Wholesale Price. In any case, for purposes of calculating all amounts due Licensor, the wholesale selling price of all Videocassettes will be deemed to be the greater of either their actual wholesale selling price or the Minimum Wholesale Price set forth in the Financial Deal Terms.

j. Free Goods: Distributor will not dispose of more than the amount set forth in the Deal Terms of Videocassettes for any Picture as promotional, discount, or free samples ("Free Goods") without Licensor's prior written permission. If Licensor does permit, such Videocassettes will be considered as if sold at not less than the Wholesale Price set forth in Paragraph 5(d) for purposes of computing any amounts due Licensor.

k. Payment of Costs: Distributor will be solely responsible for and will pay all costs of exploiting and distributing Videocassettes embodying any Picture, including costs of manufacturing, advertising, publicizing, packaging, shipping, and music royalties.

l. Sell-Off Period: During the last six (6) months of the Term, Distributor will not manufacture Videocassettes in excess of those reasonably anticipated to meet normal customer requirements. During the three (3) month period following the end of the Term for each Picture, Distributor will have the non-exclusive right to sell off its then-existing inventory of Videocassettes for such Picture. At the end of the three (3) month period, Distributor will, at Licensor's election, either sell its remaining Videocassettes and their packaging to Licensor at Distributor's cost, or destroy them and provide Licensor with a customary certificate of destruction.

   m. Import/Export Restrictions: Distributor will not import, or authorize importation of, Videocassettes embodying any Picture into the Territory other than the specific Materials provided by Licensor. At no time will Distributor export, or authorize exportation of, Videocassettes embodying any Picture out of the Territory.

13. TELEVISION EXPLOITATION OBLIGATIONS

   a. General: In exploiting the Free TV and Pay TV Licensed Rights, Distributor will abide by the following exploitation requirements in addition to any other exploitation requirements in this agreement.

   b. Usage Reports: Intentionally deleted.

   c. Commercials: Distributor may insert and permit others to insert commercial announcements within the Picture. The televising of the Picture must have stopped completely before showing the commercial messages, and it must be clear to the television audience that such commercial messages are not part of the continuity of the Picture. Distributor will televise the Picture as delivered without any alterations or deletions except those specifically permitted or required by Licensor. Distributor will televise all credits, trademarks, copyright notices, trade names, and other symbols of the Picture appearing on the Materials furnished by Licensor, including but not limited to Licensor's logo. Distributor will not authorize or permit any copying or duplication of the Picture or any part of it. Distributor will not make any cuts, changes, or insertions in any materials furnished by Licensor, except to the extent necessary to conform to censorship and time requirements.

   d. Payment of Costs: Intentionally deleted.

14. MUSIC

   a. Cue Sheet: Licensor will supply Distributor promptly after Delivery with available music cue sheets listing the composer, lyricist, and publisher of all music embodied in each Picture. Distributor will as necessary promptly file with the appropriate governmental agency or music rights society in the Territory a copy of the music cue sheets supplied by Licensor without making any changes in them.

b. Synchronization Royalties: Licensor (or a third party other than Distributor) will be responsible for acquiring all rights necessary to synchronize the music contained in the Picture on its original negative in the country of production. Licensor does not represent or warrant that such synchronization license will be recognized as valid under the local law of any country in the Territory. To the extent that local law or the rules of any local music performance or mechanical rights society requires payment of any royalty with respect to music embodied in the Picture or synchronized with its soundtrack, Distributor will be solely responsible for such payment.

c. Performance Royalties: Distributor will be solely responsible for obtaining all licenses and paying all mechanical royalties arising from Distributor's distribution, exhibition, performance, or other exploitation in the Territory of all music embodied in the Picture.

d. Mechanical Royalties: Distributor will be solely responsible for obtaining all licenses and paying all mechanical royalties arising from Distributor's distribution, exhibition, performance, or other exploitation in the Territory of all music embodied in the Picture.

e. Publishing Royalties: As between Licensor and Distributor, Licensor will be solely entitled to collect and retain the publisher's share of any music royalties arising from Distributor's exploitation of any Picture under this Agreement.

15. SUSPENSION AND WITHDRAWAL

a. Licensor's Right: Licensor may in its absolute discretion suspend Delivery or exploitation of any Picture or withdraw any Picture: (a) if Licensor determines that its continued exploitation might infringe the rights of others, violate any law, or subject Licensor to any liability; (b) if Licensor determines that its Materials are unsuitable for the manufacture of first-class commercial quality prints or other exploitation materials; or (c) due to Force Majeure.

b. Effect of Suspension: Distributor will not be entitled to claim any damages or lost profits for any suspension. Instead, the Term for any suspended Picture will be extended for the length of any suspension. If any suspension lasts more than three (3) consecutive months, either party may terminate this Agreement with respect to such suspended Picture on ten (10) days' notice, in which case the Picture will be treated as a withdrawn Picture as provided in Paragraph 15(c).

c. Effect of Withdrawal: If any Picture is withdrawn or this Agreement is terminated with respect to a Picture after a period of suspension, then Licensor may either substitute a mutually satisfactory Picture of like quality or refund an equitable portion of any unrecouped payments made by Distributor to Licensor. Distributor's sole remedy will be to receive this substitute or refund. In no case may Distributor collect any "lost profits" or other damages.

d. "Force Majeure": "Force Majeure" means any fire, flood, earthquake, or public disaster; strike, labor dispute, or unrest; unavailability of any major talent committed to the Picture; unavoidable accident; breakdown of electrical or sound equipment; failure to perform or delay by any laboratory or supplier; delay or lack of transportation; embargo, riot, war, insurrection, or civil unrest; any Act of God including inclement weather; any act of legally constituted authority; or any other cause beyond the reasonable control of Licensor.

16. DEFAULT AND TERMINATION

a. Distributor's Default: Distributor will default if: (i) Distributor becomes insolvent or fails to pay its debts when due; (ii) Distributor makes any assignment for the benefit of creditors, or seeks relief under any bankruptcy law or similar law for the protection of debtors, or suffers a petition of bankruptcy to be filed against it or a receiver or trustee appointed for substantially all of its assets; (iii) Distributor breaches any term, covenant, or condition of this Agreement or any other agreement between Licensor and Distributor; or (iv) Distributor attempts to make any assignment, transfer, or sublicense of this Agreement without obtaining Licensor's consent as required by Paragraph 19.

b. Notice to Distributor: Licensor will give Distributor written notice of any claimed default. If the default is incapable of cure, then Distributor will be in default immediately upon receipt of Licensor's notice. If the default is capable of cure, then Distributor will have thirty (30) days after its receipt to cure any non-monetary default, and fifteen (15) days after its receipt to cure any monetary default. If the default is incapable of cure, or if Distributor fails to cure within the times provided, then Licensor in addition to any other rights or remedies may terminate this Agreement, as to any or all Pictures licensed, effective immediately upon sending notice to such effect to Distributor, without refunding or rebating any amounts whatsoever to Distributor, Licensor being entitled to retain such amounts by way of partial liquidated damages. Licensor may then proceed against Distributor for legal and equitable relief, including suspending delivery of any Picture(s) and declaring all unpaid amounts due Licensor immediately due and payable.

c. Licensor's Default: Licensor will default if it fails to abide by any material requirement of this agreement imposed on Licensor. Default by Licensor is limited to the particular Picture to which the default applies. No default as to one Picture will be a default as to any other Picture, nor will a default by Licensor as to any one agreement be a default as to any other agreement.

d. Notice to Licensor: Distributor will promptly give Licensor written notice of any claimed default. Licensor will have thirty (30) days after its receipt to commence and diligently pursue cure of such default. Only if Licensor fails to do so may Distributor proceed against Licensor for available relief.

e. Resolution of Disputes: If Licensor elects, any dispute under this Agreement will be resolved by arbitration under the AFMA Arbitration Rules of the AFMA, as they may be in effect as of the date arbitration is sought, in _____. The parties agree that they will abide by any decision rendered in such an arbitration, and that any court having jurisdiction may enforce such a decision. Otherwise, Distributor submits to the exclusive jurisdiction of the federal or state courts in _____, USA, as an appropriate forum for resolving disputes. Distributor agrees to accept service of process for judicial proceedings by registered mail, and if service cannot be so effectuated, agrees that service by first-class mail on the Secretary of State of the State of _____ will be deemed service on Distributor.

17. ANTI-PIRACY PROVISIONS

a. Notice Requirements: Distributor will include in each copy of each Picture distributed under its authority the copyright notice and anti-piracy warning supplied by Licensor. Where Theatrical rights are being exercised, a "copy" of a Picture will mean all negatives and release prints of the Picture. Where Home Video & Commercial Video Rights are being exercised, a "copy" of a Picture will mean all masters, Videocassettes, and their packaging of the Picture. Where Free TV and Pay TV rights are being exercised, a "copy" will mean all negatives, masters, prints, cassettes, tapes, or discs of the Picture as distributed to telecasters.

b. Copyright Notice: Unless otherwise indicated by Licensor, the copyright notice on each copy of each Picture must read exactly as follows:

"© 20_____   All Rights Reserved"

c. Basic Anti-Piracy Warning: The anti-piracy warning on each copy of each Picture must read substantially as follows:

WARNING: THIS MOTION PICTURE IS PRO-TECTED BY LAW. Any unauthorized copying, hiring, lending, distribution, exporting, importing, dissemination, exhibition, or public performance is prohibited by law. Violators will be subject to investigation by the FBI, Interpol, and other police agencies and to criminal prosecution, civil penalties, or both.

d. Video Anti-Piracy Warning: Where Home Video or Commercial Licensed Rights are being exploited, the anti-piracy warning on each copy of each Picture must also include the following additional phrase:

Licensed only for use in the following countries:

_____

e. Home Video Anti-Piracy Warning: Where Home Video Rights are being exploited, the anti-piracy warning on each copy of each Picture must also include the following additional phrases:

AUTHORIZED FOR PRIVATE HOME USE ONLY.

f. Enforcement: Distributor will take all reasonable steps necessary to protect the copyright in each Picture to prevent piracy. Licensor may participate in any anti-piracy action using counsel of its choice. Licensor's expenses will be reimbursed from any recovery in equal proportion with Distributor's expenses. If Distributor fails to take necessary anti-piracy action, Licensor may, but will not be obligated to, take such action in Licensor's or Distributor's name, with all recoveries belonging to Licensor.

g. New Technology: If technology that inhibits the duplication of Videocassettes or that causes significant distortion in the Videocassette picture becomes in common use for the protection of Videocassettes from unauthorized duplication or exhibition, then Distributor will apply such technology to all Videocassettes of the Picture manufactured under Distributor's authority, the cost of such to be paid by Licensor.

18. DISTRIBUTOR'S INDEMNITIES

Distributor will indemnify and hold harmless Licensor (including Licensor's officers, directors, partners, owners, shareholders, employees, and agents) against all claims and expenses (including reasonable attorneys' fees) and liabilities due to Distributor's failure to abide by any restriction on the exercise of any rights granted and for each breach of any of Distributor's obligations, representations, or warranties set out in this Agreement. Distributor will remain responsible for honoring Distributor's indemnities despite any assignment or sublicense allowed by Licensor pursuant to Paragraph 19.

19. ASSIGNMENT AND SUBLICENSING

a. Distributor's Limitation: This Agreement is personal to Distributor. Except as provided in subparagraph 19(b), Distributor may not assign or transfer this agreement, or sublicense or use an agent to exploit any of the rights granted to Distributor, whether voluntarily or involuntarily, without prior written consent of Licensor in Licensor's sole discretion. An assignment or transfer of a controlling interest in Distributor's capital stock or other evidence of ownership will be deemed an assignment, transfer, or sublicense for which Licensor's consent must be given. If Licensor does consent to any assignment, transfer, sublicense, or agent, then this Agreement will be binding on such authorized assignee, transferee, subdistributor, or agent but will not release Distributor of any of Distributor's obligations under this Agreement.

b. Exception: Distributor may transfer or assign this Agreement to any wholly owned subsidiary or to any affiliated company that is wholly owned by any company which wholly owns Distributor. In that case, all references to Distributor in this Agreement will include such subsidiary or affiliated company.

c. Licensor's Rights: Licensor may freely assign, transfer or sublicense any of its rights under this Agreement, but no such assignment, transfer, or sublicense relieves Licensor of its obligations under this Agreement, unless it is to a company that acquires all or substantially all of Licensor's stock or assets.

20. MISCELLANEOUS PROVISIONS

a. Separability: In case of any conflicts between any term of this Agreement and any material law, ordinance, rule, or regulation, the latter will prevail.

b. No Waiver: No waiver of any breach will be a waiver of any other breach of the same or any other provision. No waiver is effective unless in writing. The exercise of any rights will not be deemed a waiver of any other right or of any default of the other party.

c. Remedies Cumulative: All remedies are cumulative, and resort to one will not preclude resort to any other at any time.

d. Notices: All notices and payments will be sent to the parties at the addresses specified in the Deal Terms, either by telex, telegram, or first-class mail, postage pre-paid. Either party may change its place for notice by notice to the other given in conformance with the above.

e. Entire Agreement: This Agreement contains the entire understanding of the parties regarding its subject matter, and supersedes all previous written or oral understandings or representations between the parties regarding its subject matter, if any. Each party expressly waives in favor of the other any right to rely on such oral understandings or representations, if any there may be.

f. Modification: No modification or amendment of this Agreement will be effective unless in writing, signed by both parties.

g. Captions: Captions and paragraph headings are for convenience only.

h. <u>Terminology:</u> As used in the Agreement, "and" means all of the possibilities in any combination, and "either . . . or" means only one of the possibilities. "Including" means "including without limitation."

i. <u>Governing Law:</u> Unless otherwise stated in the Deal Terms, this Agreement is governed by and interpreted under United States Copyright Law and the Laws of the State of _____.

Parties may disagree about the meaning of terms used in their agreements. The following standard AFMA terms are generally accepted in the industry. They are used to interpret whatever document they are attached to.

AFMA INTERNATIONAL
<u>SCHEDULE OF DEFINITIONS</u>

A. **Cinematic Rights Definitions**

Cinematic means *Theatrical, Non-Theatrical,* and *Public Video* exploitation of a Motion Picture.

Theatrical means exploitation of a Motion Picture Copy only for direct exhibition in conventional or drive-in theaters, licensed as such in the place where the exhibition occurs, that are open to the general public on a regularly scheduled basis and that charge an admission fee to view the Motion Picture.

Non-Theatrical means exploitation of a Motion Picture Copy only for direct exhibition before an audience by and at the facilities of either organizations not primarily engaged in the business of exhibiting Motion Pictures, such as in educational organizations, churches, restaurants, bars, clubs, trains, libraries, Red Cross facilities, oil rigs and oil fields, or governmental bodies such as in embassies, military bases, military vessels and other governmental facilities flying the flag of the licensed territory. Non-Theatrical does not include Commercial Video, Public Video, Airline, Ship, or Hotel exploitation.

Public Video means exploitation of a Motion Picture Copy embodied in a Videogram only for direct exhibition before an audience in a "mini-theater," an "MTV theater," or like establishment that charges an admission to use the viewing facility or to view the Videogram, and that is not licensed as a traditional motion picture theater in the place where the viewing occurs.

B. **Pay-Per-View Rights Definitions**

Pay-Per-View means *Non-Residential Pay-Per-View, Residential Pay-Per-View* and *Demand View* exploitation of a Motion Picture. *Pay-Per-View* does not include any form of *Pay TV* or *Free TV*, nor any form of making the Picture available over the Internet.

Residential Pay-Per-View means the broadcast of a Motion Picture Copy by means of an encoded analog signal for television reception in homes or similar permanent living places where a charge is made to the viewer for the right to use a decoding device to view the broadcast of the Motion Picture at a time designated by the broadcaster for each viewing.

Non-Residential Pay-Per-View means the broadcast of a Motion Picture Copy by means of an encoded analog signal for television reception in hotels or similar temporary living places where a charge is made to the viewer for the right to use a decoding device to view the broadcast of the Motion Picture at a time designated by the broadcaster for each viewing.

Demand View means the transmission of a Motion Picture Copy by means of an encoded analog signal for television reception in homes and similar permanent living places where a charge is made to the viewer for the right to use a decoding device to view the Motion Picture at a time selected by the viewer for each viewing.

C. **Ancillary Rights Definitions**

Ancillary means *Airline*, *Ship*, and *Hotel* exploitation of a Motion Picture.

Airline means exploitation of a Motion Picture Copy only for direct exhibition in airplanes that are operated by an airline flying the flag of any country in the licensed territory for which Airline exploitation is granted, but excluding airlines that are customarily licensed from a location outside the licensed territory or that are only serviced in but do not fly the flag of a country in the licensed territory.

Ship means exploitation of a Motion Picture Copy only for direct exhibition in sea or ocean-going vessels that are operated by a shipping line flying the flag of any country in the licensed territory for which Ship exploitation is granted, but excluding shipping lines that are customarily licensed from a location outside the licensed territory or that are only serviced in but do not fly the flag of a country in the licensed territory.

Hotel means exploitation of a Motion Picture Copy only for direct exhibition in temporary or permanent living places, such as hotels, motels, apartment complexes, co-operatives or condominium projects, by means of closed-circuit television systems where the telecast originates within or in the immediate vicinity of such living places.

D. **Video Rights Definitions**

Video means *Home Video* and *Commercial Video* exploitation of a Motion Picture.

Home Video means *Home Video Rental* and *Home Video Sell-Thru* exploitation of a Motion Picture.

Home Video Rental means exploitation of a Videogram embodying a Motion Picture that is rented to the viewer only for non-public viewing of the embodied Motion Picture in a linear form within a private living place where no admission fee is charged for such viewing.

Home Video Sell-Thru means exploitation of a Videogram embodying a Motion Picture that is sold to the viewer only for non-public viewing of the embodied Motion Picture in a linear form within a private living place where no admission fee is charged for such viewing.

Commercial Video means direct linear exhibition before an audience of a Videogram embodying a Motion Picture at the facilities of either organizations not primarily engaged in the business of exhibiting Motion Pictures, such as in educational organizations, churches, restaurants, bars, clubs, trains, libraries, Red Cross facilities, oil rigs and oil fields, or governmental bodies such as in embassies, military bases, military vessels, and other governmental facilities flying the flag of the licensed territory, but only to the extent that such exploitation is not otherwise utilized in the licensed Territory as a form of Non-Theatrical exploitation. Commercial Video does not include Non-Theatrical, Public Video, Airline, Ship, or Hotel exploitation, nor any form of making the Picture available over the Internet.

E.   **Pay TV Rights Definitions**

Pay TV means *Terrestrial Pay TV*, *Cable Pay TV*, and *Satellite Pay TV* exploitation of a Motion Picture. *Pay TV* does not include any form of *Pay-Per-View* nor any form of making the Picture available over the Internet.

Terrestrial Pay TV means over-the-air analog broadcast of a Motion Picture Copy by means of encoded Hertzian waves for television reception where a charge is made: (i) to viewers in private living places for use of a decoding device to view a channel that broadcasts the Motion Picture along with other programming; or (ii) to the operator of a hotel or similar temporary living place located distant from where the broadcast signal originated for use of a decoding device to receive a channel that broadcasts the Motion Picture and other programming and retransmit it throughout the temporary living place for viewing in private rooms.

Cable Pay TV means originating analog transmission of a Motion Picture Copy by means of an encoded signal over coaxial or fiber-optic cable for television reception where a charge is made: (i) to viewers in private living places for use of a decoding device to view a channel that transmits the Motion Picture along with other programming; or (ii) to the operator of a hotel or similar temporary living place located distant from where the broadcast signal originated for use of a decoding device to receive a channel that broadcasts the Motion Picture and other programming and retransmit it throughout the temporary living place for viewing in private rooms.

Satellite Pay TV means the uplink analog broadcast of an encoded signal to a satellite and its downlink broadcast to terrestrial satellite reception dishes of a Motion Picture Copy for television viewing located in the immediate vicinity of their reception dishes where a charge is made: (i) to viewers in private living places for use of a decoding device to view a channel that broadcasts the Motion Picture along with other programming; or (ii) to the operator of a hotel or similar temporary living place located distant from where the broadcast signal originated for use of a decoding device to receive a channel that broadcasts the Motion Picture and other programming and retransmit it throughout the temporary living place for viewing in private rooms.

F.   **Free TV Rights Definitions**

Free TV means *Terrestrial Free TV*, *Cable Free TV*, and *Satellite Free TV* exploitation of a Motion Picture. *Free TV* does not include any form of *Pay-Per-View,* nor any form of making the Picture available over the Internet.

Terrestrial Free TV means over-the-air analog broadcast by Hertzian waves of a Motion Picture Copy for television reception in private living places without a charge to the viewer for the privilege of viewing the Motion Picture, *provided* that for this purpose government television assessments or taxes (but not a charge for Pay-Per-View or Pay TV) will not be deemed a charge to the viewer.

Cable Free TV means the originating analog transmission by coaxial or fiber-optic cable of a Motion Picture Copy for television reception in private living places without a charge to the viewer for the privilege of viewing the Motion Picture, *provided* that for this purpose neither government television assessments nor taxes nor the regular periodic service charges (but not a charge for Pay-Per-View or Pay TV) paid by a subscriber to a cable television system will be deemed a charge to the viewer.

Satellite Free TV means the uplink analog broadcast to a satellite and its downlink broadcast to terrestrial satellite reception dishes of a Motion Picture Copy for television viewing in private living places located in the immediate vicinity of their reception dishes without a charge to the viewer for the privilege of viewing the Motion Picture, *provided* that for this purpose government satellite dish or television assessments or taxes (but not a charge for Pay-Per-View or Pay TV) will not be deemed a charge to the viewer.

G. **Video Use Definitions**

Cassette means the same as Videocassette.

CD means a Compact Disc.

Compact Disc means a combined optical and electronic analog storage device designed to be used in conjunction with an electronic device that causes a Motion Picture to be visible on the screen of a computer monitor or television for private viewing in a substantially linear manner. A Compact Disc does not include any type of VideoDisc or DVD.

Disc means an electronic analog or digital storage device designed to be used in conjunction with an electronic device or a computer that causes a Motion Picture to be visible on the screen of a television or computer monitor for private viewing in a substantially linear manner. A Disc includes a VideoDisc, Compact Disc, or a DVD, but not a Videocassette.

DVD means a digitally encoded electronic storage device that conforms to the DVD Specification for Read-Only Disc, version 1 (August 1996) or its successor and that is designed for use in conjunction with an electronic device or computer in a way that causes a Motion Picture to be visible for private viewing on the screen of a computer monitor or television. DVD includes Digital Versatile Discs and related DVD-enabled peripherals such as DVD-ROM devices and DVD-RAM devices, but does not include any type of Compact Disc or VideoDisc.

Laser Disc is a type of VideoDisc.

VCD means Video Compact Disc.

Video Compact Disc means a type of compressed analog VideoDisc designed to be used solely on a special-purpose electronic device that is solely dedicated for private viewing of a Motion Picture on the screen of a television in a substantially linear manner.

Videocassette means a VHS or Beta cassette or comparable analog magnetic storage device designed to be used with a reproduction apparatus that causes a Motion Picture to be visible on a television screen for private viewing in a substantially linear manner. A Videocassette does not include any type of VideoDisc or Compact Disc.

Videogram means any type of Videocassette, Compact Disc, Disc, DVD, or VideoDisc, but only to the extent use of the specific type of electronic storage device is authorized in the Agreement by the parties.

VideoDisc means a laser or capacitance disc or comparable analog optical or mechanical storage device designed to be used with a reproduction apparatus that causes a Motion Picture to be visible on a television screen for private viewing in a substantially linear manner. A VideoDisc does not include any type of Compact Disc or DVD.

H.   **Other Rights Definitions**

Compact Disc Interactive when used as a Right is a type of Interactive Multimedia Right and when used to describe a Work is a type of Interactive Multimedia Work.

CDI means the same as Compact Disc Interactive.

Dubbed means a new Version of the Picture in which the voices of performers on the soundtrack are replaced with the voices of other performers speaking dialogue in an Authorized Language.

Interactive Multimedia means exploitation of an Interactive Multimedia Work by means of a computing device that allows the Interactive Multimedia Work to be directly perceived and manipulated by the user of the computing device and that either stores the Interactive Multimedia Work on the user's computing device or accesses a Copy of the Interactive Multimedia Work by electronic means from another computing device interconnected with and located in the immediate vicinity of the user's computing device.

Interactive Networked Multimedia means exploitation of an Interactive Multimedia Work over the facilities of a communications system that allows the user of a computing device to engage in two-way transmissions over the system to access the Interactive Multimedia Work, irrespective of the operator of the system or the means by which signals are carried, and that stores a Copy of the Interactive Multimedia Work for transmission over the system at a place distant from the place where the user's computing device is located.

Internet means exploitation of a Motion Picture over the interconnected facilities of a publicly available packet-switching communications system that allows the user of a computing device to engage in two-way transmissions over the system through which the user obtains access to a Motion Picture Copy stored in digital form at a place distant from the place where the user's computing device is located.

Interactive Multimedia Work means a Work consisting primarily of a presentation communicated to a user through the combination of two or more media of expression, whether textual, audio, pictorial, graphical, or audiovisual, where a significant characteristic of the presentation is the ability of the user to manipulate the content of the presentation by means of a computing device in real time and in a nonlinear fashion.

Live Performance means performance of a Motion Picture or its Underlying Material by live players, whether by reading, performance, musico-dramatic rendition, or pantomime, where the performance occurs directly before a live audience or is broadcast live and without prerecorded material directly to the public, but excluding performances less than fifteen (15) minutes in length done for the purpose of advertising or publicizing the Motion Picture.

Mail-Order means Home Video Sell-Thru exploitation in which the sale occurs by placing an order for and receiving delivery of the Videogram through use of the postal service or other shipping service and not at a retail establishment. Ordering a Videogram over the telephone or through the Internet is not Mail-Order.

Merchandising means distribution and sale of tangible goods, other than Copies of a Motion Picture or any of its Versions, that are based on or utilize the title of the Picture, the names, likenesses, or characteristics of artists in their roles in a Motion Picture, or physical materials appearing in or used for a Motion Picture and that are made for sale to the general public. Merchandising does not include Interactive Multimedia, Interactive Networked Multimedia, Internet, or Publishing rights.

Near-Demand View means multiple regularly scheduled transmissions in a short time period over related transmission facilities of a Motion Picture Copy by means of an encoded signal for television reception in homes and similar permanent living places where a charge is made to the viewer for the right to use a decoding device to view the Motion Picture at one of the scheduled transmission times selected by the viewer for each viewing.

Near Video-On-Demand means Near-Demand View.

NVOD means Near Video-On-Demand or Near-Demand View.

Parallel Tracked means embodying a Copy of the Original Language Version of the Picture in a Compact Disc or DVD that also contains a Dubbed or Subtitled Version of the Picture.

Pay-Cable TV means the same as Cable Pay TV.

Publishing means exploitation of hard-cover or soft-cover printed publications of a novelization of a Motion Picture or artwork, logos, or photographic stills created for use in the Motion Picture that are included in such novelization.

Subtitled means a new Version of the Picture in which a translation of the dialogue into an Authorized Language appears on the bottom of the screen.

VOD means Video-On-Demand.

Video-on-Demand means the same as *Demand View*.

I. **Additional Definitions**

Affiliate means any Person, including any officer, director, employee, or partner of a Person controlled by, controlling, or under common control with a Party.

Availability Date means the first day after the end of the Holdback Period for a Licensed Right. If the Availability Date refers to a category of Licensed Rights, it refers to the first date on which Distributor may exploit any Licensed Right in the category. For example, the Pay TV Availability Date is the first date on which Distributor may exploit the Pay TV Terrestrial, Pay TV Cable, or Pay TV Satellite Right.

Broadcast means the communication to the public of a Motion Picture by means of wire, cable, wireless diffusion, or radio waves that allows the Motion Picture to be viewed on a television. Broadcast means the same as telecast or diffusion.

Compulsory Administration means any Law under which: (i) Secondary Broadcasts are subject to compulsory license; (ii) cable systems or other Persons may make Secondary Broadcasts without first obtaining authorization from rightsholders or Persons making originating broadcasts; or (iii) rightsholders may only grant or withhold authorization for Secondary Broadcasts through collective management societies or collective contractual agreements.

Copy means the embodiment of a Motion Picture in any physical form, including film, tape, cassette, or disc. Where a specific medium is limited to exploitation by a specific physical form (for example, to Videograms), then Copy with respect to such medium is limited to such physical form.

Exhibition means the same as public performance.

First English Release means, with respect to each Licensed Right, the date on which a Motion Picture is first made available to the public through the exercise of such Licensed Right in the major country within the Region whose recognized official language is English or, if there is no such country in the Region, in the United States.

First Release means the earliest of: (i) the date on which the Picture must be released as designated in the Deal Terms;

or (ii) the date on which the Picture is first made generally available to the paying public in the Territory, either through exhibition in cinemas, sale of Videograms, or telecast; or (iii) six (6) months after Notice of Initial Delivery.

First Theatrical Release means the date on which the Picture is first made generally available to the paying public in cinemas in the Territory, excluding festival and awards screenings.

First Video Release means the date on which Videograms embodying the Picture is first made generally available for sale to or rental by the paying public in the Territory.

First Negotiation means that, *provided* that Distributor is then actively engaged in the distribution business on a financially secure basis, Licensor will negotiate with Distributor in good faith for a period of ten (10) days regarding the matter for which Distributor has a First Negotiation Right before entering into negotiations regarding the matter with any other Person. If no agreement is reached within this time period, then Licensor will be free to stop negotiations with Distributor and then to negotiate and conclude an agreement regarding the proposed matter with any other Person on any terms.

Licensed Channel means the specific transmitting service of an identified broadcast service designated in the Deal Terms.

Licensed Telecasts means the total number of Authorized Runs and Playdates specified in the Deal Terms.

Law means any statute or ordinance, whether municipal, state, national, or territorial, any executive, administrative, or judicial regulation, order, judgment or decree, any treaty or international convention, or any rule, custom, or practice with force of law.

Local Language(s) mean the primary language(s) spoken in each country of the Territory.

Motion Picture means an audiovisual work consisting of a series of related images that, when shown in succession, impart an impression of motion, with accompanying sounds, if any.

Original Language means the primary language spoken in the dialogue of a Motion Picture.

Outside Release Date means the date on which Distributor must release the Picture in the First Release Medium, if so specified in the Deal Terms.

Party means either Licensor or Distributor.

Person means any natural person or legal entity.

Playdate means one or more telecasts of the Picture during a twenty-four (24) hour period over the non-overlapping telecast facilities of an authorized telecaster such that the

Picture is only capable of reception on televisions within the reception zone of such telecaster during such period.

Principal Photography means the actual photographing of a Motion Picture, excluding second-unit photography or special effects photography, requiring the participation of the director and the on-camera participation of a featured member of the principal cast.

Multi-Plexing means transmission of a Motion Picture over related broadcast channels supplied by the same broadcaster or pay service.

Remake means a new Motion Picture derived from an existing Motion Picture or its Underlying Material in which substantially the same characters and events as shown in the existing Motion Picture are depicted.

Rights means rights, licenses, and privileges under copyright, trademark, neighboring rights, or other intellectual property rights with regard to any type of exploitation of a Motion Picture or its Underlying Material, including the rights to duplicate, adapt, distribute, perform, display, and make available in accordance with the customary requirements of each specific licensed media.

Rights Management Information means a copyright notice along with any other information embodied in a Motion Picture Copy that identifies the copyright owner, producer, author, writer, director, performers, or other persons who have contributed to the making of the Picture, or that identifies any authorized terms and conditions for licensing of the Motion Picture or its use.

Run means one (1) telecast of the Picture during a twenty-four (24) hour period over the non-overlapping telecast facilities of an authorized telecaster such that the Picture is only capable of television reception within the reception zone of such telecaster once during such period. A simultaneous telecast over several interconnected local stations (*i.e.*, on a network) constitutes one (1) telecast; a telecast over non-interconnected local stations whose signal reception areas do not overlap constitutes a telecast in each station's local broadcast area.

Secondary Broadcast means the simultaneous, unaltered, and unabridged retransmission by a cable, microwave, or telephone system for reception by the public of an initial transmission, by wire or over the air, including by satellite, of a Motion Picture intended for reception by the public.

Sequel means a new Motion Picture derived from an existing Motion Picture or its Underlying Material in which a character, event, or locale depicted in the existing Motion Picture or its Underlying Material is shown engaged in or as the subject of substantially new and different events than those depicted in the existing Motion Picture.

Underlying Material means the literary and other material from which a Motion Picture is derived or on which it is based, including all versions of the screenplay, all notes, memos, direction, comments, ideas, stage business, and other material incorporated in any version of the Motion Picture, and, to the extent necessary rights and licenses have been duly obtained, all existing novels, stories, plays, songs, events, characters, ideas, or other works from which any version of the Motion Picture is derived or on which it is based.

Version means an adaptation of a Motion Picture that is not accomplished by merely mechanical reproduction or use of minimal originality but instead uses original artistic or intellectual expression to create a new Work in its own right that contains materials or expressions of authorship not found in the original Motion Picture.

Work means an original expression of authorship in the literary, scientific, or artistic domain whatever may be the mode or form of its expression.

CHAPTER 4

ATTRACTING INVESTORS

Many filmmakers begin their careers by persuading private investors to back them. Indeed, unless you are a star like Kevin Costner or Barbra Streisand, it is rare for a major studio to finance a beginning filmmaker. Banks will not lend money without substantial collateral. Loans based on pre-sales are difficult to obtain because territory buyers want packages with name actors from an experienced director. That leaves most filmmakers looking to Mom, Dad, and whatever they can scrape up from friends, relatives, and MasterCard. While such resources have financed many films, distributor's expectations have risen over the years. With a glut of independent motion pictures available, many distributors are not interested in acquiring a feature unless it 1) is shot on 35mm stock with name actors; or 2) wins an important film festival.

Thus, filmmakers are forced to raise increasingly large sums of money to produce more ambitious movies if they hope to secure distribution. As digitally shot motion pictures gain greater acceptance, some production costs may decline. Nevertheless, numerous producers are chasing a small number of name actors. This competition has driven up the price of talent, even for low-budget indie films.

As a result, the ability to woo investors has become a critical skill—one that is not taught in film school. Perhaps the best preparation for an aspiring filmmaker would be to enroll in business school and learn the intricacies of high finance. Even if you didn't learn much, you would graduate with a class of MBAs who would eventually earn large incomes and become good prospects to invest in your films. Better yet, go to dental school.

Most filmmakers have an aversion to fundraising. Like other "artists," they would prefer that someone else deal with the unsavory task of raising money. But filmmakers without personal wealth or a rich uncle may have no choice but to beat the bushes for cash. Most underestimate the difficulty of raising funds. Joel and Ethan Coen spent a year raising the budget for *Blood Simple*. First they produced a slick trailer. Then they contacted everyone they knew who could potentially invest. Many of their friends who promised to back them didn't come through. But the Coen brothers were shrewd networkers. Those prospects who were unable or unwilling to invest were asked to suggest other candidates. Whenever they found an interested investor, they would visit them and show their trailer.

The Coen brothers discovered that the motive for people to invest in film has little to do with its financial merits. There are no special tax breaks. As will be discussed later, film is a risky investment. Yet there are many reasons people invest in film. The primary motivation is usually based on their attraction to the glamor of the movie business. Perhaps they think moviemaking will be exciting and fun. They may be turned on by the enthusiasm and passion of the filmmaker. They might want to rub shoulders with the "stars." They may have a special interest in a topic. They may seek to impress their friends by inviting them to a screening of "their" film. They may desire an "executive producer" credit, a role for their niece, or a role for themselves.

Prime prospects are middle-class professionals: doctors, lawyers, and dentists. Most working-class folks can't afford to invest in a movie. Wealthy individuals are difficult to approach unless you have a pre-existing relationship with them. They have investment advisors who tend to be financially conservative people immune to stardust. They analyze investments according to financial criteria, under which movie proposals fare poorly.

The ideal investor is a doctor who makes several hundred thousand dollars a year and has substantial assets. He can lose his entire investment and the loss will not affect his lifestyle. This year instead of going to Las Vegas for a week and blowing ten grand, he is going to invest in a film in the hope that the experience will be more entertaining—it certainly won't be less of a gamble. Investors who will suffer if they lose their investment should always be avoided.

Film investments have a bad reputation, and deservedly so. There are instances where investors were cheated and lost everything. Consequently, investors who have been burned or have heard of such horror stories may be unwilling to consider film-related investments. A filmmaker needs to be persuasive and have done his research if he hopes to raise funds. One needs to convince a prospect that film can be an intelligent investment for a small portion of the potential investor's portfolio. While film investments are risky, the potential return from a hit can be enormous. Not only can the film earn revenue from box office receipts, but there are also ancillary sources of income. These sources include revenue from television, home video, merchandising, music publishing, soundtrack albums, sequels, and remakes.

As an attorney who represents both film investors and filmmakers, I have found that investors usually have a limited understanding of how films are produced, marketed, and distributed. Moreover, filmmakers often don't know how to structure their proposal in a way that makes it attractive to an investor.

In order to give filmmakers insight into the thinking of investors, let me offer you my checklist for investors contemplating a film investment. This checklist is designed to help investors protect themselves from con artists and unscrupulous individuals. It is my belief that if a filmmaker understands an investor's perspective, the filmmaker will be better able to address these concerns. This checklist is condensed; the full list is available on my website at www.marklitwak.com. So let's take a look at things from the investor's point of view:

CHECKLIST FOR FILM INVESTORS

DUE DILIGENCE: Thoroughly investigate the reputation and track record of anyone with whom you contemplate doing business. Speak to producers and investors who have worked with a candidate. Check court records in order to discover any lawsuits.

FULL DISCLOSURE: Federal and state security laws are designed to protect investors. Offerings to the public usually require prior registration with the SEC or a state agency. Private placements are limited to persons with whom the offeror has a pre-existing relationship. Even if registration is not required, the anti-fraud provisions of the security laws require that the offeror make full disclosure of all facts that a reasonably prudent investor should know before investing. The information disclosed should include a detailed recitation of all the risks of developing, producing, and marketing a movie. Avoid any offering that appears to violate this requirement by making a less than full and truthful disclosure of all relevant information.

TRACK RECORD: Do not back a production team that does not possess the proven skill needed to make a professional-looking movie. Avoid first-time filmmakers unless you are convinced that they have the requisite ability. You are safer backing filmmakers with experience making shorts, television movies, commercials, music videos, or industrial films. Partner with people of integrity who have the skills, expertise, and resources that you need.

IDENTIFY THE POTENTIAL MARKET FOR THE FILM: As explained in the next chapter, there is a limited market, and modest revenue, to be earned from most shorts, documentaries, black-and-white films, and foreign-language pictures. Distributors and exhibitors remain prejudiced against motion pictures shot on videotape. Certain themes, topics, and genres can be a difficult sell. Films containing explicit sex may not pass censorship boards in certain countries. Films without name actors can be difficult to market.

AVOID DIRECTORS WHO ARE OBLIVIOUS TO AUDIENCE APPEAL: The director is the key person who will determine whether the final product is marketable. If a filmmaker shows no concern about making a movie with audience appeal, you can expect a film whose exhibition may be limited to family and friends. This is not to say that you should only invest in low-brow fare. A well-made "art" film can win awards and return a handsome profit. Filmmakers should consider the nature of a film's intended audience. I once watched a wonderful *Lassie*-type film spiced with four-letter words. I explained to the filmmaker that his film would never sell in the family market because of the vulgar language, and it was too soft a story to appeal to adults. The film was never distributed.

CONGRUENCE OF INTERESTS: It is best to invest in an endeavor where everyone shares its risks and rewards. A filmmaker who receives a large fee from the budget may prosper from a picture that returns nothing to the investor. It is better to back a filmmaker willing to work for a modest wage and share in the success of the endeavor through deferments or profit participation. An investor can take comfort investing in a movie on the same terms as a producer or distributor, where all parties recoup at the same time. Beware of investing in a project where others benefit even if you lose.

UNDERSTAND THE PARAMETERS OF A FAIR DEAL: Usually investors recoup all of their investment from first revenues before payment of deferments or profits. Often investors recoup 110% or more of their capital in order to compensate them for loss of interest and inflation. Profits are declared after payment of debts, investor recoupment, and deferments. Profits are generally split 50/50 between the producer(s) and the investors. Thus, investors who provide 100% of the financing are entitled to 50% of the profits. Third-party profit participants (*e.g.*, the writer, director, and stars) are paid out of the producer's 50% share of profits.

OBTAIN ALL PROMISES IN WRITING: Do not rely on oral assurances from others. If a distributor promises to spend $50,000 on advertising, get the commitment in writing. If there is not enough time to draft a contract, ask for a letter reiterating the promise. Retain copies of all correspondence, contracts, and any promotional literature given to induce you to invest. If a filmmaker makes fraudulent statements, you will have a much stronger case against him if the misrepresentations are in writing.

Avoid filmmakers who make handshake deals. Such individuals may neglect to secure the written agreements needed to maintain ownership of their motion picture. In order to have a complete chain of title to a film, one needs written contracts with many parties—including actors, writers, and composer. Filmmakers who fail to pay attention to such legal formalities lack the professionalism needed to succeed.

PROVIDE FOR ARBITRATION: Include a clause providing that any disputes are resolved through arbitration rather than litigation, with the prevailing party entitled to reimbursement of legal fees and costs. Arbitration is usually quicker and less expensive than litigation. The parties meet with an arbitrator in a hearing room. Each side is given the opportunity to present documents and witnesses. The rules of evidence do not apply. Counsel may represent parties, or they may choose to represent themselves. Disputes are resolved within a matter of months.

INTEREST ON LATE PAYMENTS: Remove any incentive for a producer or distributor to retain funds due you. Courts may not be able to award pre-judgment interest to a prevailing party unless there is a provision in the contract providing for it or a specific statute that allows it. Thus, if you become embroiled in a dispute with a distributor who is unlawfully holding $100,000 due you, and after four years of litigation you win the case, the court may award you $100,000 in damages but no interest. During those four years the distributor invests your money and earns interest. Under such circumstances, the distributor has an incentive to delay payment.

COMPLETION BOND: A completion guarantor is an insurance company that insures a production against budget overruns by issuing a completion bond. Before issuing the policy, the completion bond company will review the production person-nel, script, and budget, and determine whether they think the script can be produced within the shooting schedule and pro-posed budget. The completion bond company diligently re-views the project because if the film goes over budget, the bond company is financially responsible. Having a completion bond should give some comfort to investors. If there are cost over-runs, the investors will not be called upon to invest more money or end up owning an unfinished film.

TAKE AN ACTIVE ROLE: As a shareholder in a corporation, or a limited partner in a partnership, an investor has very limited control over how a film is produced. Investors desiring limited liability in corporations and partnerships had to be willing to pay the price of accepting limited control. With a limited liability company (LLC), however, an investor can be one of the managers of the enterprise yet maintain limited liability. Thus, the investor can have a vote on critical decisions such as approval of the script, cast, budget, and the terms of distribution agreements. By being actively involved in the production, an investor will be better able to monitor the performance of the filmmaker and discover problems while there is time to remedy them.

MAKE SURE FUNDS ARE SPENT ON PRODUCTION: During fundraising, it is common for the filmmaker to set up an escrow account to hold investor funds. The money stays in the account until the filmmaker raises the minimum necessary to produce the film. If the filmmaker cannot raise enough money, the funds are returned to the investors. By depositing money in an escrow account, investors are protected because they know none of their capital will be spent unless and until all the money needed to produce the film has been raised.

After funds are released for production, there should be a system of checks and balances to ensure that all monies are properly spent and accounted for. A budget and cash-flow schedule should be approved beforehand. Production funds should be placed in a separate, segregated account and not commingled with a filmmaker's personal funds. Two individuals should sign all checks withdrawing significant funds from the account. Investors may want to be one of the signatories or they may want to select one of the signatories.

OBTAIN AN ADVISOR: Have an experienced entertainment attorney review all documents. Make sure the filmmaker has adequate representation in his dealings with third parties. Filmmakers may be very capable in the arena of production yet be unsophisticated in business matters. They can be badly taken advantage of if they attempt to negotiate a distribution deal without assistance. Since the investor shares in revenue after a distributor deducts its fees and expenses, if the filmmaker negotiates a bad deal, the investor suffers.

A skilled attorney or producer's rep who represents many filmmakers may have added clout in negotiations. Such a person is aware of how much distributors will pay to license films and the concessions they are willing to make. By virtue of the representative's relationships with festival directors and acquisition executives, attention can be drawn to a film that might otherwise get lost in the crowd.

PROTECT THE MASTERS: The production company should retain possession of all master elements. Film negatives and other masters materials should not be delivered directly to a distributor for reasons explained in Chapter 6. Instead, the materials should be deposited in a laboratory and the distributor given a lab access letter.

OBTAIN AND REGISTER A SECURITY INTEREST: A security interest gives the secured party rights in designated collateral. A bank, for instance, has a security interest in the form of a mortgage when it makes a home loan. If the house is sold, the bank loan must be repaid from the proceeds. In the movie and television industry, lenders may want to secure their financial interests by obtaining a security interest in certain collateral, such as the film negative and master materials.

Likewise, investors may want to ensure that distributors grant the owner of the film a security interest. The collateral here is the proceeds derived from exploitation of the film. By having a security interest, the owner will have superior rights to unsecured creditors. In the event that a distributor goes bankrupt, its assets will be auctioned off to pay creditors. One of the distributor's assets may be the right to distribute your film and any revenue generated from it. If the filmmaker has a security interest, then proceeds derived from the film will be paid to the filmmaker first, as a secured creditor, before payment is made to the distributor's unsecured creditors (*e.g.*, the office supply store). When several parties register security interests, there may be a conflict, and some parties may need to subordinate their interests to others. The guilds often ask for a security interest to ensure that their members are paid, but they may be willing to subordinate their interests to a bank making a production loan.

It is important not only to have a written security agreement but also to record it. The distribution agreement should have a clause granting the filmmaker a security interest. Long- and short-form security agreements are signed by the parties, as well as a UCC-1 form, which is recorded with the Secretary of State where the collateral or distributor is located. The security interest should also be recorded with the Copyright Office at the Library of Congress in Washington, D.C. If you are not knowledgeable about security interests, it is advisable to retain an attorney to assist you.

DON'T INVEST MORE THAN YOU CAN AFFORD TO LOSE: Investing in a film is a highly risky endeavor. If a film doesn't appeal to audiences, or is not marketable, one's investment can be entirely lost. Unlike some other products, one cannot reduce the price of a ticket and expect a line to materialize at the box office. Moviegoers will not watch bad films, even if they are offered them for free. Consequently, investors should never invest more than they can afford to lose.

CHAPTER 5

TACTICS AND STRATEGY IN ARRANGING DISTRIBUTION

The growth in independent cinema provides moviegoers an alternative to Hollywood's mainstream fare. As the majors increasingly homogenize their product in an attempt to create pictures for a mass audience, the independents have become the source for most quirky, offbeat, and controversial films. Unsurprisingly then, indie films receive more than their fair share of critical acclaim and awards.

Over the past two decades there has been a dramatic increase in the number of indie films produced, inspired by such trailblazers as John Sayles, Spike Lee, and Ed Burns. Many persons who might have previously aspired to write the great American novel now dream of making their own film, but the flood of independent films has created a buyer's market. Industry observers estimate that there are currently 800 to 1,000 independent pictures produced in the United States each year. This estimate does not include "independent" films financed by Miramax, Fine Line, or other studio subsidiaries.

Filmmakers often do not realize how difficult it is to secure distribution for a film. Many naively assume that if they just make a good film, distribution will fall into place. Unfortunately, this is usually not the case. Indeed, the biggest obstacle to success is not producing a film but securing its distribution. The marketplace is so glutted with product that distributors can afford to be choosy. Most distributors are not interested in films without name actors, and they are reluctant to distribute films shot on anything other than 35mm stock (although there is a growing acceptance for digital movies).

Many filmmakers are so caught up in their passion for telling their story that they spend little time considering the financial and marketing aspects of moviemaking. One's leverage in negotiating a distribution deal is a function of whether distributors perceive a film as desirable. While I don't advise filmmakers to slavishly imitate whatever is fashionable or popular at the moment, one should not completely ignore commercial realities either. Here is a quick summary of how many distributors view the marketplace.

HOW MUCH IS MY FILM WORTH?

Shorts

The market for short films is very limited, and producing shorts is usually a money-losing endeavor, notwithstanding the fact that shorts cost less to make than features. HBO and other cable channels license shorts to fill gaps in their schedule. A number of Internet companies such as Atom Films and CinemaNow distribute shorts on a revenue-sharing basis, but so far there is not much revenue to share. Film festivals play shorts but don't pay for the privilege—indeed the filmmaker often has to pay to apply. So making a short film can help filmmakers learn their craft, earn them a credit, and add some impressive footage to their reel, but shorts don't generate much revenue. A well-made short, however, can persuade investors to back a filmmaker wanting to produce a feature. Sometimes the "short" is a trailer for an upcoming feature.

Documentaries

I love documentaries. Unfortunately, many distributors never acquire documentaries because the market for them is limited and revenue modest. You may have noticed that only a handful of documentaries are theatrically released in the United States each year, and independent documentaries are almost never broadcast by the major networks. The market abroad, especially in television, is better. Many documentaries are funded through grants, but even with such financial assistance, it is difficult for documentary filmmakers to make a living. Revenue from the non-theatrical market (*i.e.*, schools, civic groups) has declined. At one time a documentary on a topic that was curriculum-related could generate significant receipts. Schools might purchase a 16mm print for $800, providing a healthy profit margin. Today, there is little demand for 16mm prints or 3/4-inch videos. Most licensees want a VHS cassette or DVD and expect to pay not much more than what Blockbuster charges its consumers. At this price point, most independent documentary filmmakers cannot survive. The most lucrative documentary work is producing for news programs (*e.g.*, *60 Minutes*), reality shows, or cable channels (*e.g.*, HBO, Discovery). Much of this work is produced in-house or commissioned before production.

Black/White Films

If you are Woody Allen or Martin Scorsese, you can produce a black-and-white ("B/W") film and obtain distribution. If you are a beginning filmmaker, you will find it extremely difficult to arrange distribution for your B/W film. Even if you attract a distributor, the market for B/W films is tiny. Many television buyers will not even consider licensing B/W movies. My advice: Save your B/W project for later in your career. Or, shoot your film on color stock and develop it in B/W. This gives you the option of going back and developing your film in color if you cannot distribute the B/W version.

Foreign-Language Pictures

While American indie filmmakers face many obstacles in selling their pictures, foreign filmmakers have an even bigger mountain to climb. The potential market for French- or German-language films, for instance, is much smaller than for English-language pictures. The language of many of the major buyers (*e.g.*, United States, United Kingdom, Australia, Canada) is primarily English. Even in countries where English is not spo-ken, moviegoers have grown accustomed to a steady diet of English-language films that are dubbed or subtitled.

In most countries, American films dominate the box office. More tickets are sold for American movies than for locally produced fare. Consequently, the words "Made in America" have come to represent quality entertainment to moviegoers world-wide. This connotation has rubbed off on American indie films.

Filmmakers considering making a film in any language other than English should realize that unless the film wins film festival awards and garners glowing reviews, potential revenue may be modest. Although occasional foreign-language films such as *Crouching Tiger, Hidden Dragon, Life Is Beautiful,* and *Like Water for Chocolate* attain hit status, most foreign-language pictures will not obtain much, if any, distribution in the United States, and may be difficult to license elsewhere.

Motion Pictures Shot on Video

Distributors remain prejudiced against motion pictures shot on videotape. They prefer films shot on 35mm stock, although quality films shot on 16mm or Super 16mm stock may obtain distribution. The reality is that many independent features will never be exhibited in theaters. They will be viewed on televi-sion and on videocassette or DVD. Thus, there is no technical reason why most motion pictures cannot be shot on video, especially the new digital formats that provide high-resolution images. There is the prestige factor, however. Films shot on 35-mm are still considered the most professional.

Of course, motion pictures shot on video can be transferred to film. The resolution of the picture may not be as sharp as if originally shot on film, but if the transfer is good and the story involving, many viewers will not notice. The cost of the transfer must be taken into account when weighing whether to shoot on video or film. In my opinion, it makes sense to shoot on video in two instances: 1) If you are shooting a documentary or improvised drama and need to be able to shoot a lot of footage without running up a huge bill. There are significant cost advantages that can be gained because if you do not capture what you want, you can hit the rewind button and reuse the stock. Moreover, not only is tape inexpensive but there are no developing costs and you can immediately view what you shot to see what you captured; and 2) If you own a video camera and cannot afford to make your motion picture any other way.

Most filmmakers who shoot on film edit on video. After finishing their final cut on video, they may ask themselves whether they should incur the expense of manufacturing a film negative before they have secured distribution. Films finished on video can be screened in theaters with video projectors. Many screening rooms in Los Angeles and New York have this capability. The latest high-end digital projectors provide extremely fine resolution, comparable to 35mm film. George Lucas's latest *Star Wars* installment was shot entirely on a digital medium, although it was transferred to film because most theatres cannot project digitally. Another reason to create a film print is to participate in film festivals, although many festivals have begun using digital projectors. Of course, if your film is not arty enough for the festival circuit, you may want to forego manufacturing a print and exhibit your motion picture to potential distributors via video projection or by sending out videocassettes or DVDs. Once you have secured distribution, if a theater owner wants to exhibit your picture, you can then pay for creation of a film print.

Taboo Topics

Certain themes, topics, and genres are difficult to sell. Religiously themed pictures can readily offend audiences. Cerebral comedies can be difficult to export because the humor may not translate well—people in other cultures may not get the joke. Slapstick humor, on the other hand, travels better. Films with a great deal of violence tend to shunned by European television, a prime market for independents. Films with a lot of sex or nudity may not pass censorship boards in certain countries.

Family Films

There is an unfilled demand for films that can be seen by the entire family. *Air Bud*, a film about a dog who plays basketball, was a huge hit. Nevertheless, few independent filmmakers appear interested in making such films, preferring instead to produce dark, edgy films. The major drawback of making family films is that they are not perceived as having much artistic merit. Many film festivals and critics disregard them. These films can generate significant revenues, however.

No-Name Movies

Independent films without name actors are difficult to market. With so many movies to choose from, the first question buyers ask is, "Who is in it?" If none of the cast members is recognizable, the buyer's interest vanishes.

Which actors are considered names? The general rule of thumb is that if you say the person's name and your listener responds, "Who?" then the person is not a name. It is not the number of credits the actor has, nor how many well-known films the actor has appeared in, but rather how recognizable the person's name is to the public. Sandra Bullock became a name after appearing in one hit film, *Speed.* Other actresses may have more credits, but they do not have the same name recognition. Of course, name recognition varies around the globe. The star of an American television series may be a big name here but unknown abroad. If that series is syndicated abroad, the actor may become a name in certain countries. The best source for information about which names matter are foreign sales agents (*i.e.,* distributors who sell international rights). They sell to foreign buyers on a regular basis and know which names matter. There are also several publications that can be consulted: *The Ulmer Scale* (www.ulmerscale.com) and *The Hollywood Reporter*'s "Star Power" (213) 525-2087.

HOW DISTRIBUTORS EVALUATE A FILM

Filmmakers are often dismayed when they observe how pictures are bought and sold at a film market. The atmosphere is more akin to a fish market than an art gallery. Most buyers do not spend much time contemplating the artistic merits of a film. They need to buy a lot of product quickly. They rush from one screening to another like contestants on *Supermarket*

Sweep. They may license films on the basis of trailers, posters, and cast without viewing the entire film. Or they may hit the fast-forward button and quickly scan the movie. They often buy in bulk, purchasing packages of films. Motion pictures are a commodity, and they are evaluated in a fairly crude fashion. Even buyers of art films are bottom-line oriented. They just serve a different market.

The primary concern of buyers is simply: Can I make money with this film? Which leads directly to the query: "How can I sell this to subdistributors and/or the public?" The marketability of the picture is of paramount concern. A brilliant film that is difficult to market is less desirable than a mediocre film with marketable elements.

Distributors typically market indie films in several ways:
1) NAME ACTORS: "Who is in it?" is the first question that most foreign buyers ask. Sometimes a name director, such as Quentin Tarantino, will suffice instead of name actors.
2) FESTIVALS: Movies that have won acclaim at major festivals can be marketed on that basis. You don't have to be a marketing genius to recognize that placing a banner across your poster proclaiming: "Winner, Sundance Film Festival" will attract an audience.
3) REVIEWS: Reviews by the trade papers (e.g., *Variety, Hollywood Reporter, Screen International*) and major media, such as *The L.A. Times, N.Y. Times,* or *Ebert & Roeper,* are useful in marketing a film. Quotes from such critics are often included in advertising.

If an independent film does not have one or more of the above elements, many distributors will pass on it. It is not that they do not like the film—they may think it is wonderful but they do not see an obvious way to market it. Much to the chagrin of the filmmaker, who has struggled for years to create a masterpiece, if a distribution executive cannot quickly discern how to sell a picture, he will move on to the next candidate. The distributor has no investment—financial or emotional—in films they acquire from others.

Thus, the filmmaker's quandary. Since many low-budget independent films are not high-concept, and may not have much sex or action, they must rely on good word of mouth to build an audience. But one cannot generate word of mouth unless one's film has been released. If no distributor is willing to take the financial risk of marketing the picture, the film may never find its audience. Of course, a filmmaker could book the film into theatres directly, by either renting the theatre ("four-walling") or entering into a "service deal" with a distributor. These arrangements, however, require the filmmaker to finance the cost of prints and advertising, which can amount to more than the production budget. Many indie filmmakers are broke by the time they complete their film.

Sometimes a controversial or newsworthy film can be distributed on the basis of publicity generated upon release. But do not think that because you made a great-looking film on a minuscule budget that this is newsworthy. That is old news.

If you want to interest distributors in your film, figure out how to market it. Make the distributor's job easy. If you are passionate about your story, you should be willing to brainstorm to come up with a good title and a marketing hook. Then persuade distributors that your campaign will work. It may be helpful to prepare a professional-looking one-sheet, poster, and/or trailer. By doing the heavy thinking for them, distributors are able to immediately see how to promote your film.

One of the few books to explain how different types of movies are marketed is *Movie Marketing: Opening The Picture and Giving It Legs* (Silman-James Press, 1998), written by my wife, Tiiu Lukk. The book explains how different movies were marketed using case studies. Among the films profiled are *Four Weddings and a Funeral*, *Pulp Fiction*, *GoldenEye*, *Hoop Dreams*, and *The Brothers McMullen*.

SOURCES OF REVENUE

Theatrical

You might think a $500,000 film presents a great bargain for a domestic distributor, but that is not the way they see it. The fact that a film was made inexpensively, and can be acquired for little or no advance, is of limited weight. Distributors are more concerned about recouping their marketing costs. The cost of prints and advertising may exceed the cost of production. Consequently, most low-budget indie films do not receive a theatrical release in the United States. Those that are released may receive very limited exposure, perhaps playing on a few screens in eight or ten cities. Some pictures will play in New York, receive bad reviews, and perform poorly at the box office and not travel any further.

Home Video

The current home video market generates less revenue for producers than it used to. At the birth of the home video industry, retailers were desperate to acquire product to fill their shelves, and even mediocre B-movies sold briskly. Today, the industry has consolidated. If the large chains like Blockbuster do not order your picture, potential sales are limited. Most retailers fill up on A-titles from the major studios, and have little room left for indie films. They prefer films that have had a theatrical release and the attendant publicity and public awareness that such a release generates. Video store consumers tend to select pictures they heard about when they were released theatrically.

When indie films are released to the home video market, sales are frequently modest. Under what is sometimes referred to as a "standard" distribution formula, the home video distributor deducts a distribution fee from gross revenue, and then recoups the cost of advertising and duplication. If anything remains, it is remitted to the filmmaker. An alternative formula is a royalty-based deal. Here the filmmaker might receive 20% or more of the price of the cassettes sold, less any returns. Thus, assuming the videos are sold to retailers at a "rental price" of $40.00 per cassette, and 10,000 sales are made, gross revenues would amount to $400,000. A 20% royalty would earn the filmmaker a payment of $80,000. It bears noting that today many indie films are lucky to sell 5,000 copies, wholesale prices vary greatly, and have been falling in response to the availability of DVDs selling at lower prices.

Retailers have traditionally bought VHS cassettes at two price points: rental and sell-through. Those sold to retailers with the intention that they will be rented to consumers sell for approximately $40 wholesale. Those sold to retailers intended for sale to consumers are often priced at $10 or less per copy. Keep in mind that videos sent to retailers are usually sold on a consignment basis with the retailer able to return any unsold items for a complete refund or credit. In the past few years many distributors have entered into "revenue-sharing" deals with retailers. Under these deals the cassettes are supplied to the retailer at a minimal cost and the retailer and distributor share whatever revenue is generated.

There has been a tremendous amount of growth in the DVD format, which has been priced for sell-through (approximately $20-$25 retail price per DVD). As more consumers buy DVD players there will likely be less demand for the VHS cassette format.

Television

A few indie films are licensed to HBO, Showtime, or Lifetime for significant sums. But most cable and broadcast buyers pay meager fees for independent films, and they are not interested in most indie titles at any price. The channels most interested in indie fare, the Independent Film Channel and The Sundance Channel, have limited subscriber bases. The Sundance Channel will pay as little as $7,500 to license a film for an 18-month window. A more desirable indie film might fetch $20,000-$30,000.

Foreign

For many low-budget independent features, most of the money that the filmmaker will receive is derived from foreign sales. A few well-made features, without big-name actors or festival acclaim, have been able to generate $1 million or more in foreign sales. With bigger names, greater sales can be expected. Of course, every year there are a few low-budget films that exceed all expectations: The $60,000 black-and-white film *Pi* won Sundance and received a large advance and a U.S. theatrical release.

If a filmmaker is dealing with an honest distributor, and all the loopholes in the distribution agreement have been closed, most of the revenue generated from foreign sales should flow to the filmmaker. For example, if foreign sales amount to $1 million, and the distributor is entitled to a distribution fee of 20% plus recoupment of expenses of $75,000, the filmmaker will receive

$725,000 as his share of revenue. If the film was made for $500,000, the filmmaker is in great shape.

Many independent filmmakers will have a different experience: They may not be able to secure any distribution; or they enter into a deal but sales are so modest that after the distributor deducts fees and costs, little or no revenue is returned to the filmmaker; or the distributor engages in creative accounting or fraud, cheating the filmmaker out of his share of revenue.

INCREASING YOUR LEVERAGE

When a distributor negotiates with a filmmaker to acquire film rights, the distributor often has a lot of clout, and the filmmaker may be desperate to make a deal. This is a perilous situation for the filmmaker. If you accept a bad deal, you may not be able to repay investors, making it difficult to raise funds for your next project.

Filmmakers should orchestrate the release of their film to the marketplace to maximize their leverage so as to secure a desirable deal. In order to secure favorable terms, one needs a strategy designed to generate distributor interest. This may entail generating positive word of mouth within the industry. This "buzz" or "heat" can be encouraged by filmmakers who work the festival circuit and mount campaigns on behalf of their films.

FILM FESTIVALS

Festivals can be a cost-effective way to introduce films to distributors. But all festivals are not equal. Some are much better launching pads than others. Certain festival directors have reputations for selecting films that go on to great critical acclaim and/or box office success. Other festivals have different ambitions; they may focus on the work of regional filmmakers, or exhibit films that have already secured distribution. These festivals may be more interested in obtaining popular programming than in helping filmmakers secure distribution.

Since acquisition executives have time to attend relatively few of the many festivals staged each year, they prefer those festivals that premiere the best films. The top festivals want to attract industry executives because they know that their presence will make their festival more worthwhile for filmmakers seeking distribution. Consequently, festivals compete with each other to premiere the best new films.

A film can only premiere once in each territory or region, and participation in one festival may make the film ineligible for selection in others. For instance, Sundance has a policy of accepting films into competition that are U.S. premieres and have not been shown in more than two international festivals. Note that Sundance does not count such markets as the IFP, as festivals, and Sundance has other sections that do not require a U.S. premiere.

Generally speaking, for independent filmmakers with feature-length films seeking distribution, the top festivals are: Telluride, Sundance, Slamdance, Hamptons, New York, Mill Valley, and Seattle. Also significant are AFI, Austin, Fort Lauderdale, Hollywood, Los Angeles, Palm Springs, Santa Barbara, and SXSW. The most important European festivals are Berlin, Cannes, and Venice. The chief Canadian film festival is Toronto, although Vancouver and Montreal are first-rate. For documentaries, Amsterdam IDFA, Hotdocs Toronto, and Marseille are vital gatherings of filmmakers and distributors. Although not a festival, the IFP Market, held each September in New York, has become a launching pad for independent films, although as of 2002 this market will focus on works-in-progress and documentaries rather than on completed narrative films. The important television markets include MIP, MIP-COM, and NATPE.

There are many festivals, each with its own selection criteria and point of view. Some are specialized and concentrate on one type of film such as documentaries, shorts, or animation, while others focus on particular subject matter such as stories of interest to the Gay and Lesbian, Ecological, and Jewish communities; other festivals exhibit a broad range of motion pictures. Consequently, the decision of which festivals to enter will depend on the nature of the film. A list of festivals can be found in the Resources section (page 309). More up-to-date information can be obtained online at my website: Entertainment Law Resources (www.marklitwak.com). The several good books about festivals including *The AIVF Guide to International Film & Video Festivals* by Kathryn Bowser, *The Ultimate Film Festival Survival Guide* by Chris Gore, and the *Variety Guide to Film Festivals* by Steven Gaydos.

Here is a brief summary of some of the festivals important to independent filmmakers:

Sundance

Over-crowded, over-hyped, and over-rated would best describe this festival. Sundance has become for independent film what the Academy Awards are for the major studios: an opportunity to generate a lot of publicity to promote one's film. Many of the specialty companies, almost all of which are now subsidiaries of the majors, spend gobs of money throwing parties, flying in stars, handing out promotional items in an attempt to generate press and a positive buzz about their pictures. Since the town is filled with 600 journalists searching for something to write about, it is not difficult to generate publicity. One gambit is for a distributor to pick up rights to a film before Sundance but not announce the acquisition until the festival so that it appears the distributor discovered it then and beat out its competitors. Or the distributor could just pay a large advance to make a splash.

The fact that many Sundance films receive little, if any, distribution is often overlooked. Many Sundance films appeal to festival programmers, but distributors shun them as too uncommercial for the general public. For those filmmakers that win an award or are the subject of a bidding war, the festival can be a springboard to success. Many filmmakers, however, get lost in the crowd. The festival shows more than 100 features and about 60 shorts. This is a festival at which it is important to have a publicist, since competition is intense, and indie filmmakers are competing against the publicity machines of the specialty distributors. While lesser festivals do not have the cachet of Sundance, the competition is less intense and one's chances of making a splash are greater. Foreign-language films often receive more attention at Berlin, Cannes, or Venice.

Sundance has been a poorly organized event. Until 2003, one could not buy individual tickets over the internet. If one is fortunate enough, and wealthy enough, to have the privilege of paying $3,000 to buy a priority pass, or $2,500 for a fast pass that lets you enter a theater without purchasing individual tickets, the experience is tolerable. However, Sundance only sells a limited number of such passes. The next alternative is to buy a limited pass, which allows you to obtain a package of tickets. You cannot select your films while attending the festival—you must call weeks beforehand at an appointed hour and try to order tickets based on the descriptions in the catalog. Too bad if you change your mind once you arrive and hear about a film that intrigues you. And when you try to order tickets, you often can't obtain the ones you want. Another possibility is to stand in line at the box office in Park City to try to buy any available tickets.

Since the theatres are scattered about town, one is constantly rushing from one venue to the next. In 1998, significant improvements were made. The hospitality center was moved off Main Street, relieving congestion downtown. The new Eccles Theater at the high school significantly expanded the number of tickets available. An improved local transportation system helped festival-goers travel from one venue to another. Of course, many of those who go to Park City during Sundance spend their time skiing and partying, rather than viewing films. The festival has become a giant networking event.

Slamdance

Slamdance was established in 1995 by a bunch of disgruntled filmmakers who decided to launch their own festival after their films were rejected by Sundance. They called their festival "Slamdance '95, Anarchy in Utah—The First Annual Guerilla International Film Festival," with the motto: "By Filmmakers, For Filmmakers." The festival takes place in Park City at the same time as the Sundance festival. Over the years Slamdance has grown. It now receives more than 1,300 submissions competing for about 40 slots. The films vary widely in quality, but screenings are well-attended by agents and distributors. In 2001 the festival moved off Main Street in Park City and relocated to the Silver Mine a short distance away. A lot of the energy on the streets left with it. By 2003 the festival had returned to Main Street. Slamdance has historically had an antagonistic relationship with Sundance, which views the upstart festival as an annoyance and an event that exacerbates congestion in Park City.

Telluride

This is a film lover's festival. Films are selected solely on artistic merit. It does not matter if the films are independently made or major studio fare. Telluride is not obsessed with premieres, although there are many. The primary concern here is to show great films. The festival does not attempt to become a promotional event for distributors. Press are allowed to attend, but they must purchase a pass just like everyone else. This greatly reduces the media's presence. Indeed, paparazzi are actively discouraged. Many movie stars and directors attend, and they appreciate the fact that they can stroll about town without a dozen photographers flashing cameras in their face.

This is a very well-organized event. You can buy a pass for $500 that allows you to attend any screening just by showing up 30 minutes before show time. Numbers are passed out so you do not have to remain in line to maintain your place. You can sit at a nearby café and sip a cappuccino until it is time to enter the theater. The most popular movies are scheduled for additional screenings. The venues are all within easy walking distance of the hospitality center. Badges are mailed to participants weeks before, so you do not have to wait in long lines to register.

Unlike most festivals, the films that are shown at Telluride are not announced beforehand. It's a grab bag. Participants show up on the strength of the festival's reputation for showing interesting films. Telluride has a great track record for picking pictures that have gone on to receive critical acclaim. The festival has evening outdoor screenings (bring a tarp to put on the ground and a flashlight to find your way home on the unlighted side streets), seminars, and a picnic. The dress is casual—you only need to bring your blue jeans and boots.

Telluride itself is a charming town, and the residents and festival staff are cheerful and helpful. You really feel welcome here. Indeed, the town closes down the main thoroughfare for the opening-night food "feed." Of course, with 5,000 participants, this festival does not have to deal with the overwhelming logistical problems that face Sundance with its 20,000 spectators.

Cannes

This is one of the most glamorous—and perhaps most important—festival in the world. It takes place on the French Riviera
in May and is the occasion for numerous parties and gala film
premieres. The French take film very seriously, and this is an
event where it is a good idea to bring a tuxedo or formal gown.
In the evening, stars walk up a red carpet while the photographers snap their pictures.

Films are shown in a number of different sections. The main
competition and *Un Certain Regard* operate under the auspices of
the official festival. Two important sidebars are the films in the
Director's Fortnight, which are selected by the Société des Réalisateurs
de Films (Film Directors' Society), and the films shown in the
Semaine de la Critique (French Critics' Week), which are selected
by the Syndicat Français de la Critique de Cinéma (French Union of
Movie Critics). There are relatively few U.S. films participating in
the festival and sidebars. Those selected tend to be independent
films from favored auteurs and a few major studio features accompanied by big stars. The programmers favor diversity and will
program a mediocre Mongolian or Iranian picture, even if it means
passing up an exceptional American indie.

The Cannes market runs alongside the festival. The market is
comprised of distributors conducting business from booths in
the Palais (the exhibit hall) or hotel rooms on the Croisette
(the seafront main road). While the festival focuses on the art
of film, the market is pure commerce, and the films exhibited
tend to be more commercial than those in the festival.

Berlin

Of the major European festivals, the Berlin International Film
Festival (the Berlinale) is the most arty. Berlin does not have the
glitz and glamour of Cannes, nor the heritage of Venice, but it is
a very important event, especially for art-house fare. Some
3,500 journalists from 70 countries attend. The European Film
Market runs alongside the festival, providing an opportunity for
buyers and sellers to conduct business. In 2000 the festival
moved to a new location on Potsdamerplatz. Bring warm clothes
as Berlin in the winter can be quite cold.

Venice

Begun in 1932, this is Europe's oldest film festival. For 2001, the festival created two parallel competitions. One section awards the "Lion of the Year," while the other awards the traditional "Golden Lion." The festival is well-attended by the press and offers a wide variety of films from Bollywood to Hollywood and everything in between.

Toronto

Toronto is generally considered the top Canadian festival and one of the most important North American festivals. It has become an important venue for acquisition executives, and a large number of films are screened. There are separate industry/press screenings, and the festival is accommodating to independent filmmakers as well as to industry bigwigs. The festival is well-organized and offers a wide variety of fare as well as seminars and roundtable discussions. Screenings are attended by enthusiastic audiences in a cosmopolitan city known for lots of film fans. Many of the films shown have distribution in place.

Montreal

Montreal is to Toronto as Telluride is to Sundance. While Toronto is a bigger and more commercial and glitzy event, Montreal focuses on more arty and international fare. In 2001 the festival showed 388 features from 66 countries. Attending this festival is always a pleasure. The city of Montreal is beautiful, and the theaters are within walking distance of each other. There is also a modest film and television market that is held during the festival.

Other notable international festivals include San Sebastian in Spain, Karlovy Vary in the Czech Republic, Tokyo International, Melbourne, Sydney, Deauville, Hong Kong, Pusan, Locarno, and London.

WORKING THE FESTIVAL CIRCUIT

Filmmakers participating in a festival or market should come early and bring plenty of marketing materials. If you show up the day of your screening and find that your picture is playing to a half-empty theater, then you have not done your homework. Screenings at major festivals in prime slots may sell out on their own, but lesser festivals may benefit from the filmmaker's efforts to build an audience.

Launching a film at a festival is somewhat like mounting a military campaign. You need troops and ammunition. One should prepare professional one-sheets (8.5x11-inch mini-posters) and several full-size posters, and consider other promotional items such as T-shirts. Filmmakers often mail invitations to acquisition executives weeks before their screening. Publicity stunts are sometimes staged to call attention to one's film. Usually it is helpful to have your stars present.

In 1994, I attended the IFP Market as a representative of the film *Unconditional Love*. The film is about a young painter searching to find his artistic vision while being involved in several romantic relationships. It is a classy art-film without any name actors in it. I met with the filmmaker and his collaborators beforehand and we plotted a strategy.

FILM FESTIVAL WEBSITES

SUNDANCE FILM FESTIVAL
  www.sundance.org
HAMPTONS INTERNATIONAL FILM FESTIVAL
  www.hamptonsfest.org
NEW YORK FILM FESTIVAL
  www.filmlinc.com/nyff/nyff.htm
MILL VALLEY FILM FESTIVAL
  www.cafilm.org/nav0_3.html
SEATTLE INTERNATIONAL FILM FESTIVAL
  www.seattlefilm.com
TELLURIDE FILM FESTIVAL
  www.telluridefilmfestival.com
SLAMDANCE
  www.slamdance.com
HOLLYWOOD FILM FESTIVAL
  www.hollywoodawards.com
LOS ANGELES FILM FESTIVAL
  www.lafilmfest.com
FT. LAUDERDALE INTERNATIONAL FILM FESTIVAL
  www.fliff.com
NORTEL PALM SPRINGS INTERNATIONAL FILM FESTIVAL
  www.psfilmfest.org

(CONTINUED)

We devised a professional full-color glossy one-sheet with still photos from the film, a beautiful poster, and a press kit with photos, a synopsis, bios, and other information about the film. We also decided to create a unique giveaway item: a small artist's sketch pad with the film's artwork and screening times on the cover. This article was effective because it was thematically related to the film, it was unique (not the usual button, hat, or T-shirt), and it was useful. Indeed, throughout the festival, acquisition executives used the pad to take notes, and it continually reminded them of the film.

The filmmaker was on excellent terms with his cast and crew. Ten of his collaborators attended the market at their own expense. The editor, composer, co-producers, and several of the stars of the film pitched in and passed out leaflets, asked nearby store owners to display the film's poster, and invited acquisition executives to attend the screenings. As a result of this effort, 57 buyers attended the first screening and positive word-of-mouth spread. The film was subsequently invited to the Hamptons Film Festival, where the director and his team repeated their efforts. It won the top prize at Hamptons, which included a $110,000 grant of services toward the filmmaker's next project. The film was subsequently acquired for domestic and foreign distribution.

BALANCING RISKS AND REWARDS

In negotiating the distribution deal, the relative bargaining power of

---

FILM FESTIVAL WEBSITES (CONTINUED)

BERLIN INTERNATIONAL FILM FESTIVAL
   www.berlinale.de
CANNES INTERNATIONAL FILM FESTIVAL
   www.festival-cannes.fr
VENICE FILM FESTIVAL
   www.labiennale.org/en/cinema
TORONTO INTERNATIONAL FILM FESTIVAL
   www.e.bell.ca/filmfest
VANCOUVER INTERNATIONAL FILM FESTIVAL /
   FILM & TV TRADE SHOW
   www.viff.org
MONTREAL WORLD FILM FESTIVAL
   www.ffm-montreal.org
INDEPENDENT FEATURE FILM MARKET (IFP MARKET)
   www.ifp.org
FOR A MORE COMPLETE LIST OF FESTIVALS SEE THE RESOURCES CHAPTER, OR VISIT MY WEBSITE, www.marklitwak.com.

the parties is determined by the appeal of the film and how much financial risk each party wants to bear.

When major studios produce and distribute a film, they usually bear most, if not all, of the financial risk. The distributor typically acquires a project at script stage and has no way of knowing whether the completed film will realize its potential. Typically, the studio pays for development, production, and distribution. The filmmaker may receive a handsome fee for his services and a modest share of net profits. "Net Profits" are defined in such a manner, however, that there is little chance the filmmaker will ever see any "back-end" compensation.

On the other hand, when a film has been developed and produced independently, the filmmaker accepts most of the risk. A distributor viewing a completed film is in a better position to judge its quality than when making a decision based on a script (although the distributor will not know how effective the marketing will be, or how audiences will respond). Consequently, with an impressive film in hand, the filmmaker may be able to negotiate a more lucrative deal than what could be obtained at the script stage. Of course, if the film turns out poorly, no distributor may want it, and the loss will be borne entirely by the producer and his investors.

Some projects are financed by investors with a distribution agreement in place before production commences. The distributor may have no obligation to pay for the film until it has been completed and delivered according to the delivery schedule. At this time, the distributor will make payment, either to the filmmaker or to a bank to repay the producer's production loan.

THE ACQUISITION/DISTRIBUTION AGREEMENT

Even filmmakers with low-budget pictures with limited commercial appeal can usually improve upon a distributor's initial offer. An experienced negotiator can obtain certain changes just for the asking. While you cannot blame a distributor for sending you their dream contract, there is no reason to uncritically accept it. Many terms are negotiable.

It is rare for an independent filmmaker to sell his copyright outright to a distributor. Usually the filmmaker licenses specified distribution rights for a term of years. Once the term expires, the rights revert to the filmmaker. In a typical deal, the distributor secures the right to distribute the movie in one or more media (*e.g.*, theatrical, home video, television). The distributor pays for all distribution, advertising, and marketing costs. Both parties share revenue derived from the film. Most deals allow the distributor to retain a percentage of gross revenues as a distribution fee, and to recoup certain designated marketing expenses from film revenues, with the remaining balance, if any, paid to the filmmaker. I will call this formula a "standard" distribution deal, although many terms vary, but all of these deals calculate the distributor's fee as a percentage of gross revenues. Another type of deal, sometimes referred to as a "50/50 net deal," allows the distributor to first recoup its expenses from gross revenues, and then share the remaining balance 50/50 with the filmmaker.

Which type of deal is best for a filmmaker? That depends on how much revenue is generated, the extent of expenses incurred, and the amount of distribution fees. If $1,000,000 is generated in gross revenues, a standard distribution deal (with a 25% distribution fee and recoupment of $100,000 in expenses) would generate $650,000 for the filmmaker. Under a 50/50 Net deal (with the same gross revenue and recoupable expenses), the filmmaker would receive $450,000. But if the film only generated $400,000 in revenue, and the standard distribution fee was 35% with recoupable expenses of $150,000, the filmmaker would receive $110,000 under the standard distribution deal, but $125,000 under a 50/50 Net deal. Most deals are more complicated to assess because they cover multiple media, and the distributor's fee varies by media (*i.e.*, 35% for theatrical, 25% for broadcast television). Thus, it behooves the filmmaker to take pencil to paper and figure out how much he will likely receive under different revenue and expense scenarios.

The distributor may agree to give the producer an advance toward his share of revenue. The producer can use this money to pay production debts, recoup expenses or repay investors. Obviously, producers prefer large advances because they may never receive any subsequent revenue. The reputations of some independent film distributors for creative accounting are worse than those of the major studios.

As previously mentioned, independent filmmakers are more likely to receive back-end monies than studio-employed filmmakers because on most independent films the distributor has not provided production financing and thus is not entitled to recoup production costs and any overhead or interest charges on them. On the other hand, the independent filmmaker is obliged to repay his investors from whatever revenues are received from the distributor, while the studio-employed filmmaker can keep all fees for himself.

The distributor will want to pay as modest an advance as possible, and may strongly resist giving an advance greater than the cost of production. That is why filmmakers should not disclose their paltry budgets before concluding their distribution deals. You may feel justly proud of making a great-looking picture for $400,000, but if the distributor knows that is all you have invested, you will find it difficult to obtain an advance beyond that. Better to keep your budget confidential, recognizing that production costs may not be readily discernible from what appears on the screen. Assuming that the distributor has not financed production, it has no right to examine your books. What you have spent is between you, your investors, and the IRS. In the next chapter, we will discuss the terms of the distribution agreement in greater detail.

Acquisition agreements can be negotiated before, during, or after production. Sometimes distributors become interested in a film after viewing it at a film festival and observing audience reaction. Many distributors send one or more acquisition executives to major festivals to scout for films.

It is not difficult to alert acquisition executives to the existence of your film. Once a start date has been announced, do not be surprised if they begin calling you. They will track the progress of your film so that they can see it as soon as it is finished—and before their competitors can view it. To ensure that acquisition executives are aware of your film, send a press release announcing your project to the trade papers and magazines (*Hollywood Reporter* (323) 525-2000; *Daily Variety* (323) 857-6600; *Filmmaker* (212) 983-3150; *MovieMaker* (310) 231-9234; and *The Independent* (212) 807-1400). These publications will include your project in their listings of films in development, preproduction, and production. Likewise, you should list your film with Film Finders (323) 308-3484, a company that tracks films for many distributors.

Tactics and Strategy

1) NO SNEAK PREVIEWS: It is best not to screen your film for distributors until it is complete. Executives may beg to see a rough cut. They may assure you, "Don't worry. We are professionals. We can envision what the film will look like with sound and titles." Do not believe them. Most people cannot extrapolate. They will view your unfinished film and perceive it as amateurish. First impressions last. The community of acquisition executives is small, and they congregate frequently at industry screenings. One acquisition executive bad-mouthing your film can cause a lot of damage.

The only reason to show your film before it is complete is if you are desperate to raise finishing funds. The terms you can secure under these circumstances will be less than what you could obtain with a finished film. If you must show a work-in-progress, exhibit it on an editing console. People have different expectations watching a film on an editing console than when it is projected in a theater. If you must send out cassettes of an incomplete film, label it so that your viewers are reminded that they are viewing a work-in-progress. Your label might say: "Avid output, not color-corrected, temp sound." Always include the name of a contact person and phone number on all cassettes.

2) SCREEN IT BEFORE A CROWD: It is usually better to invite executives to a screening than to send them a videocassette. If you send a tape to a busy executive, he will pop it in his VCR. Ten minutes later he will hit the pause button when the phone rings. Then he will watch another ten minutes until his secretary interrupts. After numerous distractions, he passes on your film because he feels the story is too disjointed.

You want an executive to view your film in a dark room, away from distractions, surrounded by a live audience—hopefully one that loves your film. So rent a screening room at a convenient location, invite all the acquisition executives you can, and pack the rest of the theater with your friends and relatives, especially Uncle Herb with his infectious laugh. If an executive views your film surrounded by an appreciative audience, it will undoubtedly affect his perception of it.

Perhaps the best venue for exhibiting a picture is at a film festival. If the film is warmly received, your bargaining position will be enhanced. Moreover, by participating in a festival you may generate favorable publicity. Journalists who attend festivals may write about your film. Most publications have a policy of only reviewing those films about to be released; unreleased films are not reviewed. But entertainment trade papers and selected publications may review pictures shown at a festival. A strong review can influence distributors. Of course, you also risk receiving a poor review, which might discourage distributors.

If you arrange an industry screening, screen your film in a theater that is convenient and whose location is well-known to the invitees. If the venue is out of the way, or if people get lost searching for it, you have made a poor choice. A list of popular industry screening rooms in Los Angeles and New York is in the Resource section at the end of this book and posted on my website.

When you prepare an invitation list, include only those distributors appropriate for the film. If foreign rights are taken, there is no reason to invite international distributors. Don't waste their time and be inconsiderate. Likewise, do not invite an art-house distributor to view a *Beach Blanket Bingo*-type movie. As soon as the acquisition executive realizes that your film is not right for him, he will stand up and leave. A stream of people departing your screening might influence the perceptions of those remaining.

When arranging a screening, book a theater large enough to hold everyone expected to attend but not so spacious that your viewers are sitting in a sea of empty seats. Filling out the audience with cast, crew, and friends may be a good idea— these people are likely to respond positively. That is why you may want to hold off on your cast and crew screening until you screen for distributors. Acquisitions executives, however, can usually spot a cast and crew screening—it is pretty obvious when the audience applauds during the opening credits.

Mail out invitations so that they arrive on the desks of executives 7 to 10 days before your screening. If you mail too early, your invite may get lost on a cluttered desk; send it too late and your executive has made other plans. If a well-known producer's rep, agent, or attorney represents you, have that person send out the invitations. Always mention any name actors and the identity of the director. If the director has impressive credits or background, include this information. If an executive respects any of the people associated with the film, he/she is more likely to attend. If you have a professionally designed one-sheet, send it with the invitation. If you have a good trailer, you could include a videocassette copy of the trailer with the invite.

Asking for RSVPs is usually a waste of time. Half the people who RSVP do not show up; others who do not respond will attend. You are not going to bar any legitimate executive who wants to attend, so why bother with RSVPs? Better to spend your time elsewhere. As a general rule of thumb, if you invite 75 busy executives to a screening of a low-budget, no-name film, you will be lucky to have a dozen show up. At the screening, have someone at the door collecting business cards or taking names of those attending. That way you can track which companies have seen the film and which have not.

3) MAKE THE BUYERS COMPETE AGAINST EACH OTHER: Screen the film simultaneously for all distributors. Some executives will attempt to get an early look—that is their job. Your job is to keep them intrigued until the picture is ready to show. You can promise to let them see it "as soon as it is finished." They may be annoyed to arrive at the first screening and see their competitors. But this may get their competitive juices flowing. They will know that they better make a decent offer quickly if they hope to acquire the film.

From the filmmaker's point of view, competition improves terms. Giving one distributor an early peek at your film is usually a bad idea. If the distributor passes on the film, word may get around and other acquisition executives may not bother to view your film. On the other hand, if the distributor likes the film, a preemptive bid may follow, giving you only a day or two to decide whether to accept the offer. If you decline, you may be rejecting the best deal you will ever receive. If you accept, you foreclose the possibility of better terms from another company. Thus, you will be forced to make a decision without knowing where you stand in the marketplace and what terms other companies might propose. Consequently, you need to orchestrate the release of your film to all potential buyers so as to create maximum competition, which will increase your leverage in any negotiations. Considerable diplomacy and tact is needed to conduct a bidding war without alienating the bidders. You want to firmly push each buyer to offer their best terms while maintaining cordial relations with all. Remember, you may want to produce your next project with one of the losers.

4) DO NOT GIVE AWAY YOUR FESTIVAL PREMIERE LIGHTLY: Carefully plan a festival strategy. I have seen filmmakers give their premiere to minor festivals and thereby disqualify themselves from participating in more significant ones. You can participate in the lesser festivals later. If you are turned down by an important festival, the worst that happens is that you incur a

MARKETS & FESTIVALS

MARKETS ARE DIFFERENT FROM FESTIVALS. MARKETS ARE ONLY OPEN TO THE TRADE: A MEMBER OF THE PUBLIC CANNOT BUY A TICKET TO SEE A FILM AT A MARKET OR PARTICIPATE IN IT. AT MARKETS, FILMS ARE SCREENED FOR BUYERS. ACTUALLY, IT WOULD BE MORE ACCURATE TO CALL THESE BUYERS "LICENSEES" SINCE THEY USUALLY DO NOT BUY FILMS OUTRIGHT BUT LICENSE DISTRIBUTION RIGHTS FOR A TERM IN A TERRITORY. ONE BUYER MIGHT BE A GERMAN BROADCASTER INTERESTED IN ACQUIRING FILMS TO DISTRIBUTE BY CABLE TELEVISION IN GERMANY. ANOTHER BUYER MIGHT BE A TURKISH THEATRE-CHAIN OWNER WHO WANTS TO ACQUIRE THEATRICAL RIGHTS FOR TURKEY. SOME BUYERS WANT ALL MEDIA RIGHTS (THEATRICAL, TELEVISION, AND HOME VIDEO) IN A TERRITORY, AND MAY SUB-LICENSE RIGHTS TO OTHER DISTRIBUTORS.

MARKETS ARE AN OPPORTUNITY FOR BUYERS WORLDWIDE TO CONVERGE AT ONE LOCATION TO MEET WITH SELLERS OF FILM RIGHTS. IN THE COURSE OF A MARKET, A BUYER CAN TALK TO MANY SELLERS AND VIEW MULTIPLE FILMS. DEALS MAY BE SIGNED DURING THE MARKET OR AFTERWARDS. THE MARKET IS ALSO AN OPPORTUNITY FOR SELLERS AND BUYERS TO SOCIALIZE, AND TO MEET PEOPLE WITH WHOM THEY TRANSACT BUSINESS LONG-DISTANCE.

FESTIVALS, ON THE OTHER HAND, ARE OPEN TO THE PUBLIC. ANYONE CAN BUY A TICKET TO A SCREENING, ALTHOUGH AT THE MOST POPULAR FESTIVALS, THERE MAY NOT BE ENOUGH TICKETS TO GO AROUND. FESTIVALS CAN PROVIDE A TEST OF AUDIENCE APPEAL. A FESTIVAL SCREENING MAY BE THE FIRST OPPORTUNITY FOR THE FILMMAKER TO SEE HOW MOVIEGOERS REACT TO HIS WORK. OF COURSE, FESTIVAL-GOERS TEND TO BE BETTER-EDUCATED, WEALTHIER, AND MORE AVID MOVIEGOERS THAN THE AVERAGE MOVIEGOER. NEVERTHELESS, A FESTIVAL SCREENING DOES PROVIDE SOME GOOD FEEDBACK.

(CONTINUED)

small delay in seeking distribution. No one knows which festivals passed on your film unless you inform them.

5) APPROACH BUYERS WHEN THEY ARE HUNGRY FOR PRODUCT: Distributors that acquire films for international distribution plan their activities around a market calendar. The major film markets are i) AFM in late February in Santa Monica, California; ii) Cannes in May in Cannes, France; and iii) MIFED in late October in Milan, Italy. AFM recently announced that it will move its dates to the fall, thereby competing against MIFED. It is possible that MIFED may not survive. Television markets include NATPE in the U.S.A. and MIP and MIP-COM in France.

Distributors are hungriest for product when a market is rapidly approaching and they do not have enough new inventory. A distributor may spend $90,000 or more to attend Cannes, and if it appears that the company will have nothing new to sell, the executives panic. This is the best time to approach them. But

MARKETS & FESTIVALS (CONTINUED)

FESTIVALS SERVE TWO IMPORTANT FUNCTIONS. FIRST, THEY EXPOSE FILMS TO DISTRIBUTORS. ACCEPTANCE AT A TOP FESTIVAL WILL INDUCE MANY ACQUISITION EXECUTIVES TO TAKE A LOOK AT YOUR FILM, EITHER AT THE FESTIVAL OR BY ASKING TO SCREEN IT OUTSIDE THE FESTIVAL. WINNING A TOP FESTIVAL MAY MAKE YOUR FILM HIGHLY DESIRABLE IN THE EYES OF DISTRIBUTORS, AND MAY LEAD TO A FURIOUS BIDDING WAR.

SECOND, FESTIVALS CAN BE USED TO GENERATE PUBLICITY FOR A FILM AND DRAW THE PUBLIC'S ATTENTION TO IT. THUS, ONCE DISTRIBUTION HAS BEEN SECURED, THE DISTRIBUTOR MAY WANT THE FILM IN A FESTIVAL TO BUILD AWARENESS. IF THE TIMING OF THE FESTIVAL IS NEAR THE RELEASE DATE FOR THE FILM, PARTICIPATION IN THE FESTIVAL MAY FURTHER PUBLICIZE THE PICTURE. ON THE OTHER HAND, IF THE FILM IS NOT GOING TO BE RELEASED FOR ANOTHER SIX MONTHS, PUBLICITY NOW MAY NOT BE HELPFUL, AND CAN BE HARMFUL. THAT IS BECAUSE WHEN THE FILM IS RELEASED, THE PRIOR COVERAGE WILL HAVE BEEN FORGOTTEN BY THE PUBLIC, AND THE NEWS MEDIA WILL CONSIDER THE FILM OLD NEWS. THE MEDIA MAY NOT REVIEW THE FILM AGAIN OR WRITE ARTICLES ABOUT IT.

you must give them enough time to prepare to market your film. They may need to create a trailer, one-sheet, poster, screeners, and advertising. The bumper editions of the trade papers usually have an ad deadline of 3-4 weeks before a market. These expanded editions contain product listings by distributor, as well as extensive advertising. Many distributors send mass faxes to buyers before a market, alerting them to their new films. Try to finalize your distribution deal so that your distributor has at least one month to prepare your film for the next market. A movie acquired at the last moment will often receive rushed and slipshod treatment. As a result, the film may sell poorly at the first market, which is the most important market for a picture. At the second and subsequent markets, the film is no longer new product.

You should avoid soliciting distributors to acquire your film during a market. They have spent a great deal of money to attend the market, and their focus is to make sales to their buyers, not to acquire more product. In their sales mode, they will be too preoccupied to spend much time with you unless you approach them at the end of the market when most buyers have departed. Likewise, you should not approach a distributor immediately after their return from a busy market. They have been out of the office for several weeks and have messages to return and paperwork to complete.

The best time to approach a distributor is 60-90 days before a market. Assuming a distributor wants to acquire rights to your film, it may take a month or more to negotiate a deal. For reasons mentioned later, you want a long-form contract, not a short deal memo.

6) OBTAIN AN EXPERIENCED ADVISOR: Retain an entertainment attorney and/or producer's rep to advise you and negotiate your deal. Filmmakers know about film, distributors know about distribution. Do not deceive yourself and think you can play in the other guy's arena and win. There are many pitfalls to avoid. A competent negotiator should be able to improve a distributor's terms enough to outweigh his cost.

An attorney or producer's rep who represents many filmmakers may have added clout. The distributor knows that the representative is aware of what the distributor has paid for other films, and the kind of terms previously agreed to. Moreover, a distributor may have more of an incentive to live up to the terms of a deal if it comes through a rep because the distributor will not want to jeopardize a steady flow of product from this rep.

In selecting an attorney or producer's rep, one should recognize the difference, although a few people serve both functions. An attorney is licensed by the state bar to give legal advice and negotiate on behalf of clients. Attorneys are required to comply with a complex set of ethical rules, known as the Rules of Professional Responsibility, and they can be disciplined and disbarred if they violate these rules. Attorneys tend to be more knowledgeable about legal issues than producer's reps. On the other hand, producer's reps often know more about the movie business and distribution practices than attorneys. A producer's rep, for instance, may have more technical knowledge about delivery items than an attorney.

Producer's reps are not licensed. Many are filmmakers or former filmmakers who have learned what they know from the school of hard knocks. Now they are selling their expertise and contacts to less-experienced filmmakers. In selecting a representative, you should choose someone who has experience in the independent film world—not someone who is learning on your dime.

An attorney or rep can assist a filmmaker in other ways. If the representative has relationships with film festival directors and acquisition executives, he can draw attention to a film that might otherwise get lost in the clutter. While most festival directors will not accept a film simply because it was submitted by a rep they like, they may be more willing to view a film that comes in from a rep. When a film arrives from an unknown source without any recognizable names attached, the film may be screened by volunteers or low-level staff. These people may have limited film knowledge, and may have different tastes than the festival director. If the screener passes on the film, no one else may give it a look.

INVESTIGATE THE DISTRIBUTOR

Always check the track record and experience of distributors. The savvy filmmaker will carefully investigate potential distributors by speaking to filmmakers with whom the distributor has done business. One can also check court dockets to see if a company has been sued.

Those who have worked in the film business for some time know the reputations of distributors. But there are always new filmmakers, who may have difficulty discerning the good from the bad. These filmmakers are easy prey for unscrupulous distributors. It makes no sense to spend a year or two of your time, spend your life savings, take a mortgage on your house, and beg and borrow from your friends to produce your film, and then sign it away because an executive has a pleasant manner, a nicely decorated office, and a lot of enthusiasm for your film. Some of the worst sharks are the most charming, soft-spoken, friendly people you will ever meet.

A good contract is important, but if the contract is with a scoundrel, all you really have is a piece of paper that provides some legal recourse. None of these remedies are likely to make you whole because you will have to endure considerable aggravation and expense to enforce your rights. Even if substantial damages are awarded you, you may not be able to collect if the distributor has no assets or goes bankrupt. With a film that has been partially distributed, you will find it difficult to attract another distributor. Most distributors do not want second-hand merchandise.

The only positive thing I can say about movie industry predators is that they are consistent. They take advantage of everyone. That is why it is not difficult to unmask their true identity. Ask a prospective distributor to send you their press kit. It will likely contain one-sheets from the films they have distributed. Examine the credits. Track down the filmmakers. If you cannot find them, ask the distributor for a list of all the filmmakers with whom they have done business over the past several years. Ask the filmmakers specific questions, such as: Did they receive producer reports on time? Have they been paid on time? Did the distributor spend the promotional dollars they promised?

I have established the Filmmaker's Clearinghouse, a website devoted to disseminating information about distributors. This source will provide filmmakers with information about distributors just as the Better Business Bureau reports on merchants. The Clearinghouse will enable filmmakers to share information with their peers about their experiences with distributors. A filmmaker who has had a bad experience can complain; a filmmaker who has had a positive experience can recommend the distributor to others.

The Clearinghouse is co-sponsored by the Film Arts Foundation, The Association of Independent Video and Filmmakers, and *MovieMaker* magazine. The survey form and the responses can be viewed on my website, Entertainment Law Resources, at www .marklitwak.com. The survey can be answered online, or you can photocopy the survey form reprinted below and mail it in.

FILMMAKER'S CLEARINGHOUSE
Survey and Evaluation of Distributors

THIS IS A SURVEY OF INDEPENDENT FILMMAKERS ABOUT THEIR EXPERIENCES WITH DISTRIBUTORS. THE INFORMATION WILL BE COMPILED AND A SUMMARY MAILED TO ALL PARTICIPANTS. THE RESULTS WILL ALSO BE PUBLISHED ON THE INTERNET ON THIS WEBSITE.

THIS SURVEY IS LIMITED TO FILMMAKERS (PRODUCER OR DIRECTOR) WITH FIRST-HAND EXPERIENCE DEALING WITH DISTRIBUTORS FOR THE DISTRIBUTION OF FEATURE-LENGTH FILMS FROM 1990 TO THE PRESENT. PLEASE COMPLETE A SEPARATE SURVEY FOR EACH FILM AND DISTRIBUTOR.

TITLE OF FILM: _____

DISTRIBUTOR: _____

YEAR DISTRIBUTION BEGAN: _____

PLEASE RATE YOUR DISTRIBUTOR'S PERFORMANCE ON A SCALE OF 1 TO 5, WITH 1 BEING THE POOREST AND 5 BEING THE BEST. INDICATE N/A IF THE ITEM DOES NOT APPLY:

	1 POOR	2 FAIR	3 AVERAGE	4 GOOD	5 EXCELLENT	N/A
REGULAR & TIMELY PRODUCER REPORTS						
TIMELY PAYMENTS TO FILMMAKER						
QUALITY OF MARKETING & ADVERTISING MATERIALS						
SPENT AMOUNT IT AGREED TO ON PROMOTION						
OVERALL HONESTY AND INTEGRITY						
OVERALL PERFORMANCE						

NAME: _____

ADDRESS: _____

PHONE: _____

THE NAME, ADDRESS, AND PHONE NUMBER OF PARTICIPANTS IS FOR VERIFICATION PURPOSES ONLY. THE INFORMATION WILL NOT BE PUBLISHED.

CHAPTER 6

THE DISTRIBUTION AGREEMENT

PRINCIPAL TERMS OF A DISTRIBUTION AGREEMENT

Territory

The territory is the country or region where the distributor may exploit the film. If the territory is "worldwide," that means the distributor has the right to distribute the film in any country throughout the world. Some distributors go further and seek rights throughout the "Universe." To my knowledge, no licenses have been made for exhibition of motion pictures on other planets. I once teased a distribution executive that he was being silly asking for such rights. He conceded that it was unlikely he would ever need any rights beyond Earth. Several weeks later, however, he proudly faxed me a request from NASA asking for permission to exhibit one of his movies on the space shuttle.

The world market for films is typically divided into two territorial groups: domestic and foreign. Domestic rights are defined as the United States, its territories, possessions and military bases, as well as English-speaking Canada. It makes sense to group French-speaking Canada with foreign rights because the foreign distributor may create a French-language version of the picture that can be shared by all French-speaking territories. Sometimes domestic rights are defined to include only the United States, while in other agreements the term may encompasses all of North America. It is important to pay attention to these definitions to avoid conflicts between licensees. Foreign rights are often defined as the entire world other than whatever is included in the domestic territory.

As a general rule, filmmakers should only grant a distributor rights to territories that they directly service. Few distributors, other than the major studios, serve both the foreign and domestic markets. Even the majors use subdistributors for some territories. Nevertheless, distributors often attempt to acquire as much territory and media as they can persuade a filmmaker to give them. The distributor will then assign various rights and media to subdistributors and take a fee for being the middleman. This fee may be in addition to whatever fees are deducted by each subdistributor.

For example, some domestic theatrical distributors (companies that book films in theaters) rely on other distributors to license their films in the television and home video media. Likewise, some distributors that serve the home video and television markets will contract with a theatrical distributor to obtain a theatrical release.

Similarly, most companies that serve the domestic U.S. market do not license pictures to foreign buyers. If you grant such a distributor worldwide rights, they will arrange with an international distributor to handle sales outside North America. This foreign sales company will deduct a distribution fee for its services, and from the balance remaining, the domestic distributor may take a fee as well. Obviously, the more companies subtracting fees from the revenue stream, the less proceeds flow to the filmmaker.

That is not to say that you should never allow a distributor to use subdistributors. But you need to understand how a distributor will exploit your film. One should determine which media and territories a distributor handles itself, and which it relies on subdistributors for. The way a distributor describes itself may be misleading. Two companies that call themselves U.S. home video companies may function quite differently. Some companies that license films internationally refer to themselves as "foreign sales agents," while others performing exactly the same function describe themselves as "international distributors." The only difference is the nomenclature. If a filmmaker believes that a distributor's use of a subdistributor is beneficial, then the filmmaker could seek to cap the total amount of distribution fees charged by the distributor and any subdistributors.

Most filmmakers contract with two or more distributors. Filmmakers will engage a foreign sales agent to license the film at the major international markets. The filmmaker will also enter into an agreement with one or more domestic distributors. If the film lacks name actors in the cast, the filmmaker may not be able to secure a theatrical release. In such a situation, the filmmaker will contract with companies that serve the television and home video markets. Again, care must be taken in drafting these agreements to ensure that the media and territory granted one distributor does not conflict with the rights given another.

It is often beneficial for the filmmaker to contract with several distributors. First, you are not putting all your eggs in one basket. If you rely on one distributor and it goes bankrupt, performs poorly, or is dishonest, all your potential revenue is affected. Second, by using several distributors, expenses in one territory might not be offset, or cross-collateralized, against revenues in another.

When expenses are cross-collateralized, expenses and revenue from different territories or media are combined. For example, suppose a film generates $1,000,000 abroad. The distributor has incurred $100,000 in recoupable distribution expenses, and is entitled to retain 20% of gross revenues, or $200,000, as a distribution fee. The remaining $700,000 of proceeds is to be paid to the filmmaker as his share of revenue.

Suppose, however, that in North America, the film generates $1,000,000 but incurs expenses and distribution fees of $1.5 million. So on the domestic side of the ledger, the distributor has lost money, and no revenue would be paid to the filmmaker. If the filmmaker had one distributor for both foreign and domestic territories, that distributor might be able to recoup its $500,000 domestic loss from foreign revenue. Thus, a filmmaker may benefit by having separate foreign and domestic deals so that revenue in one territory is not offset by losses in another.

Not only can expenses be cross-collateralized among territories, but expenses in one media can be crossed against revenues from another. In many instances, a distributor will lose money on a picture's theatrical release and will want to recoup such losses from home video and television revenues.

When contracting with several distributors, the filmmaker may want to acquire the right to use artwork and marketing materials developed by a distributor for use elsewhere. Since the distributor is often reimbursed the cost of creating such artwork from a picture's revenue, the filmmaker is essentially paying for the creation of these materials, and should have the right to use them.

When contracting with multiple distributors, the filmmaker needs to ensure that each distributor has access to master materials. As previously discussed, this is accomplished by depositing materials in a film laboratory and giving each distributor a lab access letter.

Media

Media is the medium by which a film is exploited. Many motion pictures are meant for initial exhibition in theatres. The theatrical time period, or "window," during which the movie will play in theatres will be short for a flop and long for a hit.

After the theatrical release, a picture may be distributed and exploited in the so-called allied and ancillary markets, which include home video, non-theatrical (colleges, community groups), pay television (HBO), network television (ABC), and television station syndication. The film may also generate revenue from merchandising, book novelization, a soundtrack album, and music publishing. The nomenclature can be confusing because so-called "ancillary" media are now the major generators of revenue. Home video and television revenue for a picture often exceed theatrical revenue. So the home video media is hardly "ancillary" in terms of profitability.

A theatrical release is still primary in one important respect. Although the theatrical release may not generate revenues that exceed its marketing costs—due to the considerable expense of print duplication, advertising, and shipping—the theatrical release creates public awareness for the film. It is the engine that pulls the train. When consumers visit video stores, the cassettes and DVDs they select first are the movies publicized during their theatrical release.

Ancillary media tend to be more profitable than theatrical media. When a distributor releases a film to television, the marketing expenses incurred are minimal. If you license a film to CBS, for example, the expense consists of manufacturing one video sub-master and shipping it to the network. The distributor does not have to pay for any advertising, since CBS promotes the movies it broadcasts. Thus, most of the revenue from television licensing flows directly to the bottom line.

Because a theatrical release is often not profitable, and because ancillary media frequently are profitable, most domestic distributors will not take on the financial risk of a theatrical release without also securing ancillary rights. Consequently, filmmakers need to carefully consider offers for ancillary distribution. If they license home video and television rights first, they may be unable to secure a theatrical release.

Of course, some movies and programming are meant for direct release to television or home video. Made-for-television movies—as well as exercise, specialty, and children's programs—can successfully recoup their costs and generate significant profits without a theatrical release.

In fashioning a grant-of-rights clause, filmmakers will want to retain rights to media the distributor is unlikely to exploit. It has become customary for distributors to seek multimedia and interactive rights, although few utilize these rights. Generally, filmmakers should only grant three media: 1) theatrical, 2) television (all forms—including pay TV, cable TV and broadcast), and 3) home video (distribution by videocassette, laser disc, and DVD). Unless a distributor makes a convincing case for greater rights, the filmmaker should reserve everything else, including dramatic (*i.e.*, play or stage rights), radio, electronic publishing, multimedia/interactive, merchandising, music publishing, soundtrack, and print publication rights. Distributors are usually granted limited non-exclusive radio and print publication rights to be used to advertise and promote the film.

Filmmakers often reserve remake, sequel, and television spin-off rights. If a distributor financed a picture, however, it may insist on ownership of its copyright, including all derivative rights. In this situation the best a producer may be able to achieve is a handsome fee for his services and a share in back-end compensation (*i.e.*, net profits). A producer with clout, or one with a highly desirable project, may be able to negotiate a bonus payment or a participation in gross or adjusted gross revenues. Sometimes revenues from merchandising, soundtrack albums, or home video sales are placed in separate revenue pools that are shared with the producer.

Term

The term is the period during which the distributor has the right to distribute the film. Distributors tend to ask for long terms in the

---

DISTRIBUTION RIGHTS CAN BE DIVIDED INTO MANY DIFFERENT MEDIA. EVERY DISTRIBUTOR CAN DEFINE MEDIA AS THEY LIKE, AND DEFINITIONS MAY VARY FROM CONTRACT TO CONTRACT. CARE MUST BE TAKEN TO CAREFULLY DELINEATE MEDIA TO AVOID ANY AMBIGUITY. HERE ARE DEFINITIONS USED IN ONE CONTRACT:

MEDIA DEFINITIONS

AIRLINE RIGHTS: THE RIGHT TO LICENSE ANY FORM OF MOTION PICTURE COPY FOR EXHIBITION IN AIRLINES FLYING THE FLAG OF ANY COUNTRY IN THE TERRITORY, BUT EXCLUDING THOSE AIRLINES THAT ARE ONLY SERVICED IN, BUT DO NOT FLY THE FLAG OF, A COUNTRY IN THE TERRITORY.

COMMERCIAL VIDEO: THE EXPLOITATION OF A MOTION PICTURE COPY EMBODIED IN A VIDEOCASSETTE SOLELY FOR THE PURPOSE OF EXHIBITING THE VIDEOCASSETTE DIRECTLY BEFORE AN AUDIENCE BY INSTITUTIONS OR ORGANIZATIONS NOT PRIMARILY ENGAGED IN THE BUSINESS OF EXHIBITING MOTION PICTURES TO THE PUBLIC, INCLUDING EDUCATIONAL INSTITUTIONS, CHURCHES, RESTAURANTS, BARS, CLUBS, TRAINS, LIBRARIES, GOVERNMENT OR MILITARY INSTALLATIONS, RED CROSS FACILITIES, AND OIL FIELDS AND RIGS. COMMERCIAL VIDEO DOES NOT INCLUDE EXPLOITATION BY THEATRICAL, NON-THEATRICAL, FREE TV, OR PAY TV MEANS. (NOTE: COMMERCIAL VIDEO USUALLY DOES NOT INCLUDE AIRLINE RIGHTS, HOTEL/MOTEL RIGHTS, OR SHIP RIGHTS, BUT SOMETIMES THE AGREEMENT PROVIDES OTHERWISE.)

FREE TV: STANDARD OVER-THE-AIR BROADCAST, OR BASIC CABLE TELEVISION TRANSMISSION, OF ANY FORM OF MOTION PICTURE COPY FOR RECEPTION ON A TELEVISION RECEIVER WITHOUT A CHARGE BEING MADE TO THE VIEWER FOR THE PRIVILEGE OF VIEWING THE MOTION PICTURE. FOR THE PURPOSES OF THIS DEFINITION, NEITHER GOVERNMENTAL TELEVISION RECEIVER ASSESSMENTS NOR TAXES NOR REGULAR PERIODIC SERVICE CHARGES (OTHER THAN A CHARGE PAID WITH RESPECT TO PAY TV) PAID BY A SUBSCRIBER TO A CABLE TELEVISION TRANSMISSION SERVICE (*I.E.,* "BASIC CABLE" CHARGES) IS A CHARGE TO THE VIEWER. FREE TV IS LIMITED TO TRANSMISSION ONLY BY GROUND-BASED DEVICES AND HERTZIAN WAVES, AND DOES NOT INCLUDE THE RIGHT TO MAKE SATELLITE TRANSMISSIONS OR CABLE RETRANSMISSIONS.

HOME VIDEO: THE EXPLOITATION OF A MOTION PICTURE COPY EMBODIED IN A VIDEOCASSETTE, DVD, OR SIMILAR DEVICE, WHERE THE VIDEOGRAM IS RENTED OR SOLD TO THE VIEWER FOR THE SOLE PURPOSE OF VIEWING THE PICTURE IN PRIVATE LIVING ACCOMMODATIONS WHERE NO ADMISSION FEE IS CHARGED WITH RESPECT TO SUCH VIEWING. HOME VIDEO RIGHTS DO NOT INCLUDE THE RIGHT TO ALLOW ANY PUBLIC PERFORMANCE, DIFFUSION, EXHIBITION, OR BROADCAST OF ANY VIDEOGRAM.

(CONTINUED)

10- to 20-year range, and sometimes they are audacious enough to ask for rights in perpetuity. It is not in the filmmaker's interest to grant a lengthy term. A distributor's enthusiasm for a film may wane as the years pass. After the first few years, the motion picture may languish in the distributor's library with little effort made to license it. This can be frustrating for the filmmaker, especially if he has the desire and ability to promote the film. The filmmaker may find himself requesting a reversion of rights from a distributor who has done a poor job of marketing the film.

HOTEL/MOTEL RIGHTS: THE RIGHT TO LICENSE THE PICTURE FOR EXHIBITION IN HOTELS, MOTELS, APARTMENT COMPLEXES, CONDOMINIUM PROJECTS, AND HOSPITALS BY MEANS OF CLOSED-CIRCUIT TELEVISION SYSTEMS WHERE THE TELECAST ORIGINATES WITHIN OR IN THE IMMEDIATE PROXIMITY OF SUCH PLACE.

NON-THEATRICAL: THE EXPLOITATION OF ANY MOTION PICTURE COPY OF 16MM OR 8MM FILM IN THE CUSTOMARY "NON-THEATRICAL" AND "SUBSTANDARD" MARKET, BY SCREENING THE MOTION PICTURE DIRECTLY BEFORE AN AUDIENCE BY INSTITUTIONS OR ORGANIZATIONS NOT PRIMARILY ENGAGED IN THE BUSINESS OF EXHIBITION MOTION PICTURES TO THE PUBLIC, INCLUDING EDUCATIONAL INSTITUTIONS, CHURCHES, RESTAURANTS, BARS, CLUBS, TRAINS, LIBRARIES, 16MM AND 8MM NON-COMMERCIAL HOME VIEWING, GOVERNMENT AND MILITARY INSTALLATIONS, RED CROSS FACILITIES, AND OIL FIELDS AND RIGS. NON-THEATRICAL DOES NOT INCLUDE EXPLOITATION BY THEATRICAL, FREE TV, OR PAY TV MEANS, OR BY ANY FORM OF VIDEOCASSETTE. NON-THEATRICAL DOES NOT INCLUDE AIRLINE RIGHTS, HOTEL/MOTEL RIGHTS, OR SHIP RIGHTS UNLESS OTHERWISE NOTED.

PAY TV: MEANS OVER-THE-AIR, CABLE, CLOSED-CIRCUIT, MICROWAVE, OR LASER TRANSMISSION USING ANY MOTION PICTURE COPY FOR RECEPTION ON A TELEVISION RECEIVER WHERE A SUPPLEMENTAL CHARGE IS MADE: (I) TO THE VIEWER FOR THE PRIVILEGE OF VIEWING ANY SPECIAL CHANNEL OR MOTION PICTURE IN A HOME, HOTEL, MOTEL, APARTMENT COMPLEX, CONDOMINIUM PROJECT, HOSPITAL; OR (II) TO THE OPERATOR OF SUCH HOTEL, MOTEL, APARTMENT COMPLEX, CONDOMINIUM PROJECT, OR HOSPITAL FOR THE OBTAINING OF SUCH EXHIBITION OR VIEWING AT SUCH PLACE. PAY TV ONLY INCLUDES THE RIGHT TO RECEIVE AND MAKE LIMITED CLOSED-CIRCUIT RETRANSMISSION WITHIN THE PLACES DESCRIBED ABOVE OF SUCH A SIGNAL ORIGINATING FROM OUTSIDE SUCH PLACES. PAY TV DOES NOT INCLUDE THE RIGHT TO MAKE ANY CLOSED-CIRCUIT RETRANSMISSION OF ANY MOTION PICTURE COPY, WHETHER EMBODIED ON ANY GAUGE OF FILM OR IN A VIDEOCASSETTE, VIDEO DISC, OR COMPARABLE DEVICE, FROM A PLAYBACK DEVICE LOCATED WITHIN OR IN PROXIMITY TO ANY HOTEL, MOTEL, APARTMENT COMPLEX, CONDOMINIUM PROJECT, HOSPITAL, OR OTHER PLACE WHERE SUCH PAY TV SIGNAL IS INITIALLY RECEIVED.

SHIP RIGHTS: THE RIGHT TO LICENSE ANY FORM OF MOTION PICTURE COPY FOR EXHIBITION IN OCEAN-GOING VESSELS FLYING THE FLAG OF ANY COUNTRY IN THE TERRITORY BUT SPECIFICALLY EXCLUDING THOSE OCEAN-GOING VESSELS THAT ARE ONLY SERVICED IN, BUT DO NOT FLY THE FLAG OF, A COUNTRY IN THE TERRITORY.

THEATRICAL: EXPLOITATION OF ANY MOTION PICTURE COPY IN 70MM, 35MM, OR 16MM FILM ONLY IN CONVENTIONAL OR DRIVE-IN THEATERS OPEN TO THE GENERAL PUBLIC ON A REGULARLY SCHEDULED BASIS WHERE A FEE IS CHARGED FOR ADMISSION TO VIEW THE PICTURE.

VIDEOCASSETTE: MEANS A VHS OR BETA CASSETTE OR ELECTRONIC STORAGE DEVICE IN ANY AUTHORIZED FORMAT DESIGNED TO BE USED IN CONJUNCTION WITH A REPRODUCTION APPARATUS THAT CAUSES A MOTION PICTURE TO BE VISIBLE ON THE SCREEN OF A TELEVISION RECEIVER. A VIDEOCASSETTE DOES NOT INCLUDE ANY LASER OR CAPACITANCE VIDEODISC OR OTHER VIDEO DEVICE.

In order to avoid such a scenario, it is usually in the filmmaker's interest to license motion pictures for a short term (one to three years). One can appreciate, however, that distributors who provide significant advances, or spend large sums on marketing, will want a longer term to ensure that they can recoup these costs. A good compromise is to give the distributor a short initial term followed by a series of automatic extensions tied to the accomplishment of performance milestones. The contract might provide, for example, if the distributor returns X dollars to the filmmaker during the initial term, then the term would be extended for an additional two years. There could be a series of such rollovers, with the total number of years capped at ten.

There is another "term" that the filmmaker needs to consider. This is the term of licenses that the distributor grants to third parties. An international distributor is often allowed to license rights to territory buyers for up to 12 years, with the license to Germany permitted to extend up to 15 years. (Germany is a major buyer of American films and often demands a longer term.) In any territory a longer license period may be granted, but this would be subject to the filmmaker's prior approval. What a filmmaker should avoid is a scenario where a distributor at the end of its term enters into long-term licenses with third parties at fire-sale prices. The distributor may figure that since it will soon lose all rights to the picture anyway, it might as well take whatever it can obtain. This will harm the filmmaker because the territories licensed will not be available for relicensing for many years. One way to protect the filmmaker from having his film encumbered by a long term for reduced fees is for the distributor and filmmaker to agree on a Schedule of Minimums that restricts the distributor from licensing rights in a territory for less than the agreed-upon minimum.

Distribution Fee

The distribution fee compensates the distributor for its efforts in distributing the film. Distributors generally receive a fee based on a percentage of their gross revenue. This maximizes their fee because it is based on a greater sum than a fee calculated on the distributor's net revenue (*i.e.*, revenue after deduction of expenses). If expenses are significant, there may be no revenue left to share with the filmmaker after a distributor has deducted its fee and recouped its expenses. That is why distributing a film may be remunerative for the distributor, while the filmmaker and his investors bear a considerable loss.

Distribution fees vary according to the territory and media. For a domestic theatrical release, a distributor may ask for 35% of its gross revenues, which is the revenue received from exhibitors. These monies are often called "rentals" or "film rentals," as they are the amounts paid by the theater owner to rent the film.

For domestic home video, several formulas are used, including a 50/50 Net deal and a royalty deal. The 50/50 Net deal allows the distributor to deduct distribution expenses from gross revenues and then share the remaining balance 50/50 with the filmmaker. The royalty approach pays the filmmaker a royalty, often in the range of 20%-25% of wholesale price for each cassette sold. Thus, for every cassette sold to a retailer like Blockbuster for $50, the filmmaker might receive $10. The distributor bears all distribution expenses. Keep in mind that the prices charged retailers for low-budget indie films vary greatly, and some films are sold to retailers at a lower, "sell-through" price (e.g., $10 less per cassette) to encourage customers to buy the cassette rather than rent it. The royalty rate may be reduced to 10%-15% for sell-through product. Another way that tapes are licensed to retailers is on a revenue-sharing basis. The retailer pays a nominal amount for each tape and agrees to share revenue generated from it with the distributor. Most of the major studios, and independent companies such as Rentrack, supply videocassettes to retailers on a revenue-sharing basis.

From the filmmaker's point of view, a royalty formula has the advantage of ensuring that the filmmaker receives some revenue even if sales are minimal. Moreover, since the filmmaker's royalty is based on the number of units sold, less returns, and the amount spent on marketing is irrelevant in calculating royalties, there is less room for creative accounting. If sales are robust, however, the filmmaker might receive more under a 50/50 Net deal, assuming the distributor has reasonable expenses and provides an honest accounting.

The distribution fee for arranging a domestic television license is often 25% of the license fee but can vary from 10%-40%. Licensing a film for television may entail little more than contacting a pay-cable channel and offering them the picture. Delivery is accomplished by shipping one video sub-master, accompanied by artwork and chain of title documents. More effort is involved in selling to the numerous pay-per-view, basic cable, and broadcast outlets. A distributor may be able to arrange for a series of licenses to different outlets, giving each a "window" to exhibit the film. Care must be taken to ensure that the windows do not conflict, and are arranged so as to maximize revenue. Once a film has been exhibited on basic cable, for example, it may not be desirable to a pay-cable channel. The order of the windows is usually: theatrical, home video, followed by television. Within the television window, the order is pay-per-view, pay cable, network broadcast television, basic cable, and broadcast syndication. However, most indie films are never licensed for a network broadcast, and the order of these windows can vary. Sometimes a network broadcaster such as ABC is willing to pay a premium to show a film earlier. Likewise, HBO has acquired a limited number of completed films and distributed them as "HBO Premieres," meaning that these films are exhibited on HBO before they are shown in theaters.

For distribution outside North America, a filmmaker will often use an international distributor, also known as a foreign sales agent, to license the picture. The sales agent will receive a distribution fee or commission ranging from 10%-40%, but often 15%-25%, of gross revenues. The sales agent will be allowed to recoup certain distribution expenses as well as deduct its distribution fee from revenues. The balance will be paid to the filmmaker.

Note that gross revenues are usually defined to be a sum less than actual gross. Actual gross is reduced by refunds, collection costs, currency conversion, wire transfer, bank fees, withholding taxes, and duplication and manufacturing expenses incurred to deliver materials.

Some countries may not permit license fees to be sent out of the country. In this event, the filmmaker's share of the frozen funds is deposited in a separate account in the foreign country in the name of the filmmaker. If these funds cannot be repatriated, the filmmaker will have to use them in the foreign country. The monies could be spent there for lodging or travel or to produce a film in that country. The completed picture could be removed from the country, and revenues generated from the film may be freely transferrable.

The license fee paid by a territory licensee usually does not include the cost of manufacturing film prints, video sub-masters, key art, and other materials that are needed by the purchaser. Typically these items are paid for separately, with the foreign buyer either paying the laboratory directly or by reimbursing the sales agent for these expenses. Note that sales agents may mark up duplication and manufacturing costs in order to earn additional revenue—a practice that may not be disclosed to the filmmaker. Moreover, if duplication costs are included in the license fee, this will inflate gross revenues, thereby increasing the distributor's commission.

Distribution and Marketing Expenses

The distribution agreement should clearly and precisely define the type and extent of expenses that the distributor is allowed to recoup. Many filmmakers are shocked to discover that much of the money generated from their film ends up being kept by the distributor as reimbursement of expenses. Some distributors will take on films that they know will generate modest revenue, knowing that whatever funds come in will be retained by the distributor and enable it to cover its operating overhead.

For example, a foreign sales company may spend $90,000 to participate in the Cannes film market. These expenses could include the rental of a suite to serve as a market office, airfare from the United States, local transportation, lodging and meals for staff, shipping, duplication of videocassettes, and entertainment of foreign buyers. If the foreign sales company is bringing 10 films to a market, the cost might be apportioned equally among the films. Thus, each filmmaker would be allocated a $9,000 market expense plus whatever promotional expenses were incurred to create posters, one-sheets, trailers, and advertising. These promotional expenses could amount to another $30,000. If the foreign sales company distributes an indie film that generates only $40,000 in license fees, the distributor would be entitled to retain all the revenue. Here's the math: $40,000 in gross receipts, less a distribution fee of 25% ($10,000), reduces the balance to $30,000. This sum is then applied to the outstanding expenses of $39,000, leaving the filmmaker with zero. Moreover, if additional revenue is generated, this revenue will first be applied to pay the foreign sales company's outstanding expenses.

While the filmmaker loses out, the distributor gains in a number of ways: First, the distributor earns a distribution fee based on gross receipts. Second, if the distributor has several of its own films to license, revenues on those films will not be reduced by a lot of expenses because much of the cost of attending the market is borne by films acquired from other producers. Third, the distributor benefits from the advertising paid for by the filmmakers. These ads often promote the distributor as much as any film. Fourth, the distributor may earn money by marking up the cost of deliverables manufactured for licensees and pocketing the profit. Fifth, the distributor may receive kickbacks from poster designers, trailer makers, or laboratories. Finally, the distributor may profit from various accounting games played with revenues and expenses. For example, expenses incurred on one film may be misapplied to another. Filmmakers can find themselves "reimbursing" the distributor more market expenses than were actually incurred.

While a filmmaker may not be able to control the expenses a distributor incurs, the filmmaker can restrict which expenses the distributor is allowed to recoup. Recoupment should be limited to out-of-pocket expenses actually incurred for the filmmaker's movie. It is often useful to categorize expenses into groups with a cap on each: 1) market expenses, 2) promotional expenses, and 3) delivery expenses. Since these terms do not have standard definitions within the industry, the contract must clearly delineate each. Any expense that falls within one category should not be counted in another.

Market expenses include costs to attend film markets such as AFM, Cannes, and MIFED, and may include television markets such as MIP, MIP-COM, and NATPE. Examples of such expenses would be airfare, lodging, meals, shipping, and telephone costs for attending a market. Market expenses should be recoupable for the first year of distribution only, and limited to markets that the distributor participates in (*i.e.*, the distributor attends, rents a suite or booth, and promotes the film). For a low-budget indie film, a distributor could be allowed to recoup $2,500–$5,000 per market with an overall annual cap of $7,500–$15,000. The distributor should agree to attend no less than three markets during the first year of distribution. No market expenses should be charged to the filmmaker for attendance in subsequent years, even though the distributor may continue to license the picture.

Promotional expenses include the cost of preparing posters, one-sheets, trailers, and advertising. The distributor should agree to a minimum amount of money to be spent (the floor) as well as a maximum cap (the ceiling). These expenses are limited to direct out-of-pocket expenses actually spent on behalf of the film. The agreement should provide that at the producer's request, the distributor will provide receipts for each and every expense or forgo recoupment. Recoupable promotional expenses should not include any of the distributor's general office, overhead, legal, or staff expenses, nor any market expenses. The filmmaker may want a provision that requires the distributor to spend the minimum amount necessary to adequately promote the film, including preparation of a trailer, poster, one-sheet, videocassette, and customary collateral material. The amount of money the filmmaker should expect the distributor to spend will depend on how much marketing materials the filmmaker can deliver. If the filmmaker, for example, has created a good poster and trailer, the cap on expenses can be reduced.

Delivery expenses include reasonable and verifiable out-of-pocket costs incurred in connection with the distribution and sale of the motion picture. Such expenses include the cost of creating sub-master tapes, duplicates of still photos, and key art requested by licensees. This category might also include reimbursement of long-distance phone calls, photocopying, fax, shipping and courier charges, clearance and brokerage fees, warehouse and handling charges, insurance, bank transfers, taxes and duties, copyright registrations and searches, and the cost of manufacturing any necessary picture elements that the filmmaker did not deliver. The category also covers duplication of screening cassettes, transfers to PAL format, dubbing, creating a foreign-language version, and manufacturing of promotional materials. As previously mentioned, some of these expenses may be borne by the territory licensees. Delivery expenses can be capped at a dollar amount or on a percentage basis (*e.g.*, 10% of Gross Receipts).

Advances and Guarantees

There are a number of reasons for filmmakers to seek an advance payment toward their share of revenues. First, if the distributor is dishonest or goes bankrupt, the advance may be the only money the filmmaker ever receives. Second, the filmmaker can immediately use the advance to pay outstanding production expenses or debts, or to repay investors. Without an advance, there may be a considerable delay until the filmmaker receives his share of revenue. When revenues begin to flow, they are applied first to reimburse the distributor its fees and expenses. Third, if a distributor has paid a substantial advance, it has more of a financial incentive to sell the film. Advances are usually recoupable but they are not refundable. In other words, the distributor can recoup the advance payment from revenues, but if the film generates insufficient revenue for the distributor to recoup, the filmmaker does not have to repay the advance.

Advances are paid upon signing of the distribution agreement, or upon inspection and acceptance of the deliverables, which are the master elements from which copies of the film will be manufactured. If the filmmaker fails to make delivery, or if the materials are defective, the distributor may have grounds to decline to pay the advance. Therefore, it is advisable for filmmakers to give a distributor a limited period to inspect materials and either approve or reject them. If the materials are defective, the filmmaker should be allowed reasonable time to cure any deficiencies—30 days should be sufficient for the distributor to have a laboratory perform a quality-control check on the deliverables. While the distributor has a legitimate concern that deliverables meet industry standards, the filmmaker does not want to provide a loophole for the distributor to avoid paying an advance by delaying inspection of materials, or raising spurious claims of defects. By providing a deadline to resolve any delivery issues, the filmmaker will be able to cancel the distribution deal and regain all rights to the film.

When an advance is paid in installments, the arrangement is often called a minimum guarantee. Of course, a guarantee is only as good as the financial health and integrity of the guarantor. If the distributor goes bankrupt, or if sales are less than expected, the distributor may renege on its obligation to pay the guaranteed amount. Distribution agreements should always specify the date by which the guaranteed amount must be paid.

In the current marketplace, many distributors will not pay advances or guarantees for low-budget films lacking name actors. The filmmaker needs to be creative in devising a formula that protects the filmmaker's interests while not imposing an unacceptable burden on the distributor. I have created a formula, which I call a "50/50 Guarantee." Under this provision, the distributor agrees to delay recoupment of its expenses and receipt of its distribution fee so that at least 50% of gross revenues are paid to the filmmaker. In other words, regardless of the amount of money a distributor may be allowed to deduct as recoupable expenses or distribution fees, at least 50 cents of every dollar received will be paid to the filmmaker. If the distributor cannot recoup all of its expenses and fees from 50% of the revenue, then it can recoup the balance due from future revenues, if any.

For example, if the distributor receives $100,000 in gross revenue, and if the distributor is due $60,000 in recoupable expenses and distribution fees, the distributor could recoup only $50,000 of the first $100,000 in revenues. The outstanding $10,000 balance due the distributor could be recouped from the next $20,000 of revenue.

This 50/50 Guarantee is advantageous to the filmmaker because it ensures that at least 50% of all revenues flow to the filmmaker. It will prevent a distributor from acquiring a film, making minimal sales, and retaining all the income. This provision ensures that the distributor shares some financial risk with the filmmaker in the form of unrecouped expenses.

Consultation Rights

Distributors may agree to give filmmakers consultation rights. This will allow the filmmaker to make suggestions about how their film should be marketed. Usually consultation rights do not oblige the distributor to follow the filmmaker's advice. Distributors often insist on having the final say because they think they have more marketing and distribution expertise than the filmmaker, and they are advancing the marketing costs.

In those rare instances when filmmakers pay for print and advertising (P&A) costs, distributors will grant them decision-making authority. These deals are often referred to as "service deals" or "rent-a-distributor" deals. They permit the filmmaker to use the distribution apparatus for a fee, often a percentage of the revenues generated. The distributor might receive a fee of 17.5% (compared to a customary fee of 35% for a theatrical release) with the filmmaker bearing all costs of advertising and marketing.

Even if a filmmaker does not control marketing, they may be able to prevent the distributor from editing or changing a film, or its title, without the filmmaker's consent. Frequently, the distributor is not allowed to modify an independent film except for those changes needed to comply with censorship purposes, or to adapt the film for television broadcast by inserting commercials, or to subtitle or dub a film for exhibition in foreign countries.

Warranties and Representations

Distributors routinely require filmmakers to warrant certain facts, and to indemnify the distributor for any losses or legal fees resulting from a breach of these promises. Since the distributor is usually not present during the production of a film, the distributor can't possibly know whether the filmmaker properly secured all the necessary rights. The distributor wants to make sure that the filmmaker has a clean "chain of title" to the work. To fully own the copyright to a film, one needs to obtain 1) rights to the underlying script and any literary property it may be based on, 2) depiction releases from the actors, and 3) work-for-hire agreements with the director, editor, cinematographer, and others who make a creative contribution. The distributor will also want the filmmaker to warrant that the film doesn't violate any third-party rights. Such violations could include infringement of another's copyright or trademark, invasion of someone's right of privacy or publicity, and defamation of another's reputation.

Astute filmmakers will, in turn, ask distributors to make some warranties of their own. A filmmaker may want the distributor to promise that it will diligently promote and license the film, that it is solvent and not in danger of bankruptcy, and that there are no outstanding lawsuits that might hamper the distributor from successfully exploiting the film. The distributor can be asked to promise that it will secure the rights needed to use artwork and advertising created by third parties for the distributor, that the distributor will not edit the film without prior written approval from the filmmaker, and that the distributor will not accept any undisclosed money or favors in return for licensing the film. Finally, filmmakers may demand warranties to preclude such unsavory practices as the misallocation of revenue from package sales, the receipt of secret rebates, and the mark-up of duplication costs.

Warranties can be "absolute" or "to the best of one's knowledge and belief." With an absolute warranty, one is making an unconditional promise, and good-faith mistakes are not a defense. Conversely, if you warrant a fact to the best of your knowledge and belief, you are making a lesser promise. You are only stating that as far as you know, the statement is true. This difference can be important in a collaborative enterprise such as moviemaking, where the filmmaker is relying on others. A filmmaker, for example, may have purchased a script from a writer who purports to own it. The filmmaker makes a movie based on this script, enters into a distribution deal, and then discovers that the script was plagiarized from another work. If the filmmaker made an absolute warranty, he will be liable to the distributor—irrespective of the fact that the filmmaker was deceived by the writer. On the other hand, if the filmmaker only promised that he had a good-faith belief that he had secured these rights, he would not be liable.

Accounting

When a filmmaker receives a one-time payment for all monies he will ever be due from a distributor, there is little need for him to have a continuing right to inspect the distributor's books and records. Under such a "buyout" deal, the filmmaker may be selling certain rights or the copyright for a flat fee paid when the deal is signed. Most of the time, however, filmmakers do not enter into buyout agreements. They prefer to retain ownership and license distribution rights for a limited term. In this case the distributor has a continuing duty to account to the filmmaker for a portion of the revenues generated from the film. The filmmaker will want the ability to review the distributor's records to ensure that he is receiving his fair share of monies.

An accounting provision will require the distributor to maintain books and records with regard to all sales and rentals of the motion picture. Monthly or quarterly accounting statements, accompanied by any amounts due, are sent to the filmmaker. The distributor should be obliged to provide a detailed breakdown, by territory and media, of all licenses, with an indication of how much revenue has been received and what remains to be collected. Expenses should be itemized. Sometimes the distributor is required to give the filmmaker copies of all licenses.

Some agreements compel the distributor to establish a separate bank account for revenues received from the filmmaker's picture. The filmmaker's signature may be required for withdrawals. The shortcoming of such an arrangement is that a distributor could accept cash or deposit checks into a different account not revealed to the filmmaker. Another measure sometimes employed to protect the filmmaker is a provision requiring the distributor to hold the filmmaker's share of funds in trust. If the distributor runs off with the money, criminal liability may ensue.

It is wise to provide for interest on past-due payments because the general American rule is that pre-judgment interest is not awarded to the prevailing party in litigation unless there is a specific statute that provides for such interest. In other words, until the filmmaker secures a favorable judgment, the interest clock does not begin to tick. If the distribution agreement provides for interest on late payments, however, the courts will award interest from the time the payment became due, which might be years earlier. The interest rate should be specified (*e.g.*, 10% per annum), and should not violate usury laws. Without an interest-on-late-payments provision, a distributor has a financial incentive to hold onto the filmmaker's money, and earn interest on it.

Arbitration

An arbitration clause requires that disputes be resolved through arbitration instead of litigation. Arbitration usually provides a quicker and less-expensive remedy. Rather than appearing in court, the parties and the arbitrator confer in an ordinary meeting room. Each side is given the opportunity to present documents and witnesses. The rules of evidence do not apply. Parties may be represented by counsel, or they can represent themselves. Usually disputes are resolved within a matter of months.

It may be advantageous for filmmakers to provide for arbitration of disputes, especially when they are the financially weaker party. Most filmmakers, if not poor when they commence production, are broke by the time the picture has been completed. If the filmmaker doesn't a have a cost-effective means of protecting his interests, he may be unable to prevent a distributor from flagrantly breaching its obligations and pocketing the film's revenue. An arbitration clause levels the playing field.

The arbitration clause should provide that the prevailing party is entitled to reimbursement of costs and attorneys' fees. Otherwise, the prevailing party may not be able to recoup these expenses.

Courts rarely overturn arbitration awards. The grounds for vacating an award are limited to extreme circumstances such as when an award is procured by corruption or fraud, or the arbitrator lacks jurisdiction.* A party cannot reverse an arbitration award simply because he disagrees with the arbitrator's decision.

If the losing party does not voluntarily comply with an arbitration award, the prevailing party can have the award confirmed by a court in the course of a brief hearing. Once confirmed, the award is no different from a judgment rendered after a full jury trial. The prevailing party (the judgment creditor) can obtain a Writ of Execution directing the sheriff to seize the judgment debtor's assets to satisfy the award.

An arbitration clause may provide that an award is final, binding, and non-appealable. Otherwise, the filmmaker might avoid the costs of litigation only to incur large legal bills on appeal. The parties should specify the venue (*i.e.*, city) for any arbitration, and they may want to agree on how many arbitrators will be used, and what qualifications they need to meet. It is common to have disputes resolved by a single arbitrator who is an entertainment attorney.

Insurance

United States distributors often require producers to purchase an Errors and Omissions (E&O) insurance policy. Foreign buy-

---

*See California Code of Civil Procedure Section 1268.2.

ers may not demand insurance as they operate in countries where litigation is less likely than in the U.S.

E&O insurance is essentially malpractice coverage for filmmakers. It protects against liability arising from the filmmaker's negligence in not securing all the rights, permissions, and clearances needed to exploit a film. The policy covers claims arising from invasion of a third party's rights, as might arise, for instance, if a film defamed someone. E&O insurance does not insure against intentional misconduct. Consequently, the policy will not cover a lawsuit arising from a filmmaker knowingly violating another's rights.

An Errors and Omissions insurance policy will pay for damages awarded against a policyholder and for the cost of mounting a legal defense. The policyholder will have to pay a deductible, which may be $10,000 or more. Before issuing a policy, insurers will require applicants to secure all necessary licenses and permissions. A copyright report and title report may be requested, as well as written agreements with all production personnel. Insurers typically ask whether the producer's attorney has reviewed and approved all the chain of title documents in accordance with the insurance company's clearance guidelines.

Often filmmakers cannot afford to purchase E&O insurance, which may cost $7,000 to $10,000 per film. The distributor may agree to purchase such a policy, and recoup its cost from gross revenues. If the distributor buys a policy, the filmmaker should make sure that he is added as an additional named insured. Some distributors obtain their own blanket E&O policy to cover all the films they distribute.

Termination

Filmmakers may want the right to terminate a distribution agreement if: 1) the distributor proves to be inept; 2) the distributor doesn't pay the filmmaker his share of revenue; or 3) the distributor loses enthusiasm for selling the picture. Distributors want to restrict a filmmaker's termination rights. Early termination can harm the distributor's reputation and financial health. The distributor may have already licensed the film to its buyers. Moreover, the distributor may have advanced marketing and advertising expenses that will not be recouped until revenue is received from licensees.

Many distribution agreements severely restrict a filmmaker's right to terminate the agreement, and restrict the remedies available, even when the distributor has breached its obligations. For example, it is common for filmmakers to waive their right to seek any remedy other than the award of monetary damages. Therefore, the filmmaker would be unable to request injunctive relief in the form of a court order to stop distribution. If the filmmaker has a right to terminate the agreement, the right is often predicated on first giving the distributor notice of its default and an opportunity to cure it. On termination, the licenses entered into by the distributor during the term will remain in force. The distributor may have a continuing right and obligation to service these deals, and may be permitted to deduct a distribution fee for its efforts.

A filmmaker may have a right to terminate if the distributor files a petition in bankruptcy, or consents to an involuntary petition in bankruptcy or reorganization under Chapter 11 of the Bankruptcy Act. A bankruptcy court, however, might not uphold such a termination right.

Filmmakers should carefully consider the consequences of discharging a distributor. Switching distributors midstream may create confusion among buyers, and result in additional distribution expenses. Moreover, it can be difficult to find a new distributor willing to take on a "secondhand" film for which the easy sales have been concluded. For those territories that remain unlicensed, the film may have been rejected by potential licensees.

Allocation of Package Revenue

Films are often licensed in packages. A Polish distributor might license a collection of 10 or 20 films from a distributor for a single fee. The Polish distributor may not care how the license fee is allocated among these pictures. The filmmaker, however, will care if his film is not allocated an equitable amount of the license fee.

If a filmmaker's movie is included in a package of films then the price allocated to each picture should be allocated on the basis of each film's commercial worth. Granted, it can be difficult to ascertain the value of each picture. If the films have been released theatrically, one could compare the relative box office receipts of each to determine their worth. One could compare the budget for each film, but this is a poor measure because the amount spent to make a film does not correlate closely to its value. What is certainly not equitable is to package a highly desirable film with an inferior one and then allocate the same amount of revenue to each.

A filmmaker could demand a provision in the distribution agreement prohibiting the inclusion of his film in any packages. But such a restriction is difficult to enforce—the filmmaker is usually not present when a license is negotiated, and therefore may not be privy to its terms. Reviewing individual license agreements may not fully disclose the circumstances of the deal. If a sales agent, for instance, offers to license a desirable film for $50,000 if the buyer will pay $50,000 for an inferior one, the terms of each license agreement may not disclose this tradeoff.

While not failsafe, a clause that requires a distributor to disclose the licensee fee allocated to each film in a package is advisable.

Governing Law

The parties should specify which state's law will apply in the event of a contractual dispute. Such a provision is especially important if the parties reside in different states. A filmmaker will want to avoid procedural disputes that may delay resolution of a legal action. Since many industry disputes arise in New York or California, the law in those states is the most extensive and well-settled. Note that if an agreement provides for arbitration, the arbitrator can make a decision without reference to federal or state law.

Territorial Minimums

A filmmaker will want to preclude a foreign sales agent from licensing his film for less than its fair market value. This can be accomplished by attaching a Schedule of Minimums listing the lowest amount that the distributor can accept as a license fee for each territory.

There are several reasons why a filmmaker should insist on such minimums. By setting prices that both parties acknowledge are reasonable, there is less likelihood that either party will have unrealistic expectations.

Moreover, if a distributor licenses a package of films, the distributor may need to allocate the fee among several pictures. The filmmaker and distributor may disagree as to the relative worth of each picture. Obviously, an acclaimed film with a star is worth more than a B-movie. A Schedule of Minimums limits the distributor's discretion as to how to allocate the fee. While many distributors will allocate the fee in good faith, there may be a financial incentive for the distributor to allocate more of it to those pictures that are more remunerative for the distributor. For example, if the distributor receives different distribution fees on pictures in a package, the distributor may allocate more of the license fee to those pictures that pay larger distribution fees.

Another reason for establishing minimum prices is to prevent the distributor from licensing the film at fire-sale prices near the end of its distribution term. When a distribution agreement is about to expire, the distributor may be willing to unload the film at whatever price can be secured. Such an agreement, however, could preclude the filmmaker from re-licensing the film for many years.

Schedules usually list both "asking" and "accepting" prices. Some schedules have separate listings for each media, listing, for example, minimums for a video-only sale, a television-only sale, and an "all rights" license.

ACCESS TO MASTER MATERIALS

Filmmakers should retain possession of their master elements. In other words, they should not deliver original film negatives, video masters, sound masters, artwork, still photos, or slides directly to a distributor. Instead, distributors should be given a lab access letter enabling them to order copies of the motion picture so they can fulfill orders; or in the case of artwork, photos, and slides, duplicates should be delivered.

There are many reasons for a filmmaker to retain possession of master materials:

1) If lost or damaged, it can be quite expensive to replace masters, if they are replaceable.

2) In the event of a dispute, it is best to have control over one's materials. If a distributor defaults, the filmmaker may have the right to terminate the agreement and make other distribution arrangements. If the filmmaker, however, doesn't have access to his own materials, he will not be able to engage a new distributor.

3) If a distributor goes bankrupt, the filmmaker will want to avoid having to extricate her materials from bankruptcy proceedings.

4) A filmmaker may need to give several distributors simultaneous access to master materials. Typically, independent filmmakers enter into multiple distribution deals. One deal may be with an international distributor (a.k.a. foreign sales agent) to distribute the film outside North America. One or more deals may be made with domestic distributors for distribution in different media in North America. The best solution when dealing with several distributors is to place materials in a professional laboratory, giving a lab access letter to each distributor.

5) One can better monitor how many copies are being manufactured by keeping masters in a laboratory and having the lab report on its duplication activities. Suppose that at the end of one year, the lab discloses to the filmmaker that ten film prints have been made. A review of producer reports from the distributor, however, only indicates eight sales. This is a red flag that sales may have been made that were left off the producer report. Remember that distributors do not order copies unless they have licensed the film and received payment. Typically, distributors receive full payment before they ask the lab to manufacture a duplicate and ship it to the licensee. Another method used to discern where one's film is being distributed is to register the music on its soundtrack with a music publisher (which could be a publishing company the filmmaker establishes). The publisher will enter into agreements with ASCAP, BMI, or one of the other music collection agencies. These agencies collect public performance royalties when a film is exhibited on television in the United States, and in

theatres and on television abroad. Therefore, if royalties from Thailand have been remitted, this would alert one that a license for Thailand had been concluded, or the film was being pirated.

In selecting a laboratory to deposit materials, select one that charges competitive rates and has experience duplicating films for international buyers. Licensees in certain countries are notoriously finicky and may reject films on the grounds of poor technical quality. It is also a good idea to select a lab that is not the lab ordinarily used by the foreign sales agent. A lab in the habit of fulfilling orders for this foreign sales agent may forget that the filmmaker, not the sales agent, is the owner of the film and has to grant authority for the sales agent to duplicate a film. Moreover, such a lab might inadvertently release the master to the distributor. The filmmaker should always deliver the master directly to the laboratory after the laboratory and filmmaker have signed a lab access letter. The film should be held in the name of the filmmaker or his company.

The lab access letter should include language permitting the filmmaker to receive copies of invoices for items duplicated at the request of the sales agent. Some filmmakers insist that the laboratory ship copies directly to territory buyers.

The distributor will probably insist that access be irrevocable for the term of the distribution deal. The distributor will want continued access in order to fulfill orders as they arise from its licensees. A sample lab access letter is included at the end of this chapter.

Return of Materials

Upon expiration of the distribution term, any film-related materials in the possession of the distributor should be turned over to the filmmaker. If the distributor has created artwork, cassettes, posters and other marketing materials, the filmmaker may want to take possession of these items. Moreover, during the distribution term, the filmmaker may want the right to use artwork developed by one distributor to be used outside of that distributor's territory. For instance, if a foreign sales agent has designed a great poster, the filmmaker may want to let his domestic distributor use it. Since the cost of creating this material is a recoupable expense, the filmmaker is essentially paying for it and should be allowed free use of it.

Indeed, the contract can provide that the filmmaker owns all materials created by the distributor to promote the film. These materials should be created pursuant to a written work-for-hire agreement, with the filmmaker named as the employer and owner of all rights. Thus, if a photo shoot is commissioned, the filmmaker will own the copyright to the photos. Otherwise, ownership would vest in the distributor or the photographer.

Delivery

Distribution agreements often set forth detailed technical specifications that the filmmaker needs to meet for all delivery materials. If the materials are defective, the distributor will be unable have a laboratory manufacture acceptable copies of the picture, and the distributor will not be able to service its licensees. Delivery items include chain of title documents demonstrating that the producer owns all rights to the film. If the producer has not properly secured all rights to the film, then the producer can't grant such rights to the distributor, and the distributor may be liable to third parties once distribution has commenced.

While distributors have a legitimate interest in ensuring that masters meet industry standards, distributors should not be allowed to renege on their obligations with bogus claims of defects. A distributor might decline to pay an advance, or delay payment, on the grounds of a minor technical deficiency. The distribution agreement should allow the distributor two to four weeks to inspect the materials. If the materials do not pass muster, the filmmaker should have the opportunity to cure any defects. If the distributor does not timely raise objections, it should be barred from objecting later.

LAB ACCESS LETTER

_____ (Date)

ABC Laboratory

Re: Lab Access Letter for motion picture: (Picture)

Dear:

This letter will authorize _____ (Distributor) to order copies of the film _____ (Picture) owned by _____ (Filmmaker). Distributor has the exclusive right to distribute the film in all territories except for the United States and Canada, for an initial term of _____ years with possible extensions up to _____ years.

Distributor will be solely responsible for all reproduction costs and shipping expenses for any copies it orders. Distributor or a member of its staff will contact you shortly so that you can approve their credit.

You agree to never release any master tape (whether internegative, interpositive, answer print, master videotape, audiotapes, or digital copy) to anyone other than Filmmaker, or to someone without the express prior written consent of Filmmaker. Distributor has permission to order copies of masters during the term of the distribution agreement by faxing you a purchase order.

You will send copies of all invoices for film or video copies ordered by Distributor to filmmaker at _____.
Copies of the film may be shipped directly to buyers as designated by Distributor.

Thank you for your cooperation in this matter. Please acknowledge your agreement to the foregoing terms by signing below.

Sincerely,

_____

Filmmaker

_____

AGREED TO AND ACCEPTED:

_____

Laboratory

_____

Distributor

Filmmaker Friendly Contract

The following agreement is between a filmmaker and a foreign sales agent (a.k.a. international distributor). This agreement has been the subject of negotiation, and therefore the terms presented are more balanced—and more protective of the filmmaker—than the terms initially proposed by many foreign sales agents. The custom in the industry is for the distributor to prepare this document. The filmmaker, or his representative, comments on the terms and requests changes. Often the first draft is skewed heavily in favor of the distributor. Many terms are negotiable, however. With a highly desirable picture in hand, the producer may be able to significantly improve the terms of the deal.

The commentary below is italicized.

DISTRIBUTION AGREEMENT

_____, 20__

PRODUCER FILMS, INC.
Sally Producer, Producer

_____

_____

Re: "Film title"

Agreement made and entered into as of _____, 20__, by and between DISTRIBUTION, INC., a California Corporation ("Distributor") at _____, Hollywood, CA 90069, and PRODUCER FILMS, INC., a California Corporation ("Producer") at _____. In consideration of their respective covenants, warranties, and representations, together with other good and valuable consideration, Distributor and Producer hereby agree as follows:

Commentary: It is important that the parties are accurately described. A Producer, who has produced a film under the auspices of a production company, will want that company named as a party to the contract. In this instance, the Producer would sign the agreement as an officer of the company, and not in his personal capacity. Otherwise, the Producer may be personally liable if there is a breach of the agreement.

The Producer will also want to ensure that the distributor is correctly identified. If the Distributor is a corporation, LLC, or other business entity, the Producer may check with the appropriate government agency, such as the Secretary of State, to make sure that the other party actually exists and is in good standing. The Producer will want to know precisely which entity is obligated to live up to the terms of the agreement.

1. PICTURE: Producer will deliver to Distributor the documentation, advertising, and access to the physical materials (the "Materials") set forth in the attached Delivery Schedule, relating to the 35mm motion picture, currently entitled:

"_____" (the "Picture") directed by _____ based on the script written by _____.

Commentary: The picture needs to be correctly identified.

2. RIGHTS GRANTED:

   a) Producer hereby grants to Distributor the right, title, and interest in and to the distribution of the Picture, its sound, and music in the territory (as hereinafter defined) including the sole and exclusive right and privilege, under Producer's copyright and otherwise, to distribute, license, and otherwise exploit the Picture, its image, sound, and music, for the term (as hereinafter defined) throughout the territory (as hereinafter defined) for Theatrical, Home Video, and Television media.

Such rights do not include the rights to produce other motion pictures, sequels, or remakes of the Picture or any right to produce television series, miniseries, or programs or other so-called ancillary programs or any rights reserved (hereinafter called "Reserved Rights") to Producer. Without limiting the generality of the foregoing, or any other rights granted to Distributor elsewhere in this agreement, Producer hereby grants to Distributor the following rights:

   i) Theatrical Rights: All rights in and to the manufacture, distribution, exhibition, marketing, and other exploitation of the Picture, its sound, and music, by and relating to the projection of visual images contained on positive film prints of any size or kind (including 35mm and 16mm) whether in movie theaters, drive-ins, or any other venues (herein the "Theatrical Rights") throughout the territory for the term.

Commentary: Theatrical rights are essentially the right to exhibit the film in commercial theaters. These rights generally are defined so that they do not include so called "Non-Theatrical Rights," which are for exploitation by screening the Picture directly before an audience by institutions or organizations not primarily engaged in the business of exhibition such as educational institutions, churches, restaurants, bars, clubs, government, and military installations. Theatrical and Non-Theatrical usually do not include Airline Rights, Hotel/Motel Rights, or Ship Rights.

ii) Home Video Rights: All rights in and to the manufacture, distribution, exploitation, and non-admission free home-use exhibition of the Picture, its sound, and music (whether by sale or by rental) by means of any and all forms of videocassette, videodisc, video cartridge, tape, or other similar device ("Videogram") now known or hereafter devised and designed to be used in conjunction with a reproduction apparatus that causes a visual image (whether or not synchronized with sound) to be seen on the screen of a television receiver or any comparable device now known or hereafter devised, including DVD (the "Home Video Rights" or "Video Rights").

Commentary: Home video rights are the right to view the film at home, typically on either a VHS cassette or DVD player but may also include such formats as CD-I, CD-ROM and laser discs. These rights do not include exhibition where an admission fee is charged or where there is a public performance before an audience.

Some contracts attempt to include Video on Demand (VOD) rights within the scope of home video rights, reasoning that VOD is just a new technology to permit people to view films at home. Other agreements include VOD with television rights. "Video-On-Demand" is typically defined as the transmission of a selected video image from a central video library via a television, cable, or similar electronic system with the reception at a viewing time selected by the viewer. It is available by payment of a fee in addition to whatever fee is charged for reception of a television service and/or programming channel. VOD is not much different from Pay-Per-View, which is a form of television.

iii) Free Television Rights: All rights in and to the distribution, exhibition, marketing, and other exploitation of the Picture, its sound, and music by free television utilizing means other than those provided for in Paragraph 2(a) above and including without limitation, free television, by network, or by syndicated UHF or VHF broadcast (the "Free Television Rights").

iv) Pay Television/Pay-Per-View: All rights in and to the distribution, exhibition, marketing, and other exploitation of the Picture, its sound, and music by means of "Pay Television" as that expression is commonly understood in the motion picture industry, and including without limitation, cable, wire, or fiber of any material, "over-the-air pay," all forms of regular or occasionally scrambled broadcast, master antenna, and multi-channel, multi-point distribution, satellite transmission and radio (for purposes of simulcast only), all on a subscription, pay-per-view, license, rental, sale, or any other basis ("the Pay Television Rights").

b) Advertising: Distributor shall have the right throughout the territory during the Term to advertise and publicize (or have its subdistributors advertise and publicize) the Picture by any and all means, media, and method whatsoever, including, by means of the distribution, exhibition, broadcasting, and telecasting of trailers of the Picture, or excerpts from the Picture prepared by Distributor or others, subject to any customary restrictions upon and obligations with respect to such rights as are provided for in the contracts in relation to the production of the Picture.

> *Commentary: The parties need to carefully determine which rights will be granted to the Distributor and which rights will be reserved to the Producer. It is in the Producer's interest to reserve those rights that the Distributor is unlikely to exploit. It is advisable to include a clause that specifically states that whatever rights are not granted to the Distributor are reserved to the Producer. It is customary to grant the Distributor the right to advertise and promote a picture in media that is otherwise reserved to the Producer. For example, even though the Producer reserves print publication rights, which would include the right to publish a novelization, the Distributor would have the right to use print media in the form of newspaper ads.*

c) Title: Distributor shall have the right to use the present title of the Picture. Subdistributors may change the title for distribution in their territories. No other changes to the title shall be made without Producer's written approval.

> *Commentary: The Distributor will need to allow its licensees to translate the title into another language. However, the Distributor should be restricted from unilaterally changing the title in the language in which the film was originally produced.*

d) Editing:

i) Distributor in its discretion will have the right to incorporate into the Picture preceding and/or following the main and end titles of the Picture and Trailers thereof, and in all advertising and publicity relating thereto, in such manner, position, form, and substance as Distributor may elect, Distributor's trademark, logo, and presentation announcement, and the designation of Distributor as the distributor of the Picture. Any re-edit of the credit sequence will be at Distributor's expense.

ii) Distributor's right to edit hereunder specifically excludes the right to make alterations whatsoever to the original negative and/or the Video Master of the Picture, to which Distributor shall have lab access rights (irrevocable for the term of this Agreement) for duplication purposes only. Other than changes required to meet government censorship rules, or changes made to allow for the insertion of television commercials and to meet broadcast standards and practices guidelines, Distributor shall not make any changes to the Picture without the prior written consent of Producer.

iii) Distributor hereby indemnifies Producer for any losses, including reasonable attorneys' fees, incurred as a result of any liability arising from Distributor's editing, adding, or changing material in the Picture.

> *Commentary: Distributors often request discretion to re-edit a picture. A filmmaker may be quite upset to discover that the Distributor has made creative changes. Consequently, the right to edit is often limited to making changes required for censorship purposes, to insert commercials when a movie is broadcast, and to add the Distributor's logo at the start of the picture.*

e) Licensing: Distributor has the right to grant licenses and other authorizations to one or more third parties to exercise any or all of said rights and privileges provided herein, in countries throughout the territory. The maximum term for any license granted by Distributor shall be twelve (12) years except for licensees for exploitation in Germany, which can extend for up to (15) years. Distributor may not assign its distribution rights to another sales company, or use a subdistributor to fulfill Distributor's obligations under this Agreement, without the prior written consent of Producer.

Commentary: Distributors will want the right to license the picture to its licensees. Most sales agents don't book pictures into theaters, nor do they directly control any television outlets or home video labels. A foreign sales agent is essentially a distributor that licenses a picture to other distributors. While the Producer may not want to review and approve every license agreement that the sales agent arranges, it may be unwise to give the sales agent complete discretion. It is customary for sales agents to be restricted in the length of term they can grant to licensees. Otherwise, the sales agent could license the film until the copyright expired, leaving the Producer with no residual value in his distribution rights.

f) Territorial Minimums: Producer and Distributor have established mutually agreed minimum guarantee amounts per territory (hereinafter "Territorial Minimums"). Nothing contained herein or in the schedule of Territorial Minimums shall be deemed to require Distributor in fact to obtain any such Territorial Minimums, but rather, it is the intention of the parties hereto that Distributor may not enter into an agreement for an amount less than the applicable Territorial Minimum without first obtaining Producer's approval. The Territorial Minimums for the Picture are set forth in the delivery schedule (Schedule A), attached.

Commentary: Another mechanism for limiting the sales agent discretion is to require it to license the film for no less than the minimum amounts specified in a Schedule of Minimiums.

g) No Further Rights: This agreement confers no right on the part of the Producer to use, or authorize others to use, the Picture or any of the rights granted Distributor, within the Territory, which is not authorized by the Distributor hereunder, except Producer shall have the right to exhibit the Picture in festivals, industry screenings, and screenings for non-profit and/or educational purposes.

Commentary: The Distributor does not want the Producer to interfere with any of the rights granted to the Distributor.

3. RESERVED RIGHTS: All other rights not expressly granted herein, including but not limited to electronic publishing, print publication, Internet distribution, music publishing, live television, radio, and dramatic rights are reserved to the Producer.

Commentary: As mentioned above, it is advisable for the Producer to include a provision that all rights not granted to the Distributor are reserved to the Producer, and to spell out some of the reserved rights to avoid any doubt as to what has been granted and what has been reserved.

4. TERRITORY: The territory (herein "Territory") for which rights are granted to Distributor consists of the World (in all languages) with the exception of the United States, its territories, possessions, and military bases, and English-speaking Canada.

Commentary: The territory can be an individual country ("Sweden") or a region ("Europe"). Typically, a foreign sales company obtains the right to distribute a picture in the entire world except for North America. The North American rights are often defined as the United States and English-speaking Canada. A producer will often contract with one or more domestic companies for exploitation of rights in the U.S. and Canada. Care must be taken to make sure that the grants to various distributors do not conflict. Sometimes the holder of U.S. rights also requests rights to Puerto Rico, Bermuda, and other entities that may have been included in the grant to the foreign sales company.

5. TERM: The rights granted to Distributor under this Agreement will commence on the date of this Agreement and continue thereafter for two (2) years (the "Initial Term"). If Distributor pays Producer $800,000 or more in the Initial Term, Distributor shall automatically have the right to extend the term for another two (2)-year term (the "First Extended Term"). During this First Extended Term (and additional terms if further extended), Distributor shall have the option of extending the term for additional two (2)-year periods (up to a total term of no more than ten (10) years) if the following thresholds are met:

First Extended Term: If $1.4 million cumulatively has been paid to Producer during the Initial and First Extended Terms, then Distributor may extend the term another two (2) years (the Second Extended Term).

Second Extended Term: If $1.8 million cumulatively has been paid to Producer during the Initial, First, and Second Extended Terms, then Distributor may extend the term for another two (2) years (the Third Extended Term).

Third Extended Term: If $2.2 million cumulatively has been paid to Producer during the Initial and First through Third

Extended Terms, then Distributor may extend the term for another two (2) years (the Fourth Extended Term).

Fourth Extended Term: If $2.6 million cumulatively has been paid to Producer during the Initial and First through Fourth Extended Terms, then Distributor may extend the term for another two (2) years (the Fifth Extended Term).

In order to extend the term, Distributor shall notify Producer in writing of its intention at least thirty (30) days prior to expiration of the then current term.

Commentary: This term is structured so that various performance milestones determine its length. Distributors often ask for lengthy terms of 10 years or more. In many instances the Distributor loses enthusiasm for the picture as the years go by. By tying the extent of the term to the Distributor's ability to generate revenue and pay the Producer, the Producer is assured that if the Distributor gives up on a picture, the Producer will not have to wait an unduly long period of time to regain rights to the picture.

6. ADVERTISING/PROMOTION: Distributor will consult in good faith with Producer on marketing plans before any artwork is commissioned and the marketing campaign has begun. Producer will supply to Distributor the advertising and marketing materials set forth on the attached delivery schedule, Schedule A. Distributor will not disseminate any photos or bios of Producer unless Producer has approved them. If Distributor creates its own artwork and trailers for the Picture, Ownership of these materials shall vest in Producer, and Producer shall have the right to use said materials at any time for the release of the Picture outside the Territory and anywhere in the Universe after the term of this Agreement expires. Any artwork or copyrightable material commissioned by Distributor shall be created pursuant to a written contract, signed before the material is created, which states that the work is a work-for-hire and that Producer is the owner of all rights.

Commentary: Since the Distributor typically advances the costs of advertising and marketing, and believes it has more expertise in this field than the filmmaker, the Distributor usually insists on retaining complete discretion as to how these funds will be spent. Of course, since the Distributor is allowed to recoup these expenses from the film's revenues, thereby reducing the Producer's share of revenue, at the end of the day the

Producer is really paying for advertising and marketing. Consequently, the Producer may want to share authority as to how these funds are spent. Moreover, the Producer may want the right to use the Distributor's artwork outside the Territory and after the term expires. Unless the Producer insists that the artwork be created under a work-for-hire agreement, the right to use it may reside in the designer or the Distributor.

7. COPYRIGHT:

a) Producer represents and warrants that the Picture is, and will be throughout the Term, protected by copyright. Each copy of the Picture will contain a copyright notice conforming to and complying with the requirements of the United States Copyright Act as amended from time to time.

Commentary: The Distributor wants to ensure that the Producer maintains his copyright to the picture because the right to distribute the picture is part of the copyright. Under the prior Copyright Act, a copyright had to be renewed at the end of the initial term in order to extend it. That is no longer a requirement under U.S. law. A copyright notice is not legally required but is advisable.

8. PRODUCTION COSTS:

a) As between Producer and Distributor: Producer is and will be responsible for and has paid or will pay all production costs, taxes, fees, and charges with respect to the Picture and/or the Materials except as provided herein. As used herein, "production costs" will include all costs incurred in connection with the production of the Picture and the Materials, including payments to writers, producers, directors, artists, and all other persons rendering services in connection with the Picture and/or the materials, all costs and expenses incurred in acquiring rights to use music in connection with the Picture, including synchronization, performance, and mechanical-reproduction fees and union residuals.

Commentary: The Distributor often wants to acquire the right to distribute the film without any obligation to pay for its production. The Distributor does not want to discover down the road that because the Producer failed to pay for music or some other component of the film, an aggrieved party may bring suit and attempt to stop distribution of the film. If the

Producer lacks the funds to complete the picture, the parties may agree that the Distributor will advance funds that will be used for that purpose. For example, the Distributor may agree to advance the cost of acquiring music for the soundtrack, and to pay for Errors and Omissions insurance.

9. PRODUCER'S REPRESENTATIONS AND WARRANTIES: Producer warrants and represents to Distributor, to the best of Producer's knowledge and belief, as follows:

a) Producer has full right, power, and authority to enter into and perform this Agreement and to grant to Distributor all of the rights herein granted and agreed to be granted to Distributor.

b) Producer has acquired, or will have acquired prior to the delivery of the Picture hereunder, and will maintain during the term, all rights in and to the literary and musical material upon which the Picture is based or which are used therein, and any other rights necessary and required for the exploitation of the Picture, as permitted hereunder.

c) Neither the Picture nor the Materials nor any part thereof, nor any literary, dramatic or musical works or any other materials contained therein or synchronized therewith, nor the exercise of any right, license, or privilege herein granted, violates or will violate, or infringes or will infringe, any trademark, trade name, contract, agreement, copyright (whether common law or statutory), patent, literary, artistic, dramatic, personal, private, civil, or property right or right of privacy or "moral right of authors," or any law or regulation or other right whatsoever of, or slanders or libels, any person, firm, corporation, or association.

d) Producer has not sold, assigned, transferred, or conveyed and will not sell, assign, transfer, or convey, to any party, any right, title, or interest in and to the Picture or any part thereof, or in and to the dramatic, musical, or literary material upon which it is based, adverse to or derogatory of or which would interfere with the rights granted to Distributor, and has not and will not authorize any other party to exercise any right or take any action that will derogate from the rights herein granted or purported to be granted to Distributor.

e) Producer will obtain and maintain all necessary licenses for the production, exhibition, performance, distribution, marketing, and exploitation of the Picture and/or the Materials, including, without limitation, the synchronization and performance of all music contained therein, throughout the Territory during the term for any and all purposes contemplated hereunder. Producer further represents and warrants that as between the Producer and Distributor, the performing rights to all musical compositions contained in the Picture and/or the Materials will be controlled by Producer to the extent required for the purposes of the Agreement and that no payments will be required to be made by Distributor to any third party for the use of such music in the Materials or on television or in Videogram embodying the Picture other than Guild-required residual payments.

f) Producer represents and warrants that all artists, actors, musicians, and persons rendering services in connection with the production of the Picture or the materials have been or will be paid by Producer the sums required to be paid to them under applicable agreements, and the sums required to be paid pursuant to any applicable pension or similar trusts required thereby will be made by Producer, in a due and timely manner.

g) It is understood that the Producer has not obtained Errors and Omissions insurance. However, if demand is made by a sub-licensee/distributor for a certificate of Errors and Omissions insurance as indicated above, Distributor will advance such cost and recoup the expense from Gross Receipts. Producer shall be added as an additional named insured on any E&O policy.

h) The Picture was shot on 35mm film. The Picture and the television/airline version (when available) have a running time of 90 minutes and the Picture should receive an MPAA rating no more restrictive than "R." It is understood that the Picture has not received or applied for an MPAA rating. If and when it becomes necessary to receive an MPAA rating, Producer shall promptly perform any and all additional editing necessary in order to secure said MPAA rating. The expense of securing such rating shall be advanced by Distributor and recouped from Gross Receipts.

i) At the time of delivery of the Picture to Distributor, the Picture will not have been exhibited anywhere in the Territory for commercial reasons, with the exception of festivals or industry screenings.

> *Commentary: Warranties are promises. The Distributor wants the Producer to make certain promises. These warranties will need to be modified to suit the facts and circumstances. Sometimes the Picture has been previously exhibited in the Territory. Producers need to closely review the warranties requested because a breach of a warranty may give rise to liability.*

10. DISTRIBUTOR'S WARRANTIES:

Distributor warrants that:

a) Distributor has the authority to enter into this agreement, and there are and, to the best of Distributor's knowledge and belief, will be, no claims, actions, suits, arbitrations, or other proceedings or investigations pending or threatened against or affecting the Distributor's ability to fulfill its obligations under this agreement, at law or in equity, or before any federal, state, county, municipal, or other governmental instrumentality or authority, domestic or foreign.

b) Distributor is and will continue to be engaged during the Term as a distributor of motion pictures throughout the licensed territory. Distributor is not unable to pay its bills in the regular course of business, is not insolvent nor in danger of bankruptcy.

c) Distributor warrants that all payments from subdistributors and other licensees will be by check, wire transfer, letter of credit, or money order paid directly into the collection bank account established for this Picture. If cash is accepted, a copy of license agreement with the amount of the deposit will be sent to Producer. Distributor further warrants that Distributor will not accept any other consideration, whether cash, discounts on Distributor's other films, favors of any kind, or any other form of consideration, from any subdistributor or Distributor in return for licensing the Picture, unless such consideration is approved by Producer. The amount paid by Licensees shall be divided into a license fee for distribution rights and reimbursement of any duplication and manufacturing costs needed to make delivery to the licensee. Duplication and manufacturing costs shall be limited to the direct out-of-pocket costs incurred by Distributor to create delivery materials for the licensees. These expenses shall not be marked up, and the reimbursement of these expenses shall not be included in Gross Receipts.

d) Distributor will obtain any necessary clearances needed for any advertising and marketing materials created to promote Producer's film, and will employ artists and designers on a work-for-hire basis with Producer designated as the Employer and copyright owner of such materials.

e) Distributor shall diligently promote and license the Picture throughout the licensed territory.

f) The standard of quality of all Videograms, sub-masters, and other materials manufactured or duplicated by, or at the request of, Distributor shall be of a high quality.

g) Distributor shall not use the Picture, or authorize the Picture to be used, in any manner that is likely to bring Producer into disrepute or which is defamatory of any person.

h) Distributor shall not make any edits, cuts, alterations, or re-arrangements to the Picture as released without the prior written approval of Producer.

Commentary: It is not unusual for a Distributor to send a Producer a contract lacking any Distributor warranties. A Producer will want to ensure that the Distributor makes certain promises.

11. INDEMNITY: Each party hereby agrees to defend, indemnify, and hold harmless the other (and its affiliates, and its and their respective successors, assigns, distributors, officers, directors, employees, and representatives) against and for any and all claims, liabilities, damages, costs, and expenses (including reasonable attorneys' fees and court costs) arising from or related to any breach by the indemnifying party of any of its undertakings, representations, or warranties under this Agreement, and/or arising from or related to any and all third-party claims, which, if proven, would be such a breach. Each party agrees to notify the other in writing of any and all claims to which this indemnity will apply, and to afford the indemnifying party the opportunity to undertake the defense of such claim(s) with counsel approved by the indemnified party (which approval will not be unreasonably withheld), subject to the right of the indemnified party to participate in such defense at its cost. In no event shall any such claim be settled in such a way as which would adversely affect the rights of the indemnified party in the Picture without such party's prior written consent; provided, however, that Producer

hereby consents to any settlement entered into under any of the following circumstances: (i) the applicable insurance carrier authorized the settlement; (ii) the settlement relates to a claim for injunctive relief that has remained unsettled or pending for a period of thirty (30) days or longer which otherwise interferes with Distributor's distribution of the Picture hereunder; or (iii) the settlement is for not more than $10,000. All rights and remedies of the parties hereunder will be cumulative and will not interfere with or prevent the exercise of any other right or remedy that may be available to the respective party.

Commentary: The indemnity clause provides that if a party to the Agreement breaches its obligations, it will reimburse the other party any losses incurred from such a breach. The loss may include the cost of settling a lawsuit filed by a third party and any attorney fees spent in defense of a claim. Producers often specifically ask the Distributor to indemnify the Producer for any changes the Distributor may make to the picture, and for any liability arising from the Distributor's exploitation of the Picture.

---

12. DELIVERY MATERIALS: The Picture will be delivered as follows:

a) On or before _____, 20__, Producer will deliver to Distributor the materials specified in Exhibit A hereto, accompanied by a fully executed lab access letter (irrevocable for the term) for access to the Master materials. The lab access letter shall provide that at Producer's request the Laboratory will disclose to Producer a complete listing of all orders fulfilled by Laboratory for Distributor, including a description of what materials were ordered, the prices charged for the work, and to whom each order was shipped.

b) If any said materials are not acceptable to Distributor, Distributor will notify the Producer of any technical problems or defects within ten (10) business days, and Producer will promptly replace the defective materials at Producer's sole expense. Distributor shall have no right to terminate this Agreement unless and until Producer has failed to cure any such defects within thirty (30) days after notice thereof from Distributor. If no objection is made by Distributor within ten (10) business days of delivery of an item, the item will be deemed acceptable and not subject to further objection.

Distributor will supply Producer with a copy of any laboratory quality-control report that Distributor receives.

c) Producer will concurrently with the delivery of the
materials deliver to Distributor a list of contractual requirements for advertising credits to persons who rendered services or furnished materials for such Picture and a list of any
restrictions.

d) All materials delivered to Distributor shall be returned
to Producer within thirty (30) days of the end of the term.

> *Commentary: Distributors want to make sure that the Producer's
> master elements are not defective because they need to be able
> to arrange for the manufacture of copies to be delivered to
> licensees. Consequently, the distributor should have a reason-
> able opportunity to have the master materials inspected and
> checked, which is typically performed by a laboratory, which
> supplies a quality-control report. The Producer should request
> a copy of this report, which may be requested by other distribu-
> tors of the Picture.*
>
> *Distributors may allege the existence of technical defects in
> the Producer's materials, and use these real or imagined
> defects as an excuse for not paying the Producer his share of
> revenue. Requiring the Distributor to timely raise an objec-
> tion or waive their right to raise the objection later can
> prevent this abuse.*

13. ADVANCE/GUARANTEE: Distributor shall advance the
sum of $_____, which sum shall be non-refundable but
recoupable from Gross Receipts. Time is of the essence in
regard to the payment of this advance. If payment is not made
by _____, then Distributor's rights under this agreement
are void ab initio, and Distributor immediately loses its right to
distribute this Picture.

> *Requiring the Distributor to make an advance payment to the
> Producer allows the Producer to immediately realize revenue
> from the film, and repay investors their capital contribution.
> Furthermore, a Distributor that pays an advance is sharing
> financial risk with the Producer. This gives the Distributor an
> incentive to aggressively market the picture because the ad-
> vance is customarily recoupable, but not refundable. This
> means that if the Distributor is unable to generate any revenue
> from the picture, the Distributor cannot demand that the*

Producer return the advance. All other factors being equal, a Distributor will push harder to make sales on a film that it has invested in than one that is free inventory.

Instead of offering an advance, some distributors will offer to pay the Producer a Minimum Guarantee (MG). This is a minimum payment that the Producer is guaranteed to receive, but the payment may be due many months after distribution commences. From the Producer's view, an advance is prefer-able because the advance is typically paid on signing of the distribution agreement, or on complete delivery of the picture to the Distributor, while the MG may not be payable until much later. Moreover, there is a risk that, despite the Distributor's promise to pay a MG, no guarantee will be paid. If the Dis-tributor is unable to generate revenue from the film, it may give the Producer an excuse instead of cash.

14. ALLOCATION OF GROSS RECEIPTS: As to proceeds de-rived from Distributor's exploitation of all rights outlined in Paragraph 2, division of the Gross Receipts will be made as follows:

a) From the Distributor's exploitation of Theatrical, Tele-vision, Home Video, and any other Granted Rights, Distribu-tor shall deduct and retain twenty percent (20%) of Gross Receipts. From the remaining revenues Distributor may re-coup all recoupable expenses related to the prints, marketing, advertising, and sale of the Picture. The net proceeds shall be paid to Producer.

Commentary: The distribution fee, or commission, is compen-sation paid to the Distributor for its services. A foreign sales agent may license a film, and make delivery, to licensees in 50 or more countries. It the sales agent does a good job, and pays the Producer his share of revenue, the agreement benefits both parties. Most Producers do not have the relationships and expertise needed to perform the function of the sales agent.

b) Gross Receipts: As used herein, the term "Gross Receipts" shall mean all monies actually received by and credited to Distributor less any refunds, returns, taxes, collec-tion costs, and manufacturing or duplication costs. Distributor may be sent advances, guarantees, security deposits, and similar payments from persons or companies licensed by Distributor to subdistribute or otherwise exploit the Picture (which monies shall be deposited in the collection account established for this Picture). Notwithstanding the receipt of such monies, if any, and notwithstanding anything to the contrary contained herein, no such monies will be deemed to be Gross Receipts hereunder unless and until such monies are earned or deemed forfeited, or become non-returnable.

Commentary: Since the Distributor's fee is based on a percentage of Gross Receipts, the sales agent would like the definition to be as expansive as possible. The Producer, on the other hand, wants to define Gross Receipts narrowly in terms of calculating the Distributor's fee, but wants to include all possible revenue to ensure that the Producer shares in it. The above definition excludes manufacturing costs from the definition of Gross Receipts. Typically, territory licensees will pay a license fee for the right to show the film in their territory and media, and make a separate payment, or reimbursement, to the Distributor for whatever manufacturing and duplication costs are incurred to ship to the license prints, photos, artwork, and collateral material.

c) Deductions from Gross Receipts shall be taken in the following order:

1) Distribution fee of twenty percent (20%).

2) Recoupment of any recoupable Delivery Expenses incurred by Distributor.

3) Recoupment of any recoupable Market and Promotional Expenses incurred by Distributor.

4) Net Proceeds shall be paid to Producer.

15. RECOUPABLE EXPENSES: As used herein, the term expenses and/or recoupable expenses shall mean all of Distributor's actual expenses on behalf of the Picture limited as follows:

Commentary: This section restricts the amount of expenses that a Distributor is entitled to recoup from revenue generated from a film. The more expenses the Distributor is permitted to recoup, the less revenue will flow to the Producer. Obviously, the Producer wants the Distributor to spend a reasonable amount to market the film or it is unlikely to generate much interest among buyers. On the other hand, if the Distributor overspends

*and is allowed to recoup excessive expenses, very little if any
revenue will flow down to the Producer. This agreement di-
vides expenses into three categories: market, promotional, and
delivery expenses. The amount of allowable expenses for each
type is treated differently to ensure that an appropriate amount
is spent for each activity.*

a) Market Expenses: These expenses include all direct
out-of-pocket costs to attend film markets such as AFM,
Cannes, and MIFED. Such expenses include airfare, hotel,
shipping, telephone, and staff expenses incurred to attend a
film market. Such expenses shall be recoupable for the first
year of distribution only, and only for those markets in which
Distributor is actively participating (*i.e.*, Distributor attends,
rents a suite, and is actively selling the Picture). Distributor
may recoup a total of $3,500 per market attended with an
overall cap of no more than $10,000 overall market cap for
the year. Distributor agrees to attend no less than three (3)
markets during the first year of distribution. Should the
distribution term extend beyond one year, no market expenses shall be recoupable during the second and any subsequent years, unless the parties agree otherwise in writing.

*Commentary: Market expenses can be substantial, usually in
the tens of thousands of dollars. Market expenses include the
cost of registration at a film or television market (e.g., MIP,
Cannes, AFM), travel and lodging for the Distributor's staff,
rental of television, VCRs and furniture for a market suite, and
shipping of promotional materials such as one-sheets, videocassettes, and film prints. Usually these costs are apportioned among
the current films that the Distributor is marketing. There are a
number of formulas that can be used to apportion these expenses among different films. One method is to simply agree on
a dollar amount that may be spent for each market attended
with an overall cap for the first year, and no recoupment
allowed for subsequent years. Another formula is to divide
expenses among the films represented in a market. So if $90,000
was spent at a market and the Distributor represented 10 films,
each film would be charged $9,000 as its share.*

b) Promotional Expenses: These expenses include the cost
of preparing posters, one-sheets, trailers, and advertising. Distributor agrees to spend no less than $15,000 and no more than
$20,000 on promotional expenses. These expenses are limited

to direct out-of-pocket expenses actually spent on behalf of the Picture. At Producer's request, Distributor shall provide receipts for each and every expense or forgo recoupment. Recoupable promotional expenses do not include any of Distributor's general office, overhead, legal, or staff expenses or any of the aforementioned Market Expenses, or the Delivery Expenses set forth in the next paragraph. Distributor agrees to spend the minimum necessary to adequately promote the Picture, including preparation of a trailer, poster, one-sheet, videocassette, and customary promotional material, if Producer has not supplied these items. Distributor will use its best efforts to promote the Picture, and will promote the Picture in a no-less-favorable manner than any of Distributor's other films.

Commentary: Promotional expenses are defined here as out-of-pocket expenses to promote the Picture. The Distributor cannot recoup its general office, overhead, or staff expenses that it incurs in the normal course of business. Distributors will often take out full-page ads in the trade papers promoting several pictures. The cost of these ads should be apportioned among the pictures advertised.

c) Delivery Expenses: Delivery Expenses are the direct out-of-pocket costs incurred by Distributor to manufacture any of the film or video deliverables (as listed on Exhibit A) that Producer did not supply. Delivery Expenses also include the direct out-of-pocket costs incurred between markets for shipping, duplicating, delivery of marketing materials (*i.e.,* screeners) to foreign buyers. At Producer's request, Distributor shall provide receipts for each and every expense or forgo recoupment. Recoupable Delivery Expenses do not include any of Distributor's general office, overhead, legal, or staff expenses or any of the aforementioned Promotional or Market Expenses.

Commentary: While Market expenses are often recoupable for the first year of distribution only and Promotional expenses are usually incurred at the outset of distribution, delivery expenses are often incurred over many years as the film is licensed. Sometimes the Distributor will attempt to mark up the delivery costs charged by a laboratory (for instance, when licensees order materials), and pocket the difference.

16. CONTRACTS: Distributor will use exclusively AFMA deal memos and model contracts. Distributor will provide copies of all Deal Memos and contracts to Producer within fourteen (14) days of their execution.

Commentary: A Producer is dependent on the Distributor to use care in contracting with its licensees. The Producer wants to make sure the Distributor uses well-drafted agreements to secure its rights with licensees. If the Distributor relies on a vague or unenforceable agreement, and as a result the Distributor cannot collect revenue due it, the Producer will suffer. The AFMA deal memos and model contracts are widely used by those in the industry. Copies of these forms can be purchased from AFMA.

17. PACKAGE SALES: The Picture may be included in any of Distributor's package of motion pictures provided that Distributor shall make a fair and reasonable allocation of the package price to each of the pictures in the package, and provided that the price allocated to Producer's Picture shall be at least the minimum set forth in Schedule A, attached.

Commentary: There is a lot of room for abuse when a Distributor sells a package of films. No matter what the paperwork says, it is difficult for the Producer to know what was discussed when a package deal was cut. The licensee may have taken the Producer's film only because he was forced to buy a package of films, which may benefit the Producer. On the other hand, the Producer's film may have been the only picture that the buyer wanted, and by being forced to buy the film as part of a package, the Producer may have received less than what he could have received if the film had been licensed by itself. This paragraph attempts to set the standard to be used in allocating a license fee among several films in a package.

18. LATE PAYMENTS/LIEN: Producer shall hold a lien and security interest on the gross receipts and distribution contracts for the Picture. All monies due Producer shall be paid in accordance with this agreement. Distributor shall pay Producer interest on any amounts thirty (30) days past due at the lesser of 1) ten percent (10%) per annum, or 2) the maximum legal rate of interest. Time is of the essence hereof in regard to all payments due Producer.

> *Commentary: In many instances courts may not award interest on late payments unless there is a specific statute or contractual provision that permits it. A Producer who receives a payment a year after it is due has not been paid what he is entitled to.*
>
> *The Producer wants to remove any financial incentive the Distributor may have to delay payment. If the Distributor is allowed to hold onto the Producer's share of revenue for an unduly long period of time, and earn interest on it, the Distributor benefits from its breach.*

19. SECURITY INTEREST: As security for payment of Producer's share of Gross Receipts, hereunder, Distributor hereby grants to Producer a lien and security interest in all of Distributor's right, title, and interest in and to (i) all rights granted to Distributor in the Picture and its underlying material, (ii) all film elements, videotapes, sound elements, and other physical materials of any kind to be used in the exploitation of the Picture by Distributor from exploitation of the Picture by Distributor, (iii) all proceeds realized by Distributor from exploitation of the Picture, to which Producer is entitled as Producer's share of Gross Receipts hereunder. With respect to said security interest, Producer shall have all the rights, power, and privileges of a secured party under the California Uniform Commercial Code as the same may be amended from time to time. Distributor agrees to sign and deliver to Producer all such financing statements and other instruments as may be legally necessary for Producer to file, register, and or record such security interests.

> *Commentary: A filmmaker will want to protect his right to share in his picture's revenue by having the Distributor grant the filmmaker a "security interest." Such a provision will give a filmmaker preference over unsecured creditors in the event of the Distributor's bankruptcy. The secured party holds the security interest. The other party—the one who owes the obligation—is called the "debtor." The "collateral" that secures the contract is usually the Distributor's right to distribute the motion picture, including any rights it may have in film elements (e.g., master tapes) and any revenues it may receive from the exploitation of these rights.*
>
> *In addition to a security interest clause in the distribution agreement, the parties often sign separate long- and short-form security agreements, and form UCC-1. Documents should*

*be promptly recorded both with the appropriate state agency
(e.g., Secretary of State) for the state in which the collateral is
located, and with the Copyright Office in Washington, D.C.
Information and downloadable copies of the UCC-1 form are
available from the California Secretary of State at: www.ss.ca.gov/
business/ucc/ra_9_ucc_formsfees.htm.*

*Note that Distributors who provide production financing, or
pay advances to Producers, may seek to protect their interests
by having and recording their own security interests. Likewise,
a bank that loans funds for production will often insist on
securing its interest, and unions such as SAG and DGA may
want security interests to ensure that their members receive
residuals due them. In fashioning multiple security interests,
care must be taken to ensure that they do not conflict. Financiers often insist on a first-priority security interest. Unions
may be willing to subordinate their interests to a bank.*

20. DEFAULT/TERMINATION:

a) Distributor Default: If it is found and proven that
Distributor has defaulted on its obligations under this Agreement, upon notification of that fact from Producer, Distributor
will have thirty (30) days to cure said default. If the default is
not cured within the allotted period, the Producer will have
the right to initiate arbitration.

*Commentary: This provision requires the Producer to notify
the Distributor of any default, and give it 30 days to cure the
problem, before the Producer initiates arbitration proceedings.*

b) Producer Default: Distributor shall notify Producer in
writing of any alleged default hereunder. Producer shall have
thirty (30) days to correct alleged default before Distributor
will have the right to initiate arbitration.

*Commentary: This clause requires the Distributor to notify the
Producer of any default by the Producer. Once the Producer
makes complete delivery, the Producer has fulfilled most, if not
all, of his obligations under the agreement.*

c) Termination Rights: No failure by either party hereto
to perform any of its obligations under this Agreement shall
be deemed to be a material breach of this Agreement until the

non-breaching party has given the breaching party written notice of its failure to perform and such failure has not been corrected within thirty (30) business days from and after the giving of such notice. In the event of an uncured material breach, either party shall be entitled to terminate this Agreement (subject to arbitration) by written notice to the other party, obtain monetary damages and other appropriate relief, and in the case of Producer, regain all of its rights in the Picture subject to existing executory contracts and licenses respecting the Picture.

> *Commentary: Many distribution agreements severely restrict the Producer's remedies. Often the Producer waives the right to terminate the agreement or obtains injunction relief, such as a court order stopping distribution. The Producer's remedy is often limited to obtaining a monetary judgment against the Distributor. This may be quite unsatisfactory if the Distributor has no assets to pay a judgement. The clause above is more favorable to the Producer because the Producer can terminate the distribution under certain circumstances.*

d) Termination/Bankruptcy: Producer shall have the right to terminate this Agreement and cause all rights herein conveyed to Distributor to revert to Producer subject, however, to third-party agreements conveying rights in the Picture (in respect to which Producer shall be deemed an assignee of all of Distributor's rights therein in respect to the Picture), by written notice to Distributor in the event that Distributor files a petition in bankruptcy or consents to an involuntary petition in bankruptcy or to any reorganization under Chapter 11 of the Bankruptcy Act. Notwithstanding anything to the contrary that may be contained in the preceding sentence, in the event that Distributor files a petition in bankruptcy or consents to an involuntary petition in bankruptcy or to any reorganization under Chapter 11 of the Bankruptcy Act, Producer shall not be entitled to terminate this Agreement if thereafter: (1) Distributor segregates Producer's share of the monies that Distributor receives in connection with the Picture and places the monies into a separate trust account, and that such monies are not commingled with Distributor's other funds, and Producer's share of such monies shall become Producer's property immediately upon the collection by Distributor, and (2) this procedure is approved by the Bankruptcy Court. In connection with the foregoing, Distributor hereby grants to Producer a security interest in the Picture and the right to receive monies from the exploitation of the Picture ("Security Interest"). Producer may by written notice to Distributor execute against the Security Interest if and only if Distributor files a petition in bankruptcy or consents to an involuntary bankruptcy or an organization under Chapter 11 and Producer is entitled to terminate this Agreement in accordance with the other provisions of this Paragraph.

> Commentary: This clause is of questionable enforceability. Once a distributor goes into bankruptcy, the bankruptcy court takes control of the company, and it has the power to modify the terms of the distribution agreement.

21. ACCOUNTINGS:

a) Distributor will render, or cause to be rendered to Producer and his attorney, quarterly accounting statements ("Producer Reports") commencing forty-five (45) days after the first quarter in which any deposit or licensee fee has been paid for exploitation of the Picture in any portion of the Territory, for the first year of this Agreement. Thereafter, quarterly statements will be made within forty-five (45) days after the last day of Distributor's then-current fiscal accounting period. All monies due and payable to Producer pursuant to this Agreement shall be paid simultaneously with the rendering of such statements. Statements and payments shall be sent to: PRODUCER FILMS, INC., at _____ with a copy of statements to _____. Payments shall be made payable to "PRODUCER FILMS, INC."

b) Producer will be deemed to have consented to all accountings rendered by Distributor or its assignees or successors, and all such statements will be binding upon Producer unless specific objections in writing, stating the basis thereof, is given by Producer within thirty-six (36) months of Producer's receipt of each Producer Report.

c) Distributor shall keep and maintain at its office in Los Angeles County, California, until expiration of the Term and for a period of five (5) years thereafter, complete, detailed, permanent, true, and accurate books of account and records relating to the distribution and exhibition of the Picture, including, but not limited to, detailed collections and sales by country and/or buyer, detailed billings thereon, detailed playdates thereof, detailed records of expenses that have been deducted from collections received from the exploitation of the Picture, and the whereabouts of prints, trailers, accessories, and other material in connection with the Picture. Records shall be kept in accordance with Generally Accepted Accounting Principles (GAAP). Producer shall be entitled to inspect such books and records of Distributor relating to the Picture during regular business hours and shall be entitled to audit such books and records of Distributor relating to the Picture upon ten (10) business days' written notice to Distributor and provided that not more than one audit is conducted every twelve (12) months during each calendar year and further provided that such audit shall last not more than ten (10) consecutive business days once begun and does not interfere with Distributor's normal operations. Within thirty (30) days of the completion of the audit, Producer will furnish Distributor with a copy of said audit. In the event that the audit discloses that Producer has been underpaid $5,000 or more, Distributor shall reimburse Producer for all audit costs. Otherwise, all audit expenses shall be borne by Producer.

d) Relationship Between Parties: Distributor will hold the Producer's portion of Gross Receipts in trust for Producer. This agreement will not constitute a partnership or joint venture between Distributor and Producer, and neither of the parties will become bound or liable because of any representations, acts, or omissions of the other party hereto.

e) Bank Account: Producer and Distributor shall establish a separate bank account at the _____ Bank in the name of _____ Picture/Special Account ("_____") or similar account name into which any and all monies generated from the exploitation of the Picture are to be deposited (the "Special Account"). Distributor shall advise its licensees to pay all advances and royalties into said Special Account. For any monies to be withdrawn from the Special Account, two (2) signatures shall be required: one from an authorized signor of Producer and one from an authorized agent of Distributor.

Commentary: The Producer should have the right to examine the Distributor's books and records on reasonable notice, at least once a year. Records should be kept in accordance with Generally Accepted Accounting Principles (GAAP). After concluding an audit, the Producer may be required to furnish the

Distributor a copy of the results. Some agreements provide that in the event of a significant underpayment (e.g., $1,000), the Distributor shall reimburse the Producer the cost of the audit. Otherwise, audit expenses are borne by the Producer.

Distributors often try to restrict a Producer's right to contest accounting statements. If a Producer does not timely object, he may waive his right to challenge a report later. Sometimes, the period to raise an objection is quite limited, perhaps as little as 18 months. Such a provision shortens the otherwise applicable statute of limitations, which may allow five years or more to object. The Distributor wants the Producer to object promptly or waive his rights.

The difficulty for the Producer is that even though he may suspect an error, he may not be able to determine whether a mistake has been made without an expensive audit. Paying for such an audit may not seem prudent if the amount of money at stake is small. It makes no sense to spend $10,000 for an audit if one believes it may only uncover an error of no more than $5,000. On the other hand, if the Producer delays, he may relinquish his right to object later.

Rather than force the Producer to object and conduct an audit to preserve his rights, a better solution is to require the Producer to inform the Distributor of an objection before initiating legal proceedings. This gives the Distributor an opportunity to review records and resolve the dispute informally, while preserving the Producer's remedies.

22. ASSUMPTION AGREEMENT: Distributor agrees to sign the customary assumption agreements required by any Union/ Guild that are applicable to the Picture.

Commentary: The union and guilds, such as SAG, have negotiated for their members to receive certain residual payments. Residuals are payments the union member is entitled to if the work is exploited in supplemental markets. For a theatrical feature, these ancillary markets would be television and home video. Of course, nowadays more revenue is generated from the ancillary market than from the theatrical market.

The unions and guilds want their members to receive payment of residuals directly from the distributor of the motion picture rather than have the Distributor pay the Producer, who would

*then in turn pay the union members. The unions are con-
cerned, based on past experience, that some Producers don't
live up to their residual obligations.*

*The assumption agreement is an agreement wherein the Dis-
tributor agrees to make these residual payments directly to the
union. The payments come from revenues generated in the
ancillary markets. Some distributors, however, don't want to
sign a guild assumption agreement because they are concerned about having a direct contractual relationship with the
union. They don't want to expose themselves, for instance, to
having the union audit the distributor's books and records.*

*If the Producer is unable to persuade the Distributor to sign an
assumption agreement, the producer faces a dilemma. When
the Producer signed a collective-bargaining agreement with
the union, the Producer agreed to have its Distributor sign the
assumption agreement.*

23. NOTICES: All notices, correspondence, writings, and statements shall be forwarded to the addresses and numbers as
follows: PRODUCER FILMS, INC., at _____,
fax number _____, with a copy to _____,
at _____, fax number _____; DIS-
TRIBUTION, INC., at _____, fax number
_____, with a copy to _____, at _____,
fax number _____. Fax receptions shall be deemed
an acceptable mode of acceptance of all notices, writings, and
statements unless otherwise agreed. In all instances, hard
copies will follow all telephonic or fax correspondence. Both
parties reserve the right to change the address of service at
any time with notice in writing to the receiving party.

24. ASSIGNMENT: This agreement will be binding upon and
will inure to the benefit of the parties hereto and their
respective successors and permitted assigns. Producer may
assign its rights to payment of monies. Distributor may not
assign its rights without the prior written consent of Producer,
provided that nothing herein will prevent Distributor from
assigning its rights to a successor company that may arise
from Distributor merging, being acquired, or partnering with
another company.

Commentary: After one has diligently researched potential distributors, selected one, and carefully negotiated an agreement, a filmmaker will not be pleased to learn that the right to distribute the film has been assigned to a different company. A well-drafted assignment clause can prevent a distributor from transferring its rights and obligations without the prior written consent of the filmmaker.

That is not to say that a distributor should not be allowed to sub-license some of its rights. If the distributor is a foreign sales company, it will be expected to enter into a series of license agreements with territory distributors around the globe. It is not feasible, nor necessarily desirable, for the filmmaker to review and approve every sub-license agreement. But the filmmaker will not want a wholesale assignment of the distribution agreement to another company that may not have the stature, integrity, and financial ability to successfully distribute the film. Moreover, the use of subdistributors may reduce the amount of revenue received by the filmmaker. Each distributor in the chain of distribution may want a distribution fee and to recoup its expenses.

Before entering into an agreement, a filmmaker will want to ask some pointed questions to determine exactly the nature of the distributor he is dealing with. Distributors come in all formulations. Some market films in multiple media, while others may focus on theatrical, television, or home video markets. Often distributors try to obtain as broad a grant of rights as possible with the intent of using subdistributors to serve other media and markets. For example, a domestic theatrical distributor may want the right to contract with an unaffiliated home video company. Or the domestic distributor could be a home video company that wants to have a theatrical distributor book the film in theaters. Such arrangements are not always detrimental for the filmmaker. A theatrical distributor might have an overall or output deal with HBO, for example, that ensures a healthy license fee for cable television rights that far exceeds what the filmmaker might be able to secure on his own. Moreover, a domestic theatrical distributor may be unwilling to advance the cost of a theatrical release if it does not also share in ancillary revenue.

While a filmmaker should try to limit assignment by the distributor, the filmmaker will want the right to freely assign his

> *share of revenues. Most distributors will not object to such a*
> *provision provided that they are not required to send checks to*
> *numerous parties.*

25. ARBITRATION AND JURISDICTION: This Agreement shall be interpreted in accordance with the laws of the State of California, applicable to agreements executed and to be wholly performed therein. Any controversy or claim arising out of or in relation to this Agreement or the validity, construction, or performance of this Agreement, or the breach thereof, shall be resolved by arbitration in accordance with the rules and procedures of the American Film Marketing Association, as said rules may be amended from time to time with rights of discovery if requested by the arbitrator. Such rules and procedures are incorporated and made a part of this Agreement by reference. If the American Film Marketing Association shall refuse to accept jurisdiction of such dispute, then the parties agree to arbitrate such matter before and in accordance with the rules of the American Arbitration Association under its jurisdiction in Los Angeles before a single arbitrator familiar with entertainment law. The parties shall have the right to engage in pre-hearing discovery in connection with such arbitration proceedings. The parties agree hereto that they will abide by and perform any award rendered in any arbitration conducted pursuant hereto, that any court having jurisdiction thereof may issue a judgment based upon such award, and that the prevailing party in such arbitration and/or confirmation proceeding shall be entitled to recover its reasonable attorneys' fees and costs. The arbitration will be held in Los Angeles and any award shall be final, binding, and non-appealable. The parties agree to accept service of process in accordance with the AFMA Rules. The parties further agree that if an arbitration award is awarded against Distributor, and Distributor fails to pay the award after it is confirmed by a court, the AFMA market-barring rule will apply against _____ as an officer of Distributor, and _____ agrees to sign the AFMA Rider attached to this agreement (attached as Exhibit B).

> *Commentary: Most entertainment industry arbitrations are*
> *conducted under the auspices of either the American Arbitra-*
> *tion Association (AAA) or AFMA, a trade organization repre-*
> *senting the interests of international distributors. The AAA has*

*a well-defined system of procedural rules and numerous of-
fices across the USA and in many other countries. AFMA is the
entity that organizes the American Film Market (AFM). AFMA
arbitrations usually occur in Los Angeles, but they can be held
during an international film market or in a foreign city. All
AFMA arbitrators are experienced entertainment attorneys.
AFMA arbitration fees are reduced if one of the parties to the
dispute is an AFMA member.*

*A unique feature of AFMA arbitration is that if the claimant
wins an award, and the respondent refuses to comply with its
terms, the claimant can have the respondent barred from
participating in future AFMs. This remedy is particularly valuable if the respondent is a company with its assets abroad and
difficult to reach under the authority of U.S. law. The threat of
being barred from the American Film Market might persuade
a recalcitrant distributor to comply with an award. There have
been instances, however, where respondents have sought to
avoid awards against them by abandoning their companies—
often shell corporations with no assets—and then establishing
new companies. Conducting their business under this unsul-
lied entity, they attempt to exploit another wave of victims,
expecting to abandon their current companies when the law
catches up with them.*

*To preclude such abuses, AFMA has created a personal binder
that can be enforced against a company's executives. If the
filmmaker is able to persuade an executive to sign such a
binder and his company fails to comply with an arbitration
award, the executive can be personally barred from future
AFMs. A sample binder (Exhibit B) is included at the end of
this contract.*

26. ENTIRE AGREEMENT: This Agreement is intended by the
parties hereto as a final expression of their Agreement and
understanding with respect to the subject matter hereof and
as a complete and exclusive statement of the terms thereof
(unless amended in writing by both parties) and supersedes
any and all prior and contemporaneous agreements and
understanding thereto. This Agreement will be understood in
all respects to lay under the jurisdiction of California law and
the laws of the United States of America. All parties agree that
because of the specialized interest of this Agreement pertaining to entertainment that it is in both parties' interests that

confirmation of any arbitration award, and any other matters of law, be submitted to the jurisdiction of the U.S. District Court for the Central District of California, or the Superior Courts in Los Angeles County. The parties waive their rights to transfer such actions to any other jurisdictions and will be bound by the decisions of such courts.

In the event of any conflict or action between the parties, the prevailing party shall be entitled to recoup its reasonable attorneys' fees and court costs and expenses from the non-prevailing party.

Paragraph headings in this Agreement are used for convenience only and will not be used to interpret or construe the provisions of this Agreement.

IN WITNESS WHEREOF, the parties have executed this Agreement as of the date hereof.

DISTRIBUTION, INC.

By: _____

Its: _____

ACCEPTED AND AGREED:

_____

Ms. Sally Producer on behalf of
PRODUCER FILMS, INC.

EXHIBIT A

DELIVERY REQUIREMENTS

Delivery of the Picture shall consist of Producer making delivery, at Producer's expense, to either Distributor or a laboratory designated by Producer (with a lab access letter given to Distributor) for all the items set forth below.

I. PICTURE ITEMS

1. <u>Original Picture and Soundtrack Negative:</u>

   (a) <u>Original Picture Negative:</u> The original first-class, completely edited, color 35mm film-stock Picture negative, fully timed and color corrected.

   (b) <u>Original Optical Soundtrack Negative:</u> A first-class, completely edited, 35mm film-stock optical soundtrack negative (including combined dialogue, sound effects, and music made from the original magnetic print master described in Paragraph 5 below) conforming to the original negative and answer print. The soundtrack is to be in stereo.

   (c) <u>35mm Low-Contrast Print:</u> One (1) first-class 35mm composite low-contrast print fully timed and color-corrected, manufactured from the original action negative and final soundtrack, fully titled, conformed, and synchronized to the final edited version of the Picture (if available).

   (d) <u>Color Interpositive Protection Master:</u> One (1) color-corrected and complete interpositive master of the Picture, conformed in all respects to the answer print for protection purposes without scratches or defects (if available).

   (e) <u>Color Internegative/Dupe Negative:</u> One (1) 35mm internegative manufactured from the color interpositive protection master conformed in all respects to the delivered and accepted answer print without scratches or defects (if available).

The elements listed in Subparagraphs (a) (b) (c) (d) and (e) above are to be without scratches or injury, so that clear, first-class, composite positive prints can be made therefrom in order to properly exhibit and perform the Picture, and to properly produce the recorded sound of the Picture and the musical compositions included in the score thereof in synchronization with the photographic action in the Picture.

2. Interpositive Masters of the Textless Background:

(a) Master Negative

(b) One set of first-class, completely edited, color-corrected 35mm interpositives or fine grains (made from the original Picture negative described in Paragraph (1)(a) above (if available).

(c) Corresponding daily prints (to be held with outtake trims) of the following:

(i) all main titles and end title backgrounds, without lettering;

(ii) background of any forewords and/or scenes carrying superimposed titles, without lettering (if available); and

(iii) backgrounds of any inserts, without lettering, where text must be replaced in foreign languages (if available).

(d) In addition, one (1) overlay-title 35mm internegative (first-class completely edited color) of main and end titles and any forewords (if available). Should the text of any titles and/or inserts as photographed for theatrical release printing extend beyond the "Safe Title Area" for television (as specified by the Society of Motion Picture and Television Engineers), then Producer shall provide Distributor with an alternate original 35mm negative (if available) of each such title and/or insert, photographed to the precise length and with the same lettering style and background of the theatrical title or insert and which can be printed by normal laboratory procedure within the limits of the "Safe Title Area" for television.

3. Videotape Master: A Videotape master of the original motion picture and television version thereof, meeting the specifications set forth in Section III of this Exhibit.

4. Answer Print: One (1) first-class 35mm answer print, fully timed and color-corrected, manufactured from the original action negative and original optical soundtrack negative, fully titled, conformed, and synchronized to the final version of the Picture.

5. M&E Track: One (1) 35mm state-of-the-art magnetic sound-track master, including the music track and the 100% fully filled effects track on separate channels where the effect track

contains all effects, including any effects recorded on the dialogue track. This M&E track shall also include a third separate dialogue guide track with no Spanish dialogue in the M&E tracks. If the Picture is to be released with stereophonic sound, Producer shall deliver an additional 35mm stereophonic dubbing four-channel magnetic soundtrack minus any Spanish dialogue or narration, for use as an M&E track with surrounds if surrounds were recorded and in Dolby if the Picture is in Ultra-Stereo.

6. Magnetic Print Master: One (1) 35mm 3-track stereo magnetic master of the dubbed soundtrack of the Picture on 10002 reels from which the optical soundtrack negative was made.

7. Sound Tracks: Separate dialogue tracks, sound effects tracks, and music tracks, each recorded on 35mm magnetic tracks from which the magnetic print master was made.

8. Complete Materials to Create Trailer: A Beta SP sub-master of the entire Picture.

9. Music Masters/Tracks/Dubbing Set-Up Sheets:

(a) The uncut original music masters in the form (e.g., number of tracks) in which they were recorded or, at Distributor's election, a first-generation copy thereof of selected takes of each musical sequence of the Picture, regardless of whether such selected takes are in the Picture;

(b) The synchronized magnetic tracks of music, sound effects, and dialogue, as set up for dubbing; and

(c) Copies of dubbing set-up sheets (e.g., all "cue sheets").

II. DOCUMENTATION

1. Continuity Script: Delivery of two (2) copies of the dialogue cutting continuity (in English), being an accurate transcript of dialogue, narration, and song vocals and description of action of the trailer as finally edited for release, conforming to the format of release scripts used by Distributor, from which such scripts may be printed. Each scene shall be numbered. There shall be a margin of 2 inches on the left side of the page. Masters to be typed so text will appear when printed on pages with dimensions of 8.5x11 inches.

2. <u>Title Sheets:</u> One (1) typewritten list of all words appearing visually in the Picture suitable for use in translating such words into another language.

3. <u>Music Cue Sheets:</u> Two (2) copies of a music cue sheet showing the particulars of all music contained in the Picture, including the sound equipment used, the title of each composition, names of composers, publishers, and copyright owners, the usages (whether instrumental-visual, vocal, vocal-visual, or otherwise), the place and number of such uses showing the footage and running time for each cue, the performing rights society involved, and any other information customarily set forth in music cue sheets.

4. <u>Dubbing Restrictions:</u> A statement of any restrictions as to the dubbing of the voice of any player, including dubbing dialogue in a language other than the language in which the Picture was recorded.

5. <u>Copyright Information:</u> Upon Distributor's request, information as to the copyright proprietor(s) of the Picture and appropriate copyright notice to be affixed to reproductions of the Picture and packaging of such reproductions, as well as copies of all copyright registrations, assignments of copyrights, and/or copyright licenses in Producer's possession (or in the possession of Producer's agents or attorney) pertaining to the Picture or any component element thereof (including but not limited to copies of all synchronization and performance licenses pertaining to music contained in the Picture).

6. <u>Chain of Title:</u> Upon Distributor's request, copies of all certificates of authorship, licenses, contracts, assignments, and the written permissions from the proper parties in interest, establishing Producer's "Chain of Title" with respect to the Picture and all elements thereof and permitting Producer and its assigns to use any musical, literary, dramatic, and other material of whatever nature used by Producer in the Production of the Picture, together with Copyright and Title search reports and Opinion prepared either by Thompson & Thomson, Dennis Angel, Esq., and/or Brylawski, Cleary & Leeds. "Chain of Title" materials must be suitable for filing with the United States Library of Congress and reasonably suitable to Producer's primary lender indicating that Grantor has full right, title, and interest in and to the Picture and all underlying property.

7. Screen Credit Obligations: A copy of the screen credit obligations for all individuals and entities affiliated with the Picture.

8. Paid Ad Credit Obligations: A copy of the Paid Advertising Credit obligations for all individuals and entities affiliated with the Picture.

9. Billing Block: A copy of the approved credit block to be used in paid advertising of the Picture.

10. Name and Likeness Restrictions: A copy of all name and likeness restrictions and/or obligations pertaining to all individuals and entities affiliated with the Picture.

11. Talent Agreements: If requested, a copy of all contracts with the cast, director, cinematographer, screenwriter(s), producer(s), and author(s) (or other owner of the underlying material, if applicable).

12. Certificate of Origin: One Certificate of Origin of the Picture.

13. Music License and Composer Agreement: Copies of Music Licenses (synchronization and mechanical) and composer's agreement.

14. Publicity and Advertising Materials:

(a) Color Slides: At least fifty (50) color slides (35mm color transparencies) and any available prints of black-and-white still photographs and accompanying negatives, and at least twenty-five (25) color still photographs and accompanying negatives depicting different scenes from the Picture, production activities, and informal poses, the majority of which depict the principal members of the cast. A notation identifying the persons shall accompany each slide and events depicted and shall be suitable for reproduction for advertising and publicity purposes. Where a player has still approval, Producer shall furnish Distributor with only approved photos and shall provide an appropriate written clearance from the player.

(b) Synopses: One (1) copy of a brief synopsis in the English language and in such other language as such synopsis exists (one typewritten page each) of the story of the Picture.

(c) <u>Statement of Credits:</u> The statement of credits applicable to the Picture, including verification of the writing credits by the appropriate Writers Guild and photocopy excerpts of all of Producer's obligations (taken from the actual contract) to accord credit on the screen, in advertising, and on recordings; and excerpts as to any restrictions as to use of name and likeness.

(d) <u>Cast:</u> One (1) copy of a list indicating the name of the character portrayed by each player and a complete description of the character.

(e) <u>Crew:</u> One (1) copy of a list indicating each member of the crew and his/her function.

(f) <u>Titles:</u> One (1) typewritten list of the main credits and end titles of the Picture.

(g) <u>Miscellaneous:</u> At least one (1) copy of all advertisements, paper accessories, and other advertising materials, if any, prepaid by Producer or by any other party in connection with the Picture; and art elements and transparencies necessary to make proofs thereof.

(h) <u>Website Materials:</u> Artwork, text, bios, and any other background material needed by Distributor to market the Picture on its website.

(i) <u>Press Books:</u> Two hundred (200) press books, including biographies (one to three typewritten pages in length) of key members of cast, individual producers, director, cinematographer, and screenwriter.

(j) <u>Production Notes:</u> If requested, a copy of the production notes of the Picture prepared by the unit publicist, including items relating to: underlying work (original screenplay, book, etc.), places where the Picture was photographed, anecdotes about the production, and background of the new Picture.

15. <u>Editor's Script Notes and Editor's Code Book</u>

16. <u>Final Shooting Script:</u> If requested, one (1) copy of the final shooting script of the Picture.

17. <u>MPAA Rating Certificate:</u> It is understood that the Picture has not received nor applied for an MPAA rating. If and when it becomes necessary to receive an MPAA rating, Producer shall make application for the rating, and recoup expense from sales/licensing revenues.

18. <u>Shooting Script</u>

19. <u>Laboratory List:</u> A list of the names and addresses of all laboratories used and to be used for production and post-production of the Picture (including, without limitation, sound labs, optical labs, special effects labs, etc.), and a list of all physical elements of the Picture in the possession of each such laboratory.

20. <u>Title Report:</u> One current (no more than 60 days old) title report showing that the title of the Picture is available for use without infringing any other person's or entity's rights.

21. <u>Copyright Report</u>

22. <u>Copyright Certificate:</u> Two (2) U.S. copyrights (stamped by the Library of Congress). If the copyright application has not yet been received from the Library of Congress, then Producer shall deliver a copy of the Form PA application, along with a copy of the cover letter and two (2) copies of the Copyright Certificate to Distributor when received from the Library of Congress. If application has not been made, Distributor shall apply for the U.S. copyright at Producer's expense.

III. VIDEO SPECIFICATIONS

1. <u>Type of Videotape:</u> The Master Videotapes (to be made only from the original 35mm low-contrast print, interpositive, or internegative) of the Picture and the television version are to be of broadcast-quality D2 NTSC-format tape (and access to D2 PAL-format tape), containing the M&E tracks in two parts.

2. <u>Video Specifications:</u>

   (a) Peak luminance must not exceed 100 IRE.

   (b) Pedestal level must be 7.5 IRE for all signals.

   (c) Peak chrominance level must not exceed 110 IRE.

   (d) Color burst must be present at all times, including stereochrome recordings.

   (e) Color subcarrier phase must be continuous across edits (color frame edits).

   (f) Stability is requested in both the sync and control-track signals.

   (g) Great care must be taken to achieve the highest possible video S/N (SNR).

(h) Video signal timings must meet EIA standards.

3. Audio Specifications:

(a) The Picture must be recorded in stereo.

(b) The audio test signal during color bars must be a 1kHz tone at zero dB (zero db 4dBm) on both audio channels.

(c) The Audio recording level must be well balanced between the two VTR audio channels.

(d) There will be no audio modulation during "run out."

(e) Great care must be taken to achieve the highest possible audio S/N ratio.

(f) Channel 1 of video masters shall contain stereo left of the final soundtrack and channel 2 shall contain stereo right of the final soundtrack.

(g) Channel 3 of video masters will contain M&E left and channel 4 will contain M&E right.

4. Time Code Specifications:

(a) The SMPTE time code must be of the drop mode.

(b) The first frame of Program material must have SMPTE time code of 00:00:00:00.

(c) The recording level of the SMPTE time code is zero (0) VU.

5. Film to Tape Transfer:

(a) The program material must be transferred from negative or internegative, or low-contrast print with interlock for the highest quality.

(b) The Picture must be ultrasonically cleaned, inspected, and evaluated prior to the transfer process.

(c) Action or audio break-up between reels is unacceptable.

(d) Anamorphic kinescope prints must be panned and scanned to ensure maximum letterbox and pan positions for monitor viewing.

(e) "T.O.P.S.Y." scene-by-scene color correction is desirable. Cynamic gain, gamma, and color enhancement should be applied where required.

(f) Textless background shall be attached to the tail of each feature master. At 23:53:30:00, non-drop SMPTE time code must begin with 75% color bars and 1kHz tone oscillated to both audio channels. At 23:54:30:00, black bursts must run with no modulation until the beginning of program material at 00:00:00:00, with three (3) minutes of black prior to beginning of Picture.

Black bursts must be initiated for a minimum of ten (10) minutes at end of program material. No audio modulation.

6. Aspect Ratios: The Picture shall not be in an aspect ratio other than the standard theatrical 1.85:1 without Producer's prior written consent. No elements shall be "letterboxed" without Distributor's written consent.

7. Quality Control Requirements: Distributor may, at its own option and its own cost, perform one quality-control test on each element supplied by Producer. Producer shall be liable for the cost of all quality-control tests after the initial quality-control test of all elements replaced because of failure to conform to Distributor's technical quality requirements.

SCHEDULE A
TERRITORIAL MINIMUMS

Territory	Minimum Acceptable
French Canada	
UK	
Australia/New Zealand	
South Africa	
East Africa	
West Africa	
West Indies	
EUROPE	
Germany/Austria	
Switzerland w/Germany	
France	
Italy	
Spain	
Benelux	
Scandinavia	
Iceland	
Portugal	
Greece	
FAR EAST	
Japan	
Korea	
Taiwan	
Hong Kong	
Singapore	
Brunei	
Malaysia	
Indonesia	
Philippines	
Thailand	
India	

Territory	Minimum Acceptable
Sri Lanka	
Pakistan	
China	
LATIN AMERICA	
Argentina/Paraguay/Uruguay	
Brazil	
Mexico	
Chile	
Columbia	
Venezuela	
CENTRAL AMERICA	
Ecuador	
Peru/Bolivia	
Dominican Republic	
MIDDLE EAST	
Lebanon	
Turkey	
Israel	
EASTERN EUROPE	
Bulgaria	
Czech Republic	
Hungary	
Poland	
Croatia	
Serbia	
CIS	
Romania	

EXHIBIT B

AFMA RIDER TO INTERNATIONAL DISTRIBUTION
AGREEMENT

Licensor: _____

Distributor: _____

Picture: _____

Territory: _____

Contract Reference Code:

Date: _____

The Undersigned, in order to induce the Licensor to enter into the "Agreement" with the Distributor for the Picture in the Territory with the date and Contract Reference Code listed above, executes this Rider to the Agreement and agrees and confirms as follows:

1. Arbitration

The Undersigned agrees that the Undersigned shall be a party respondent in any arbitration and related court proceedings that may be originally brought or brought in response by the Licensor against the Distributor under the Agreement. The Undersigned shall have the right to raise in such proceedings only those defenses available to the Distributor. No failure of Licensor to resort to any right, remedy, or security will reduce or discharge the obligations of the Undersigned. No amendment, renewal, extension, waiver, or modification of the Agreement will reduce or discharge the obligation of the Undersigned. The Undersigned waives all defenses in the nature of suretyship, including without limitation notice of acceptance, protest, notice of protest, dishonor, notice of dishonor, and exoneration. Subject to Paragraph 2 below, any award or judgment rendered as a result of such arbitration against the Distributor shall be deemed to be rendered against the Undersigned. In the event that Licensor shall obtain an award for damages against Distributor, Licensor shall receive a similar award against the Undersigned.

2. Remedies

Notwithstanding anything in this Rider, in the event of an award against the Distributor, Licensor shall have no remedy against the Undersigned other than the remedy provided under the Market Barring Rule of the American Film Marketing Association. In that regard, the Undersigned hereby agrees to be bound by the provisions of the Market Barring Rule with respect to the Agreement, as though the Undersigned were the Distributor. Licensor confirms that its only remedy against the Undersigned in the event of breach of the Agreement by, and an arbitration award for damages against, the Distributor shall be application of the Market Barring Rule, to the same extent that the Market Barring Rule may be applied against the Distributor. Licensor waives any and all other remedies of every kind and nature that it may have with respect to the Undersigned's inducements and agreements herein.

3. Assignment

This Rider will inure to the benefit of and be fully enforceable by Licensor and its successors and assigns.

4. Governing Law

This Rider will be governed by and interpreted in accordance with the Agreement, including without limitation the arbitration provisions, governing law, and forum provisions therein stated.

The Undersigned confirms that service of arbitration notice, process, and other papers shall be made to the Undersigned at the address first set forth in the Agreement pertaining to Distributor, unless otherwise set forth below.

WHEREFORE, the Undersigned and the Licensor hereby execute this Rider as of the date first set forth above.

UNDERSIGNED:

Name: _____

Signature: _____

LICENSOR:

Name: _____

Signature: _____

CHAPTER 7

WHEN A DISTRIBUTOR DEFAULTS

Many years ago I represented a filmmaker who entered into an agreement with a small home-video distributor. The company had a decent reputation, and since there were no other offers for this $80,000 movie, a deal was struck. The filmmaker was promised a $40,000 advance for U.S. home video rights. The advance was payable in four installments over the course of a year. After the second installment was received, the distributor was acquired.

The new owners stopped making payments to my client. There was no question that the company owed another $20,000, and that my client had fulfilled all of his contractual obligations. The only excuse offered was that the company was experiencing "financial difficulties." We suggested small monthly payments to retire the balance due. Payments were promised but never made. We initiated arbitration, quickly won an award, confirmed it in court, and obtained a writ of execution directing the sheriff to seize the company's film library. Miraculously, the distributor's cash-flow problems immediately disappeared, and full payment was received. But that was not the end of the matter. When I negotiated the agreement, I included a clause enabling my client to demand accelerated payments on default, interest on late payments, and reversion of all distribution rights. So the distributor not only had to pay the balance due with interest, but it forfeited its right to distribute the film. We re-licensed the picture to another home video distributor and received another $40,000 advance, thereby enabling the filmmaker to repay his investors. The film is an example of a picture that performed poorly in exhibition but did great in litigation. Ironically, if the first distributor had not defaulted, the filmmaker would not have been able to re-license the film and repay his investors.

There are honest distributors, but there are also a fair number of disreputable distributors who will look for any real or imagined excuse to avoid paying a filmmaker his share of revenue. Distributors know that the relatively small amounts at stake may not be enough to justify legal proceedings. Most independent filmmakers have limited financial resources, and most, if not all, of that will be spent to complete the film. Attorneys are not inclined to take on such cases on a contingency fee basis (*i.e.*, the attorney gets a percentage of the recovery rather than being paid an hourly rate). That's why it is often wise to provide for arbitration. With arbitration, disputes can be settled without the expense and delays typical of litigation. The arbitration clause should provide that the prevailing party be reimbursed attorneys' fees and costs.

Filmmakers need to exercise great caution when negotiating distribution agreements. Even if the filmmaker thoroughly trusts the executives at a distribution company, the contract is signed with a company, and companies can be sold. Your friend who manages the company today could be gone tomorrow. Therefore, filmmakers need ironclad protections no matter which individuals may be running the company.

One of my recent cases concerned a dispute with a home video distributor. The filmmaker made an oral agreement with the distributor and delivered his film. The distributor began to advertise and promote the picture. Six weeks later, before any paperwork had been signed, the company reneged on the deal and pressured the filmmaker to renegotiate its terms.

To protect yourself from such tactics, make sure all promises are in writing. Do not deliver any materials until you have received a fully executed copy of the contract. Always retain possession of your film negative and master elements by providing a lab access letter instead of the actual master elements as explained in Chapter 6.

SELECTING A DISTRIBUTOR

Filmmakers may not have the luxury of choosing a distributor to their liking. In many instances, only one or a handful of distributors express interest. The terms may range from bad to worse. But assuming one has a choice, here are some factors to consider:

1. **Media:** Which media (*e.g.*, theatrical, television, home video) does the distributor serve? Is the distributor an unnecessary middleman, or does it provide valuable resources and expertise? Any company can call itself a distributor. What services does this entity provide? To what extent does it use subdistributors? If subdistributors are used, do they take an additional commission?

2. **Territory:** What geographical area does the distributor serve? American independent filmmakers often use multiple distributors: a foreign sales company for international sales and a domestic distributor(s) for release in North America.

3. **Reputation:** Has the distributor left a trail of unhappy filmmakers in its wake? Is the distributor known for distributing films of a similar genre, budget, and stature? Does the distributor have a good reputation among its licensees or exhibitors?

4. **Advance/Minimum Guarantees:** What is the amount of any advance? When is it payable, and what conditions need to be satisfied? When are minimum guarantees payable? Will the distributor pay this guarantee if the film is not successful?

5. **Division of Proceeds:** How will revenues be shared? How much does the distributor take in fees or commission? Can the distributor recoup any of its overhead or staff expenses? Are there caps on marketing and distribution expenses?

6. **Marketing:** Is there a guaranteed marketing commitment? What is the minimum amount the distributor will spend to advertise the film? On how many screens in how many venues will the picture open? What is the marketing strategy? What kind of audience does the distributor think will be attracted to the film? What grassroots promotion efforts are planned? Will the film be entered into festivals?

7. **Consultation Rights/Final Cut:** Does the producer have any input or approval over artwork? Can the title be changed or the film re-edited without the filmmaker's approval?

8. **Financial Health:** Is the company in any danger of becoming insolvent or going bankrupt? How long has the company been in existence? How well capitalized is it?

9. **Cross-collateralization:** Are expenses from one media or territory cross-collateralized with other media or territories?

10. **Accounting:** How often does the distributor issue producer reports? How detailed are the reports? Will the distributor provide receipts to document its expenses and revenues? Is interest paid on late payments? What kind of audit rights does the filmmaker have?

11. **Ability to Collect:** How much leverage does the distributor have with exhibitors/licensees to collect revenue?

12. **Conflicts of Interest:** Does the distributor handle any competing films? Does the distributor produce its own films that might receive preferential treatment?

13. **Term:** For how long will the distributor have the right to distribute the film? What is the maximum license term that the distributor can grant to others? Are there performance milestones that must be met before the term is extended? Does the producer have the right to regain distribution rights if the distributor performs poorly or breaches the agreement?

14. **Personal Chemistry:** Does the filmmaker have a good rapport with distribution executives?

CREATIVE ACCOUNTING

Filmmakers and profit participants often lament about distributors engaging in creative bookkeeping. This is one area where filmmakers concede that studios are sufficiently imaginative in their thinking. A frequent complaint is that the studios continually devise new and ingenious ways to interpret a contract so that all the money stays in their pockets. The general consensus among filmmakers is that net profits are illusory. Rarely does a share of net profits generate hard cash.

No doubt, there are numerous instances where producers or distributors have cooked the books to avoid paying back-end compensation to those entitled to it. Expenses incurred on one movie might be charged to another. Phony invoices can be used to document expenses that were never incurred. Some ruses are subtler, and not readily apparent to the uninitiated.

The major studios determine profits for participants using their own special accounting rules as set forth in their net profit definitions. The accounting profession has generally agreed-upon rules called Generally Accepted Accounting Principles (GAAP). There are special guidelines for the motion picture industry called Financial Accounting Standards Bulletin 53 (FASB 53). These rules provide, among other things, for the accrual method of accounting. Under this method, revenues are recognized when earned, and expenses are recognized when incurred. But distributors do not necessarily follow these rules. They may use GAAP and FASB 53 when accounting to their shareholders, or reporting to their bankers, but they often resort to their own *Alice in Wonderland*-type rules when they calculate net profits for participants. They may recognize revenue only when it is actually received, while taking expenses when incurred. So if the distributor licenses a film to NBC, the distributor may not count the license fee as revenue until they actually receive it. Even when they receive a non-refundable advance, they might not count it as income until the time of the broadcast. Meanwhile, they count expenses as soon as they are incurred, even if they have not paid them. This mismatching of revenues and expenses allows the distributor to delay payment to participants. It also allows distributors to charge producers interest for a longer time on the outstanding "loan" extended to the producer to make the film.

The Art Buchwald case illuminates some of the devices Paramount used to deny payment to net profit participants. The trial judge found many of these practices to be unconscionable and therefore refused to enforce them. Paramount appealed, and the case was settled before the Court of Appeals could rule on the issue.

If Buchwald had won the appeal, the precedent would have caused severe repercussions for all the major studios. That is because Paramount's "net profit" definition was virtually identical to the definitions found throughout the industry. If Buchwald's contract was invalid because it was unconscionable, then many other contracts could be contested.

In my opinion, Buchwald may well have lost the appeal had the case been decided. The trial court judge in *Buchwald* used the doctrine of unconscionability to invalidate a contract that Buchwald was trying to enforce. Courts have traditionally embraced this doctrine only when it was used as a defense, or shield, against enforcement of an unfair contract, rather than as a sword to enforce the terms of a contract against another. Courts have typically relied on the doctrine to protect uneducated people who have been taken advantage of. If an unscrupulous door-to-door salesman sells a refrigerator for an exorbitant price to a poor, illiterate consumer on an installment plan using a boilerplate contract not open to negotiation, the judge might refuse to enforce the contract because it "shocks the conscience of the court."

Buchwald, however, was hardly a poor, defenseless victim. He was an intelligent, wealthy, and acclaimed writer represented by the William Morris Agency. If a judge was willing to rewrite his contract because it was unfair, then why not rewrite thousands of other writer contracts? Indeed, why not rewrite any unfair contract? Where does one draw the line? If any contract can be contested simply because it is unfair, then how can anyone safely rely upon the terms of a contract? How can you conduct business if you cannot be sure your contracts will be enforceable?

Under long-established precedent, courts refuse to invalidate contracts simply because they are unfair. Law students are taught the principle that even a peppercorn—something worth less than a penny—can be valid consideration. This means that if you are foolish enough to sign a contract to sell your $200 bike for a dime, do not expect a court to bail you out of a bad deal. Absent fraud, duress, or some other acceptable ground to invalidate a contract, courts do not second-guess the wisdom of what the parties agreed to.

While the trial judge in the *Buchwald* case thought the doctrine of unconscionability could be invoked to invalidate a net profit definition, it bears noting that another Los Angeles Superior Court came to a different conclusion. In reviewing the accounting practices of Warner Bros. in the *Batman* case, the judge found that the plaintiffs had failed to prove that the studio's net profits definition was unconscionable.

Regardless of whether the *Buchwald* decision would have been upheld on appeal, the dispute has had an impact on the industry. The major studios have rewritten their contracts, replacing the phrase "net profits" with such terms as "net proceeds." They want to avoid any implication that the back-end compensation promised participants has anything to do with the concept of profitability.

As a result of many highly publicized creative-accounting disputes, anyone who has clout insists on receiving either large up-front payments or a share of gross revenue. Distributors have consequently lost the ability to share risk with talent. Budgets have escalated to accommodate large up-front fees, with major stars now demanding $20 million per picture. Moreover, stars and directors have little incentive to minimize production expenses, since it doesn't affect their earnings.

Not all complaints about creative accounting concern accounting errors. Many grievances reflect the inequality of the deal itself. The studio uses its leverage and superior bargaining position to pressure talent to agree to a bad deal. The distributor then accounts in accordance with the terms of the contract and can avoid paying out any revenue to participants because of how net profits are defined. The contract may be unfair, but the studio has lived up to its terms. It is only after the picture becomes a hit that the actor bothers to read the fine print of his employment agreement. This is not creative accounting. This is an example of a studio negotiating favorable terms for itself.

Keep in mind that there is no law requiring distributors to share their profits with anyone. Indeed, in most industries, workers do not share in their employer's profits. Moreover, when a major studio releases a flop, losses are not shared; they are borne by the studio alone.

CONDUCTING AN AUDIT

Many filmmakers sign complex distribution agreements that they do not fully understand. Several years ago I was approached by a filmmaker who seemed certain that his distributor was cheating him. His film had been licensed to HBO for a large fee, and significant revenue was generated from foreign sales. Nevertheless, very little revenue was paid to the filmmaker. He asked me to investigate, and to arrange for an audit.

I reviewed the distribution contract and the distributor's producer reports. The agreement allowed the distributor to deduct virtually any expense, with no caps or limitations. The distributor was therefore able to deduct several hundred thousand dollars in expenses. The contract permitted the distributor to take 35% of gross receipts as a distribution fee. The balance remaining was split 50/50 with the filmmaker. This formula allowed the distributor to retain almost all the revenue without resorting to cheating or creative accounting. It was a terrible deal for the filmmaker. I asked him why he had agreed to these terms. He replied that the distributor told him the terms offered were "standard."

Of course, these terms are not standard, and a savvy filmmaker would never accept them. A distributor is usually allowed to recoup specified market and promotional expenses only, and the total amount of recoupable expenses may be capped. The distribution fee charged was excessive, and for the distributor to also share in the balance remaining on a film it did not provide any financing for is just outrageous. I told the filmmaker not to bother with an audit since it was unlikely it would make any difference. This was not creative accounting; it was an instance of a gullible filmmaker being taken advantage of by a more experienced distributor.

While creative accounting complaints are common, many films are not profitable by any measure, so the profit participant will not bother to audit the books. For those films that do generate significant revenue, audits often recover more than their cost, which may be $20,000 to $30,000 or more.

An audit may reveal two types of errors. The first type are clerical mistakes. A studio accountant might make a mathematical error when adding numbers. For some mysterious reason, these errors usually favor the studio. When such errors are discovered, distributors usually make corrections without much protest.

The other type of error arises from contract interpretation. The philosophy prevalent at many studios is, "When in doubt, interpret it in our favor and we will fight it out later if someone objects." Despite the great care taken by lawyers to draft straightforward contracts, new areas of ambiguity constantly arise. As a result, contracts have become increasingly detailed and long. Every time a lawyer thinks that his client has been taken advantage of, he tries to clarify matters in the next deal by being even more explicit. This is why signing a short-form contract may not be wise. A deal memo addresses the major issues without spelling out the details. The resulting ambiguity often does not favor the filmmaker because in a dispute the distributor can better afford the legal expense of contesting the point.

HOW REVENUE IS DIVIDED

Creative accounting disputes usually involve net profit participants. Those who share in the distributor's gross are less likely to become embroiled in an accounting dispute because calculating gross revenues is fairly simple—few deductions are allowed.

To understand the difference between different forms of contingent compensation, which can vary from a "net" to a "gross" deal, let's review how revenue flows from the box office to the profit participant. "Box Office Receipts" is the term for the monies that the theater owner (exhibitor) collects from moviegoers in the form of ticket sales. A theater owner is entitled to retain a portion of these revenues to cover its costs and make a profit. Filmmakers and talent do not share directly in box office gross, although sometimes they may be entitled to receive bonus payments tied to box office performance.

The exhibitor and distributor enter into a lengthy and complex agreement, which controls how they divide revenue. The agreement may require the exhibitor to give certain advances or guarantees to the distributor to book a film. The exhibitor might agree to play the film for a minimum number of weeks. For a major distributor releasing a wide-release picture, revenues may be split on a sliding scale beginning with a 90/10 split[1] for the initial few weeks: The distributor receives 90% of the revenue, the exhibitor 10%. In subsequent weeks the split may shift to 70/30, 60/40, or 50/50.[2] This sliding-scale formula gives the exhibitor an incentive to play the picture for a long run.

Before revenues are divided, however, the exhibitor may be allowed to deduct certain expenses. These expenses, often referred to as the "house nut," are supposed to reimburse the exhibitor its overhead costs. This figure is arrived at through negotiation, and may be more than the theatre's actual expenses. In such a case the house nut is said to have some "air" in it. The exhibitor also retains 100% of whatever revenue is

---

[1] The exhibitor typically gets to deduct his "house nut," or overhead expenses, before the split.

[2] These splits may be without any deduction for the house nut.

generated from the concession stand. This is a major profit center for theaters as a large portion of the ticket price goes to the distributor.

After the exhibitor deducts his house nut and allocates revenue according to the distribution/exhibition contract, he remits the distributor's share of monies, which are referred to as "film rentals." As a rough rule of thumb, exhibitors retain about half of all box office receipts and pay the other half as rental payments. For art-house-type pictures, exhibitors may retain a larger share of revenue, and rental payments are smaller.

The "Distributor's Gross" is comprised of rental payments from all exhibitors plus revenue from home video, television, foreign sales, and merchandising. Profit participants with a "piece of the gross" share in the distributor's gross revenue, although a few deductions—such as taxes, checking, and collection costs—are allowed off the top. Top stars and directors are usually the only people who have the clout to obtain a piece of the gross. Studios dislike these deals because gross participants share in revenue before the studio has even recouped its costs of producing the film.

To illustrate, suppose a studio gives Tom Cruise 10% of the gross from a picture. If the distributor's gross revenues from all sources are $50 million, and if the film's production, marketing, and distribution costs total $50 million, the distributor has broken even. However, Cruise is owed another $5 million in addition to whatever he was paid up front as part of the production budget. So the studio is taking a loss, while Cruise is making even more. To avoid this situation, studios prefer to pay participants a share of revenue after the studio recoups certain expenses such as advertising and duplication costs. This arrangement is called an "Adjusted Gross" or "Modified Gross" deal.

Filmmakers and studios have devised all kinds of variations on these deals, and there are no standard industry-wide definitions of "gross," "adjusted gross," or "net" deals. In some instances a participant's piece of the gross might not be payable until the movie grosses two or three times its negative cost (*i.e.*, the cost of production). The parties could also agree to allocate revenue from some sources, such as home video revenue, in separate pools and share these with participants.

The least desirable deal from the profit participant's point of view is a "Net Profit" deal. Here, so many deductions are allowed that no revenue may remain to pay participants. Although the net profit participant may not receive any money for his share of net profits, the distributor may earn substantial sums because it receives 30% to 40% of gross revenues as a distribution fee. This fee is usually far more than the actual costs the studio incurs to distribute a film. Thus, the release of a picture may be very profitable to the studio, although technically there are no "profits" to share with participants.

Net profits, if there are any, are often shared 50/50 between a studio that has financed a picture and the producer. But the producer's 50% is reduced by whatever is granted to other profit participants, such as writers, directors, and actors. Although profit participants receive their share from the producer's half of the profit pie, net profits are defined in terms of the whole (100%). Contracts will state that the writer is entitled to 5% of 100% of net profits. This means that the writer is entitled to 5% of all the net profits, although his slice of the pie comes from the producer's half. The industry defines net profits this way to avoid ambiguity. If the contract simply stated that the writer is entitled to 5% of the net profits, the question might arise, is he due 5% of the producer's half (which would amount to 5% of 50%), or is he entitled to 5% of the whole? Moreover, if the writer is to receive his share of profits from the producer's half, is this before, after, or at the same time as other profit participants receive their shares?

Net profit calculations are frequently disputed because the studio is permitted to deduct a variety of expenses as well as interest, distribution, and overhead fees. In addition, payments made to gross profit participants are deductible before calculating net profits. The payment to a gross profit participant may be considered part of the negative cost of the picture, and an overhead fee may be assessed on it. Suppose the gross profit participant earns $5 million. The studio might deduct an overhead fee of $750,000 for the task of writing and mailing a few checks. Thus, even in the absence of any creative accounting, a net profit participant is unlikely to see any profits if anyone else has been granted a gross participation

A writer's or filmmaker's share of profits may be reduced under certain circumstances. A writer's back-end compensation is often tied to whether the writer receives sole or shared writing credit. If a writer's script has been extensively rewritten and the writer, therefore, does not receive a credit, the writer may lose all of his back-end compensation. Likewise, directors may be subject to an over-budget penalty. This sum may be added to the negative cost of the picture, even if the studio was responsible for the film going over budget.

As mentioned earlier, participation in gross receipts is usually reserved to big stars and famous directors. Even here, the participant doesn't really share in true or "first dollar" box office gross. These agreements usually allow the following deductions: 1) the cost of converting foreign currency into U.S. dollars; 2) the expense of checking attendance at theatres; 3) collection costs, including attorney and auditor fees; 4) residual payments made pursuant to union/guild agreements; 5) trade dues to the MPAA; 6) taxes imposed on the picture (but not on the distributor's income taxes); and 7) sometimes the cost of co-op advertising that is shared by the exhibitor and distributor.

CREATIVE ACCOUNTING PITFALLS

Calculating Gross

The distributor's "gross revenues" or "gross receipts" are usually defined as the amount of revenue received from all sources. As noted already, a few deductions may be permitted when calculating the gross—namely refunds, collection costs, and certain taxes. Since the distributor's distribution fee is typically a percentage of gross revenues, the distributor has an incentive to include as much revenue as possible for purposes of enhancing its fee. On the other hand, any deductions allowed will reduce the amount of money shared with profit participants.

A number of games are played in calculating gross revenues. Sometimes a distributor will try to reduce gross receipts by not reporting revenue until it has been received in the United States in U.S. dollars. If revenue is earned in foreign currencies that are not freely transferable out of that country, the parties have to decide how such frozen funds will be shared. A filmmaker could ask that his share be placed in a separate bank account in his name in the foreign country. These funds could then be spent in that country by the filmmaker.

Certain foreign taxes paid by a distributor may entitle a distributor to a commensurate tax credit on its U.S. tax return. Some governments impose a remittance tax on money taken out of their country. The U.S. government allows a credit on foreign taxes paid by a U.S. distributor. This credit may be as valuable as income for the distributor. Yet distributors may not take this tax benefit into account when calculating the filmmaker's share of revenue.

Filmmakers need to be alert to benefits derived from a movie that a distributor might not include in gross revenues. For example, income from a theme-park attraction based on a movie might be overlooked. Likewise, when a distributor licenses a film for television broadcast in return for free commercial time, this barter arrangement may not be recognized. When a studio contracts with a music-publishing subsidiary, only a small portion of the income generated by the subsidiary may be returned to the parent company and counted. On the other hand, if the entire amount collected by the subsidiary is counted when calculating the studio's distribution fee, that fee will be overstated. The studio may earn a fee from including a Coca-Cola commercial when it releases a picture into the home video market. Sometimes product manufacturers will pay a fee to have a product shown in a picture. A studio may license a manufacturer to produce spin-off toys and merchandise.

Inflated Bills and Overhead

If a studio uses a film lab that is a studio subsidiary, will the film processing charges be at market rates? Some studios will lend vehicles it owns to a production and mark up the costs to equal the highest daily rental-car rate that an outside company like Hertz might charge. Studio overhead charges may apply even if a film is not shot on the studio lot. This fee is supposed to compensate a studio for the fixed costs of running the production and for the corporate functions performed by the studio. Distributors also may charge a 10% advertising overhead charge, which is meant to reimburse the studio for the fixed costs of running its marketing department. But what if all the advertising work is contracted to outside agencies? Is it fair for the studio to receive an overhead fee? What does the contract say?

Many studios have home video subsidiaries. These subsidiaries will typically pay the studio 20% of the wholesale price per cassette/DVD as a royalty for the right to distribute the movie in the home video market. The royalty payments are included in the studio's gross receipts, from which the studio's distribution fee is deducted. Many filmmakers think it is unfair for the studio to license product to its own subsidiary for only a 20% royalty. Both the subsidiary and the parent company make a profit on home video distribution. Moreover, since the home video distributors sell to retailers on a consignment basis, the distributor often holds a reserve to cover any returns from retailers. This delays payment to those entitled to deferments or participations.

When films are exported to non-English-speaking countries, they may be dubbed or subtitled. Local practice varies. Pictures released in Japan, for example, are subtitled, not dubbed. Sometimes this expense is borne by the local licensee. Filmmakers need to know the custom in each territory to ensure that deductions are appropriate.

Interest

If the studio has financed production, it will often charge the production interest on the money "loaned" to the producer to make the film. Interest may be charged even if the movie is an in-house production funded from the studio's funds. Moreover, the studio may inflate the interest rate and charge more than what it costs the studio to borrow money. So if the studio is able to borrow money at prime, the producer may be charged prime plus two. The rationale for this markup is that the interest is fair considering what it would cost the producer to borrow the money from a bank. At the same time the studio is charging the producer interest, it may be receiving advance payments from exhibitors. This revenue is not counted against the interest being charged. Thus the studio collects interest on advances while refusing to credit it against the interest charged to the producer. Filmmakers should examine whether the studio is charging simple interest or compound interest, and the period for which interest is charged. Some studios assess interest at a daily rate based on a 360-day year. If interest is

tied to the prime rate, the filmmaker should check to make
sure it was properly calculated.

Misallocation of Expenses and Revenues

It is in the distributor's interest to allocate expenses to successful pictures to avoid or minimize payments to profit participants. Unsuccessful pictures will never earn enough to pay
participants under any circumstances. So the cost of limos,
lunches, executive travel, and other expenses incurred on flops
may find their way onto the books of hits.

Likewise, distributors may misapply revenue when they sell a
package of films. For example, HBO might license 10 films from a
studio. While HBO may not care how the package price is divided
among the pictures, profit participants will care. If too much is
allocated to flops, then less revenue will flow to profit participants,
keeping more money in the studio's pockets.

Allocation abuses can be exceedingly difficult for a filmmaker to detect. That is because the written contracts may not
conform to the deal that was struck. Let's say a studio agrees
to sell 10 films to a buyer for $10 million. The buyer may have
only wanted six of these films, and might be willing to pay $10
million for them. The studio insists on selling 10 films, including several undesirable ones. The buyer does not object
because essentially it is receiving these flops for free. The
filmmaker was not present during the negotiations, so he is
unaware of the true nature of the deal. The documents are
prepared in the form of 10 individual licenses to hide the fact
that these films were sold as a package.

Variations on this game can be played by improperly allocating box office revenue to a second-feature on a double bill, or
to a short film that precedes a feature. When studios enter into
overall or output deals with buyers, they may receive an
"exclusivity" fee, which they may not count as revenue from
any film. Similarly, if a studio receives a year-end rebate from a
laboratory, it may neglect to credit the rebate to the films.

The distributor may have an inherent conflict of interest when
allocating revenue. These conflicts increase as major studios
grow into conglomerates. When 20th Century Fox licenses one
of its features to Fox Television, how does one determine a fair

price? Or if Disney licenses a movie to its ABC subsidiary, how can the filmmaker be sure that NBC was given the opportunity to make a competing bid?

See my book *Dealmaking in the Film and Television Industry* (Silman-James Press, 2nd ed., 2002) for a sample profit-participation calculation for the movie *Three Men and a Baby*.

ACCOUNTING TERMS

Each studio can define the terms used in its agreements as it likes. There are no industry-wide definitions for "Gross," "Adjusted Gross," or "Net" deals. What one studio calls an adjusted gross deal another considers a net deal. Before you celebrate the "gross" deal you obtained, examine the fine print and see how the term is defined.

Generally, industry terms mean the following:

ADJUSTED GROSS PARTICIPATION: Gross participation minus certain costs, such as cost of advertising and duplication. Also called "Modified Gross." If many deductions are allowed, the participant is essentially receiving a "Net Profit" deal.

ADVANCES: Up-front payment that counts against monies that may be payable at some time in the future. Non-recoupable advances are payments that are not refundable even if future monies are never due.

BOX OFFICE RECEIPTS: The monies a theater owner receives from ticket sales to customers at its box office. A portion of this revenue is remitted to the studio/distributor in the form of rental payments.

DISTRIBUTION EXPENSES: May include taxes, guild payments, trade association dues, conversion/transmission costs, collection costs, checking costs, advertising and publicity costs, re-editing costs, prints, foreign-version costs, transportation and shipping costs, copyright costs, copyright infringement costs, insurance, royalties, and claims and lawsuits.

DISTRIBUTOR GROSS RECEIPTS: Revenues derived from all media, including film rentals, television sales, merchandising, and ancillary sales. In the case of home video, a parent distributor may receive a royalty from its home video subsidiary. This royalty is often 20% of the wholesale price of each videocassette or DVD sold.

DOUBLE DISTRIBUTION FEES: When a distributor uses a subdistributor and each takes a fee for the same service.

FILM RENTAL: What the theatre owner pays the distributor for the right to show a movie. As a rough rule of thumb, this usually amounts to about half of box office receipts.

FIRST-DOLLAR GROSS: The most favorable form of gross participation for the participant. The participant shares from the first dollar received by the distributor, but even here the fine print allows some deductions, such as checking fees, taxes, and trade-association dues.

GROSS AFTER BREAK-EVEN: The participant shares in gross revenues after a break-even point has been reached. The break-even point can be an agreed dollar amount or it can be determined by a formula.

GROSS PARTICIPATION: A piece of gross receipts without any deductions for distribution fees, expenses, or production costs. However, checking and collection costs, residuals, and taxes may be deductible. A "piece of the gross" is the most advantageous type of participation from the filmmaker's or writer's point of view. In an audit, it is the most easily verified form of participation. Keep in mind that the "gross" is gross film rentals, not box office gross.

NEGATIVE COST: The cost of producing a film. It may be defined to include overhead expenses, interest, and other expenses, which may inflate the amount beyond what was actually spent to make the film.

NET PROCEEDS: The term now used by major studios instead of Net Profits. Means the same thing.

NET PROFIT: What is left, if anything, after all allowable deductions are taken. This often amounts to zero. Typically expressed in terms of 100% of net profits, although payable from the producer's share (*e.g.*, out of the producer's 50%).

TELEVISION DISTRIBUTION FEE: Typically 10%-25% for U.S. network broadcast sales, 30%-40% for domestic syndication, and 45%-50% for foreign distribution. Many filmmakers consider these fees excessive since licensing to television may not require much time or expense. For television, there are minimal duplication expenses (*i.e.*, the studio sends one video copy to the buyer).

THEATRICAL DISTRIBUTION FEES: Generally between 30% and 40% of gross film rentals.

DEFENSIVE TACTICS

1. READ YOUR CONTRACT carefully, including any addendum of standard terms and conditions. Do not assume that "standard" terms are either standard or non-negotiable. Do not accept the distributor's reference in a deal memo to its standard delivery terms or standard auditing rights unless you have reviewed and approve those terms. Avoid signing short-form deal memos that do not address all essential points.

2. REDUCE OR PLACE CAPS on expense items such as overhead and interest. If a distributor is permitted to recoup expenses, try to limit these expenses to out-of-pocket costs and specifically exclude overhead, office, legal, and staff expenses. Try to cap the amount of expenses that can be allocated to your film at any one film market (*e.g.*, $10,000) and place an overall cap on all market expenses (*e.g.*, $40,000).

3. DEFINE PROFITS CAREFULLY: Always define net profits in terms of 100% of all profits. Remove any ambiguity as to whether you are sharing in the producer's share of net profits or a percentage of the whole. Review carefully how profits are calculated.

4. AUDIT RIGHTS should provide the participant with a reasonable length of time to challenge statements. A participant will not want to incur the expense of an audit until he is reasonably certain the picture can be profitable. Since revenue from markets may dribble in over many years, the participant should not be forced to either audit early or waive his rights. Also, the agreement should provide for reimbursement of audit costs and attorneys' fees if the participant successfully recovers monies owed as a result of studio accounting errors. If the distributor maintains several offices, make sure to specify that the audit can take place at the office nearest you.

5. ARBITRATION is usually preferable to litigation, especially when your opponent has more resources to finance a protracted court struggle. Make sure that the arbitration clause provides for binding arbitration and reimbursement of attorneys' fees and costs.

6. ELIMINATE OR REDUCE STUDIO DISTRIBUTION FEES, especially when the studio is using a subsidiary company as a subdistributor. For example, studios may distribute through a wholly owned home video distributor. The home video distributor

pays a 20% royalty on sales to the parent company. This revenue then goes into studio gross revenues, which are reduced further when the parent studio takes its distribution fee.

7. ADVERTISING EXPENSES should be carefully defined and should not include salaries for staff or only include salaries for staffers assigned exclusively to your picture for the time they actually worked on it. An overall cap on advertising expenses is important to prevent the distributor from "buying the gross." It can be profitable for a studio to spend money to promote a picture, but it may not be in the financial interest of profit participants. That is because the studio recoups its advertising expenses, overhead fees, and takes its distribution fee before any monies flow to profit participants. On the other hand, filmmakers may want to require a distributor to spend a minimum amount for advertising and promotion to ensure that the picture has an opportunity to find its audience.

8. REDUCE INTEREST: If a studio wants to charge the producer interest on funds spent to produce, market, or distribute a picture, try to limit or eliminate this item. One could ask that the interest be offset by whatever interest the studio earns on advances from exhibitors. It is not fair for the studio to earn interest on advances while charging the producer interest on the full outstanding negative cost. If the distributor delays payments to the filmmaker, the filmmaker should be entitled to interest on late payments.

9. SUBDISTRIBUTION fees: If the primary distributor is permitted to delegate media or markets to subdistributors, the total amount of distribution fees deducted should be capped so that they do not become excessive.

10. TAXES should be deducted from gross revenues before the studio deducts its distribution fees. Some nations assess a remittance tax on funds sent out of the country. Payment of such taxes may give the distributor a credit that can be as valuable as cash. This tax credit should either be shared with the filmmaker or counted toward the distributor's share of revenue. Note that some distribution agreements allow the studio to deduct such taxes as a distribution expense.

11. A LAB ACCESS LETTER, not the original film negative, should be given to a distributor that has acquired distribution rights to an independently produced picture. In the event of a dispute or distributor default, the filmmaker can terminate the

studio's access to the film negative. Furthermore, the filmmaker will not need to regain possession of the negative if he/she wants to arrange for distribution with another distributor.

12. PERODIC PRODUCER REPORTS should be required. Ask for monthly reports the first year, quarterly thereafter. Any payments due should accompany the reports.

13. TERM should be reasonable. What is reasonable depends on the nature of the deal. A term that is in perpetuity might be reasonable if a distributor pays a large sum to buy out all rights. If the distributor is providing a small advance, then the filmmaker should seek a short initial term in the 2-5 year range. If a distributor or sales agent asks for a longer term, a short term could be granted with automatic renewals contingent on performance. For example, the distributor is given an initial term of two years, and if the distributor pays the filmmaker a certain amount of revenue in those two years, the term is automatically renewed for additional years. The filmmaker will want to ensure that if a distributor stops selling a film that the rights will revert to the filmmaker fairly soon. The filmmaker will then have an opportunity to market the film himself, or arrange for another distributor to take over.

14. TERMINATION RIGHTS ensure that upon a distributor default the filmmaker can terminate the agreement and regain rights to her film. The filmmaker may also want a provision that the agreement will terminate immediately upon the distributor's bankruptcy or insolvency.

15. A SECURITY INTEREST in the filmmaker's share of revenue should be requested. This can give the filmmaker preference over unsecured creditors in the event the distributor goes bankrupt.

16. DISTRIBUTOR AGREEMENTS WITH OTHERS: Filmmakers may want to require the sales agent to use license agreements to maintain certain standards. Sales agents often use the American Film Marketing Association (AFMA) recommended deal memo and long-form contract when licensing rights to territory buyers. Breach of these agreements may subject a dispute to binding AFMA arbitration. AFMA arbitration provides a unique remedy: A company that refuses to pay an award can be excluded from future American Film Markets. This may be more effective than assessing monetary damages, which can be difficult to collect against a foreign company.

See my book *Dealmaking in the Film and Television Industry* (Silman-James Press, 2nd ed., 2002) for a discussion of the remedies available to filmmakers if they need to initiate legal action.

A FILMMAKER'S BILL OF RIGHTS

A reputable distributor should be willing to accept terms that protect a filmmaker's interests. Many such provisions do not cost a distributor a penny if it lives up to the terms of its agreement. A provision for interest on late payments, for example, places no burden on the distributor provided timely payments are made. Such protections encourage a distributor to live up to its obligations, and provide the filmmaker with a viable remedy if the distributor defaults.

Here is a list of some of the primary ways for filmmakers to protect their interests. This list should not be considered exhaustive. There are other provisions a filmmaker may want to include, such as clauses dealing with advances, guarantees, and reservation of rights.

1. NO CHANGES: The film should not be edited, nor the title changed, without the filmmaker's approval. Editing for censorship purposes, for television broadcast, and for a foreign release (such as translating the title) are usually permitted.

2. MINIMUM ADVERTISING SPECIFIED: The contract should specify in writing the minimum amount the distributor will spend on necessary advertising and promotion. For many films, this means that the distributor will commit to pay for the creation of a poster, one-sheet, and trailer.

3. EXPENSES SPECIFIED: There should be both a floor and a ceiling on expenses. The floor amount should be the minimum amount necessary to market the film. The ceiling should cap expenses unless the filmmaker permits additional spending. The cost to attend film markets should be limited to the first year of distribution and capped per market. Promotional expenses should be limited to direct out-of-pocket costs spent to promote the film and should specifically exclude the distributor's general overhead and staff expenses.

4. TERM: The term should be a reasonable period, perhaps up to 10 years, but not in perpetuity. The filmmaker should be able

to regain rights to the film if the distributor stops distributing it. Thus, it is best to have a short initial term, such as two years, and a series of performance milestones that must be met in order for the term to extend longer.

5. INDEMNITY: Filmmakers should be indemnified (*i.e.*, reimbursed) for any losses incurred by the filmmaker as a result of a distributor's acts, its breach of contractual obligations, and any distributor picture changes or additions that result in the filmmaker becoming liable to others.

6. POSSESSION OF NEGATIVE: The distributor should receive a lab access letter rather than possession of the original negative and other elements. The distributor should not be permitted to remove master elements from the laboratory.

7. ERRORS AND OMISSIONS (E&O) POLICY: While it is generally the filmmaker's responsibility to purchase an E&O insurance policy, distributors are often willing to advance the cost of this insurance and recoup the cost from gross revenues. In such an event, the filmmaker should be added as an additional named insured on the policy.

8. TERMINATION CLAUSE: If the distributor defaults on its contractual obligations, the filmmaker should have the right to terminate the contract, and regain rights to license the film in unsold territories as well as obtain monetary damages for the default. The filmmaker can give the distributor reasonable written notice of default, and a period to cure, before exercising his right to termination.

9. INSPECTION OF BOOKS AND RECORDS: The distributor should maintain complete books and records with regard to all sales and rental of the film, and report to the filmmaker on a regular basis. At least once a year, the filmmaker should have the right to examine the books and records of the distributor during reasonable business hours on reasonable notice.

10. SECURITY INTEREST: The distributor should hold in trust all monies due and payable to the filmmaker. The filmmaker should be granted a security interest in the proceeds from the picture to protect the filmmaker in the event of distributor bankruptcy.

11. LIMITATION ON ACTION: The filmmaker should have at least three years from receipt of any financial statement, or discovery of any accounting irregularity—whichever is later—to contest accounting errors and bring a legal action.

12. ASSIGNMENT: It is best to prohibit a distributor from assigning all its rights to a film to a different distributor unless the filmmaker consents. If assignment is permitted, the distributor should not be relieved of its obligations under the original contract.

13. FILMMAKER DEFAULT: Distributor should give filmmaker reasonable written notice of any alleged default by filmmaker, and a period to cure such default, before taking any action to enforce its rights.

14. WARRANTIES: Filmmaker's warranties in regard to infringement of third-party rights should be to the best of the filmmaker's knowledge and belief, and not be absolute.

15. SCHEDULE OF MINIMUMS: For international distributors (or foreign sales agents) who license foreign rights, there should be a schedule of minimums listing acceptable license fees per territory. The distributor is not permitted to license the film in each territory for less than the minimum without the filmmaker's prior approval.

16. ARBITRATION CLAUSE: Every contract should contain an arbitration clause ensuring that all contractual disputes are subject to binding arbitration with the prevailing party entitled to interest on late payments and reimbursement of attorneys' fees and costs. The arbitration award should be final, binding, and non-appealable.

CHAPTER 8

LOOKING FORWARD

Currently, the economic climate for independent film can best be characterized as "challenging." Filmmakers often fail to recoup their production costs, notwithstanding the modest budgets of most indie films. Although a few pictures receive a theatrical release and earn handsome returns, many struggle to obtain distribution, and most revenue is derived from television and home video. An American independent film that a few years ago might fetch $500,000 for a German license today will be lucky to secure $150,000. Since the major European buyers are licensing fewer films for smaller fees, many projects can no longer be financed through foreign pre-sales. At the same time, the decline of the stock market and economic recession has dried up equity financing.

There are several reasons for the depressed state of independent film. The accomplishment of such filmmakers as John Sayles and Spike Lee has encouraged others to follow their examples. This has dramatically increased production of independent movies, creating a buyer's market and driving prices down. Independent film has become a victim of its own success.

The dot-com bust and economic recession have forced many companies to cut back advertising, reducing revenue for broadcasters, thereby pressuring them to trim costs. The bankruptcies of several large media companies such as Kirch in Germany have decreased competition to acquire films. Moreover, in many European countries the appetite for indigenous motion pictures has grown, reducing demand for American imports.

The future, however, holds promise. The success of such recent pictures as *Memento* and *My Big Fat Greek Wedding* shows that independent films can still compete against major studio fare. Word of mouth remains the most important, and least expensive, means of promoting a film. *Greek Wedding* was produced for $5 dollars. Virtually every distributor turned down the opportunity to distribute it. The producer had to finance the picture's marketing. It went on to gross more than $241 million at the U.S. box office, out-grossing Steven Spielberg's *Minority Report* ($132 million), starring Tom Cruise. *Greek Wedding* has become the most successful independent feature of all time, demonstrating that a small film can compete in the marketplace if the public has the opportunity to see it, and falls in love with it.

During 2001, cinema attendance grew rapidly in the United States (4.6%), the European Union (9%), and in Japan (20.6%).[1] The international market for films is projected to grow, especially in such countries as China, Peru, and Venezuela. China has announced the establishment of a second distribution network. India is opening its cinema market to foreign investors and films. Some 6.65 billion tickets were sold worldwide. Three billion of these admissions were in India alone, although India has only 11,000 of the world's 100,000 screens. The 2001 worldwide box office totaled $19.4 billion, with ticket prices averaging $2.92, and the average global moviegoer attends a mere 1.6 movies a year.[2] Obviously, there is a lot of room for growth.

Technological developments including digital cameras and high-resolution digital projectors can minimize the cost of producing and distributing movies. A filmmaker can use an inexpensive digital camera to shoot a motion picture and edit the footage and add special effects with a home computer and low-cost software that at one time could only be afforded by major studios. Owners of personal computers can in effect become desktop moguls, producing slick and sophisticated programming at minimal cost. Distribution may become as simple and inexpensive as sending email.

I recently represented a filmmaker who shot a feature motion picture titled *The Poor and Hungry* on weekends using a $600

---

[1] Lange, A. "Harry, Billy, Amelie...and the Others?," CannesMarket.com (Oct. 21, 2002), www.cannesmarket.com/information/stats/default.html?langue=6002.

[2] "ShowEast's Latin Flavor," *Weekly Variety* (Oct. 14-20, 2002), p. 14.

camera purchased from a consumer appliance store. He edited his picture on a computer desktop. Although the movie was in black and white and featured non-professional actors, the picture was shown at numerous festivals to great critical acclaim. It received a nationwide broadcast on the IFC channel. The craftsmanship and success of this film helped the filmmaker gain visibility and notice, and a major studio has offered to finance his next project on a multi-million-dollar budget.

Digital cameras are especially economical if the movie is exhibited digitally and film prints do not need to be created. Moreover, film prints wear out, while digital media does not. With electronic cinema, the major studios stand to save close to a billion dollars a year on shipping and print-duplication costs. Instead of spending one to two thousand dollars per print, a movie can be beamed by satellite to theaters across the globe. The advent of digital cinemas may make the filmgoing experience possible for small audiences in remote areas where shipping a print is costly. Seven major studios recently formed Digital Cinema Initiatives, an organization that is expected to reach an agreement on uniform engineering standards for digital cinema by 2003. Until then, uncertainty about technical standards is deterring theater owners from investing in digital projectors.

Other new methods of distribution may break the major distributors' near monopoly on access to consumers. At some time in the near future, the Internet may become a widespread means for distributing motion pictures. This scares the heck out of the major studios, which are afraid that they may suffer the same file-swapping fate as the music industry. While piracy will remain a threat, there appears no way to stop the inevitable march toward Internet distribution. Short films and trailers are available today from Atom Films and IFILM. CinemaNow delivers unlimited access to 350 premium features for a fee of only $9.95 per month. Recognizing the inevitable, MGM, Paramount, Sony, Universal, and Warner Bros. are launching their MovieLink service that will offer their films on demand over the Internet. Disney and Fox have formed Movies.com, an on-demand service available through cable television.

Other companies are exploring novel ways to use the Internet. Yahoo!Movies and Filmthreat.com encourage moviegoing by making it simple for patrons to find films that interest them and locate the theaters exhibiting them. The Internet Movie Database

(IMDB.com) has made it easier for consumers to find information about independent films. MSN.com asks viewers to rate movies, encouraging the spread of word-of-mouth.

New Internet-based services such as Netflix, allow consumers to select among 13,000 different titles on DVD and have them mailed to their homes. Subscribers receive three movies at a time for $20 per month. As soon as they return a DVD in its prepaid return envelope, the next film on their list is automatically sent to them. Subscribers can view trailers, select films, and build lists online. Moreover, Netflix asks its seven million subscribers to rate films and has built a huge database, which predicts audience preferences. Based on the films their subscribers like, the service recommends lesser-known films that they might otherwise overlook. One of my clients struck a deal with Netflix to distribute copies of his film *Nice Guys Sleep Alone*, a film that received a five-city theatrical release. As a result of Netflix's recommendation, 10,400 subscribers rented the DVD, and the filmmaker earned additional revenue.

Today's media gatekeepers, the television networks and entertainment/publishing conglomerates, will lose much of their hold over access to consumers in a world of high-speed Internet access and satellite television. Indeed, the concept of a channel becomes obsolete when viewers can order any program they want on demand. Every viewer will become his or her own programmer. If your local video store does not have shelf space for the independent or foreign films you want, you may be able to order them directly over the Internet from an electronic store or library. Eventually there should be as much diversity in electronic programming as there is in printed matter. Electronic libraries will have several advantages over traditional libraries. Electronic libraries will not have to stock numerous hard copies of works nor incur substantial storage and replacement costs, and "borrowers" will never need to return anything.

Such technologies as TiVo already enable the television audience to take control of its viewing schedule. They also permit viewers to skip commercials, which will discourage advertisers from paying the large sums that presently subsidize a lot of programming.

Once video on demand becomes widely available, talented entrepreneurs should be able to profitably produce programs for niche markets. A film about trout fishing might not be economically viable to distribute with a system that requires duplication of film prints, advertising, and shipping. But distributed over the Internet, these works could generate a small, steady stream of income from viewers around the globe. How far into the future is such a scenario? Consider that 24 million Americans now have a broadband connection, according to a 2002 Pew Internet Report,[1] and their numbers are rapidly growing at an adoption rate faster than consumers embraced color TV or the VCR. Nearly one-third of American Internet users have broadband access at home, work, or school, according to a study by Arbitron.[2]

Of course, while technology can greatly reduce production and distribution costs, it does nothing to create demand for an independent producer's work. The cost of marketing and promoting an independent program may pose a substantial barrier to widespread distribution. The entertainment conglomerates will retain some advantages over independents. If tomorrow's *TV Guide* resembles the phone book, viewers will have so many choices that an individual program can be lost in the clutter. While Universal can promote its programs with full-page newspaper ads and 30-second television commercials, independents do not have the same resources.

Several technological developments on the horizon may help independents level the playing field. The development of software "smart agents" could assist viewers in navigating the Internet. These agents could learn the preferences of viewers and make suggestions. The providers of video-on-demand might collect information on viewer preferences. These lists could be used to promote the works of independent producers. Suppose a provider thinks that a new independent film will appeal to the same viewers who enjoyed *Fried Green Tomatoes*. If the provider has compiled a list of viewers who ordered that movie, those subscribers could be contacted by regular mail or e-mail. This would be much more cost-effective than advertising on network television or in a general-interest newspaper.[3]

---

[1] Horrigan, J.B. and Rainie, L. "The Broadband Difference: How Online American's Behavior Changes with High-Speed Internet Connections at Home." *Pew Internet & American Life Project* (June 23, 2002), www.pewinternet.org/reports/pdfs/PIP_Broadband_Report.pdf.

[2] "Broadband Revolution 2: The Media World of Speedies." Arbitron Inc. and Coleman (June 21, 2001), www.colemaninsights.com/onlines/broadband%20rev%202/broadband%20rev%202%20home.htm.

[3] Of course, allowing providers to compile this type of information raises privacy issues. Moreover, unsolicited e-mail may not be welcomed by recipients.

While the means for producing and distributing films has remained fairly constant for most of the twentieth century, filmmakers are now faced with a new world of opportunities and risks in a rapidly changing entertainment industry. Nobody knows for sure how well independent film will fare, but this sure is an exciting time to be a filmmaker.

APPENDIX A

DISTRIBUTION

DELIVERY CHECKLIST

TITLE OF FILM: _____

WHAT WAS MOTION PICTURE SHOT ON: ____16mm ____Super 16 ___35 mm ___Video

WHAT FORMAT WILL MOTION PICTURE BE EXHIBITED ON: ____16mm ____Super 16 ___35 mm ___Video

Please indicate which of the following elements you have on hand. If you are in the process of producing an element, please indicate when you expect completion:

COMPOSITE POSITIVE PRINT:

INTER NEGATIVE:

D-2 VIDEO:

MAIN AND END TITLES:

STILL PHOTOS (how many, color or B/W):

STILL TRANSPARENCIES (how many, color or B/W):

DIALOGUE LIST:

MUSIC CUE SHEET:

COPYRIGHT CERTIFICATE:

MUSIC LICENSES:

CREDIT LIST:

CHAIN OF TITLE REPORT:

COPYRIGHT SEARCH:

TITLE SEARCH & REPORT:

E&O INSURANCE:

M&E TRACK:

MPAA RATING CERTIFICATE:

LAB ACCESS LETTER:

ADVERTISING MATERIAL:

    ARTWORK

    ONE-SHEET

P.R. KIT: BIOS
              SYNOPSIS
              TRAILER

OTHER:

Certificate of Origin

"_____" (the "Picture")

Production Company:
Selling Company:
Director:
Cast:
Year of Production:
Year of Release:
Running Time: _____ minutes
Theatrical Film Length: _____ feet
Color: [In color or B/W]

Format: 1:85 - Theatrical Film

Sound Format: Stereo

Country of Origin: USA

LICENSOR: _____ PRODUCTIONS, INC.

BY: _____
_____ - PRESIDENT

STATE OF   )
) ss.   By: _____
COUNTY OF   )
                             Its: _____

On _____, 2003, before me personally appeared
_____, who proved to me on the basis of satisfactory
evidence to be the person whose name is subscribed to the
within instrument and acknowledged to me that she executed
the same in her authorized capacity, and that by her signature
on the instrument the person, or the entity upon behalf of
which the person acted, executed the instrument.

WITNESS my hand and official seal.

_____
Notary Public in and for said
County and State

STATEMENT OF PRIOR DISTRIBUTION

There has been no prior distribution or exploitation of the picture, "_____" (the "Picture"). This includes any and all media (including film or video festivals or applications thereto and also includes marketing of the film at any film markets). There are no licensees or buyers who have been shown the Picture or any excerpt other than _____.

Executed effective as of the _____ day of _____, 2003.

_____ PRODUCTIONS, INC.

_____

[NAME], President

STATEMENT OF DISTRIBUTION RESTRICTIONS AND OBLIGATIONS

There are no restrictions nor obligations in any agreements entered into by _____ Inc., with third parties regarding the exploitation of the picture "_____."

Executed effective as of the _____ day of _____, 2003.

_____ PRODUCTIONS, INC.

_____

_____

[NAME], President

MAJOR DEAL POINTS:
ACQUISITION/DISTRIBUTION AGREEMENT

TITLE OF FILM/VIDEO: _____

NAME OF DISTRIBUTOR: _____

ADDRESS OF DISTRIBUTOR:

CONTACT:

PHONE: FAX:

WHICH TERRITORIES DOES DISTRIBUTOR HANDLE ITSELF,
WHICH THROUGH SUBDISTRIBUTORS?

NAME OF FILMMAKER/SUPPLIER: _____
CORP? _____

TERRITORIES COVERED:

RIGHTS/MEDIA OBTAINED:

RESERVED RIGHTS:

TERM:

    AUTOMATIC EXTENSIONS ON MEETING THRESHOLDS:

ADVANCE: AMOUNT $_____

    WHEN DUE: _____

MINIMUM GUARANTEES:

ALLOCATION OF REVENUES (Distrib. agrees to take dist.
fees and recoup from ____% of first $_____ in revenues.)

DISTRIBUTION FEE: ____ FOREIGN ____ DOMESTIC

MINIMUM/MAX. ADVERTISING SPECIFIED:

DEFINITION OF EXPENSES TO EXCLUDE GENERAL OVER-
HEAD, LEGAL EXPENSES

ARBITRATION CLAUSE

REIMBURSEMENT OF ATTY. FEES AND COSTS

    FORUM: VENUE:

WARRANTIES

INDEMNITY

POSSESSION OF NEGATIVE

E&O POLICY (Who pays, filmmaker named insured)

TERMINATION CLAUSE

RIGHT TO INSPECT BOOKS AND RECORDS

ACCOUNTING STATEMENTS: QUARTERLY___ MONTHLY____

PAYMENT OF AUDIT IF UNDERPAYMENT OF ___%.

LATE PAYMENTS/INTEREST

LIEN/SECURITY INTEREST

NO LIMITATION OF REMEDIES

FILMMAKER DEFAULT/NOTICE/CURE PERIOD

GOVERNING LAW:

WHEN IS DELIVERY DUE:

WHAT FORM SHALL PRODUCT BE SUPPLIED:

COPYRIGHT SECURITY AGREEMENT

Copyright Security Agreement ("Agreement"), dated _____, 2003, between _____ (the "Debtor"), and _____, (the "Secured Party"). Capitalized terms not otherwise defined herein have the meanings set forth in the Security Agreement executed concurrently herewith.

RECITALS

A. In connection with the [describe loan], the Debtor, among other things, agrees to grant a security interest in the Collateral to Secured Party.

B. Debtor is granting a security interest in, among other things, various intangible assets, including the Copyrights and Copyright Licenses (each as defined in Paragraph 1 below).

C. The Secured Party wishes to become a secured creditor with respect to the Copyrights and Copyright Licenses and Debtor agrees to create in the Secured Party a secured and protected interest in the Copyrights and Copyright Licenses.

AGREEMENT

In consideration of the foregoing and for other good and valuable consideration, receipt of which is hereby acknowledged, Debtor and the Secured Party hereby agree as follows:

1. The Debtor hereby grants, pledges, transfers, and conveys to Secured Party on the terms and conditions set forth in the Security Agreement and to secure Secured Party's obligations as set forth in the Security Agreement a security interest in all of its right, title, and interest now owned or hereinafter acquired in and to:

(a) All United States and foreign copyrights and rights and interests in copyrights and works protectible by copyright (including but not limited to copyrights in software and databases) and all renewals and extensions thereof, copyright registrations, and applications therefor, including, without limitation, (i) all copyrights or rights or interests in copyrights in the works listed on Schedule I attached hereto and made a part hereof, (ii) all works based upon, incorporated in, derived from, incorporating or relating to all works covered by copyright, (iii) all income, royalties, damages, claims, and payments now and hereafter due and/or payable with respect thereto, including, without limitations, damages and payments for past, present, or future infringements related to any such copyrights, all rights to sue for past, present, and future infringements related to any such copyrights, and (iv) any other rights corresponding to any such copyrights throughout the world (hereinafter collectively called the "Copyrights");

(b) All agreements providing for the grant of any exclusive right in or to Copyrights ("Copyright Licenses").

2. This security interest has been granted in conjunction with the security interest granted to the Secured Party under the Security Agreement.

3. The rights and remedies of Secured Party with respect to the security interest and granted hereby are without prejudice to and are in addition to those set forth in the Security Agreement, all terms and provisions of which are incorporated herein by reference. In the event that any provisions of this Agreement conflict with provisions in the Security Agreement, the provisions of the Security Agreement shall govern.

4. The Debtor authorizes Secured Party, upon notice to Debtor to modify this Agreement in the name of and on behalf of the Debtor without obtaining the Debtor's signature to such modification, if such modification is limited to an amendment of Schedule I to add any future right, title or interest in any Copyright or Copyright License acquired by the Debtor.

5. Except as set forth in Paragraph 4, this Agreement or any provisions hereof may be changed, waived or terminated only in accordance with the amendment provisions of the Secured Debenture.

6. Termination of Agreement. This Agreement shall automatically terminate [___] days following the indefeasible full and final payment and performance of all indebtedness and obligations secured hereunder in accordance with the provisions of the Secured Debenture. At such time, the Secured Party shall reassign and redeliver to Debtor all of the Collateral hereunder that has not been sold, disposed of, retained, or applied by the Secured Party in accordance with the terms hereof. Such reassignment and redelivery shall be without warranty by or recourse to the Secured Party and shall be at the expense of the Secured Party. At such time, this Agreement shall no longer constitute a lien upon or grant any security interest in any of the Collateral, and the Secured Party shall, at the Secured Party's expense, deliver to Debtor written acknowledgment hereof and of cancellation of this Agreement in a form reasonably requested by Debtor and

adequate for proper recording at the United States Copyright Office and the offices where any financing statements were filed. This Agreement shall continue to be effective or be reinstated, as the case may be, if at any time any payment of the principal of the Secured Debenture and any reasonable expenses incurred by the Secured Party pursuant to the Security Documents or any of the indebtedness or other obligations of the Debtor is rescinded or must otherwise be returned upon insolvency, bankruptcy, or reorganization of the Debtor, all as though such payment had not been made.

7. Governing Law. This Agreement shall in all respects, including all matters of construction, validity, and performance, be governed by, and construed and enforced in accordance with, the internal laws of the State of [_____] that are applicable to contracts entered into in such jurisdiction by citizens thereof and to be performed wholly within such jurisdiction, without regard to principles of conflict of laws.

8. Counterparts. This Agreement may be executed in one or more counterparts, each of which shall be deemed an original but all of which shall together constitute one and the same agreement.

9. Binding Effect; Assignment. This Agreement shall be binding upon and inure to the benefit of the parties and their respective successors and assigns, except that Debtor shall not have the right to assign its rights hereunder or any interest herein without the prior written consent of the Secured Party, which consent shall not be unreasonably withheld, and the Secured Party shall not have the right to assign its rights under this Agreement or any interest herein without the prior written consent of Debtor, which consent shall not be unreasonably withheld; provided, however, that the Secured Party may assign its rights hereunder to any of its Affiliates or in accordance with any bankruptcy, insolvency, or receivership of the Secured Party or any of its Affiliates pursuant to a judicial order or decree; provided, further, that in no event shall the rights hereunder be assigned to any competitor of the Debtor as determined in the reasonable judgment of the Debtor.

10. Power of Attorney. Debtor hereby appoints and constitutes the Secured Party as Debtor's attorney-in-fact to take, subject to the terms of Section [__] of the Security Agreement, any action Debtor is required to take under any of the Security Documents, including, without limitation, to (i) collect any Collateral, (ii) convey any item of Collateral to any

purchaser thereof, and (iii) make any payments or take any acts under Section [__] of the Security Agreement. The Secured Party's authority hereunder shall include, without limitation, the authority to alter any signature card of the Company at any financial institution at which Debtor maintains a cash account to the Secured Party, to endorse and negotiate, for the Secured Party's own account, any checks or instruments in the name of Debtor, to execute and receive any certificate of ownership or any document, to transfer title to any item of Collateral, and to take any other actions necessary or incident to the powers granted to actions necessary or incident to the powers granted to the Secured Party in this Agreement or the Security Agreement. This power of attorney is coupled with an interest and is irrevocable by Debtor.

11. Recordation of Copyrights. Debtor agrees to register and record, and shall register and record respectively with the United States Copyright Office, promptly after the execution of this Agreement, all Copyrights and Copyright Licenses listed on Schedule I that have not been registered or recorded with the United States Copyright Office as of the effective date of this Agreement.

12. Recordation of Security Agreement. An original signed copy of this Agreement shall be recorded with the United States Copyright Office promptly after the execution hereof, and promptly after the registration and recording of all Copyrights and Copyright Licenses pursuant to Paragraph 11 of this Agreement. In the event that it is discovered that any Copyright or Copyright License on Schedule I has inadvertently not been registered or recorded pursuant to Paragraph 11, said Copyright or Copyright License shall immediately be registered or recorded, and a memorandum or notice of a security interest therein shall be promptly recorded with the U.S. Copyright Office.

IN WITNESS WHEREOF, the parties hereto have caused this Agreement to be executed and delivered as of the date first above written.

_____ (Debtor)

By: _____

_____ (Secured Party)

By: _____

For sample Net Profits Definitions, see *Contracts for the Film & Television Industry* (Silman-James Press, 2nd ed., 1998).

APPENDIX B

PRODUCTION INCENTIVES

INCENTIVE PROGRAMS IN THE UNITED STATES

DISCLAIMER: Before relying on any of the incentive programs listed here, please consult with an attorney knowledgeable about the applicable laws and make sure to check that the provisions have not changed.

ALABAMA

Incentive information: www.alabamafilm.org/filmakerincentives.htm
Film office: www.alabamafilm.org

Brenda Hobbie, Film Office Coordinator
Alabama Center for Commerce
401 Adams Ave. Suite 630
Montgomery, AL 36104
Phone: (334) 242-4195 or (800) 633-5898   Fax: (334) 242-2077
Email: hobbieb@ado.state.al.us

Incentives:
Alabama offers sales tax and lodging tax exemptions to qualified productions.

ALASKA

Film office: www.dced.state.ak.us/trade/film/film.htm

Alaska Film Program
P.O. Box 110804
Juneau, AK 99811-0804
Phone: (907) 269-8112
Email: Alaskafilm@dced.state.ak.us

Incentives:
There is no sales tax in Alaska and there are no fees for shoots on city, borough, and state-owned property.

ARIZONA

Incentive information: www.commerce.state.az.us/Film/Incentives.htm
Film office: www.commerce.state.az.us/Film

Robert Detweiler, Director
Arizona Film Commission
3800 N. Central Ave. Bldg. D
Phoenix, AZ 85012
Phone: (602) 280-1380 or (800) 523-6695   Fax: (602) 280-1384
Email: film@azcommerce.com

Incentives:

Sales Tax Rebate

Arizona offers a 50% state sales tax rebate to motion picture and television/video production companies spending at least $1 million in qualified expenditures over a consecutive 12-month period. The rebate is also available to commercial advertising production companies spending at least $250,000 in qualified expenditures over a consecutive 12-month period. The productions must be filmed in Arizona. State sales tax is 5%. Call Christi Comanita at (602) 542-4672 early in production for more information about the rebate program.

Use Fuel Tax Exemption

Production vehicles entering Arizona for the purpose of motion picture production on location are exempt from the Use Fuel Tax. Call George Collaco, Port of Entry Supervisor, at (520) 927-6652 for more information about qualifying.

ARKANSAS

Incentive information: www.1800arkansas.com/Incentives
Film office: www.1800arkansas.com/Film

Joe Glass, Film Unit Leader
One Capitol Mall
Little Rock, AR 72201
Phone: (501) 682-7676   Fax: (501) 682-FILM
Email: jglass@1800arkansas.com

Incentives:

Arkansas offers a sales and use tax refund program rebating five cents for every dollar spent on qualifying motion picture production. Qualifying motion-picture production businesses spending more than $500,000 within six months, or $1 million within 12 months, in conjunction with the filming or producing of one feature film, telefilm, music video, documentary, episodic television show, or commercial advertisement may receive a refund of state sales and use taxes paid on qualified expenditures incurred in conjunction with the project.

CALIFORNIA

Incentive information: www.filmcafirst.com
Film office: www.film.ca.gov

California Film Commission
7080 Hollywood Blvd., Suite 900
Hollywood, CA 90028
Phone: (800) 858-4PIX (4749), (323) 860-2960   Fax: 323-860-2972

Incentives:

Refunds:

Under the Film California First Program, filmmakers can receive reimbursement of up to $300,000 to qualified productions that film on public property in California. Rebates are given for public labor and location fees for use of public properties. The program will also reimburse the cost of local law enforcement, up to $750 per day, with a maximum cap of $3,000 per production. See ww.film.ca.gov and www.filmcafirst.com. Reimbursements from the fund are on a first-come, first-served basis. The funds available fluctuate annually depending on what is allocated to it in the state's budget. A production company needs to complete production before applying.

The State Theatrical Arts Resources (STAR) program provides filmmakers with the use of state-owned surplus, such as vacant buildings, at little or no charge. The properties available can be viewed online by use of the CinemaScout (www.cinemascout.org).

Tax Breaks:

California also offers some tax incentives. There is no state hotel-occupancy tax. There is no sales or use tax on production or postproduction services on motion pictures or TV films. There is a 5% sales tax exemption on the purchase or lease of post-production equipment for qualified persons.

COLORADO

Film commission: www.coloradofilm.org

Colorado Film Commission
1625 Broadway, Suite 1700
Denver, CO 80202
Phone: (303) 620-4500   Fax: (303) 720-4545
Email: coloradofilm@state.co.us

Incentives:

Colorado hotels may offer a sales tax rebate for stays of 31 days or longer. As the rebate is discretionary, ask before booking your stay. Colorado offers no other incentive programs.

CONNECTICUT

Incentive information: www.ctfilm.com/Guide/Info/tax_exemptions.pdf
Film, Video & Media Office: www.ctfilm.com/

Guy Ortoleva, Director
Connecticut Film, Video & Media Office
805 Brook St., Building 4
Rocky Hill, CT 06067
Phone: (800) 392-2122, (860) 571-7130   Fax: (860) 721-7088
Email: info@ctfilm.com

Incentives:

Connecticut generally does not levy sales/use tax or property tax on machinery, equipment, and services leading up to the production of a film, video, or sound master recording. Once the master has been created, duplication or "non-creative" functions remain taxable.

DELAWARE

Film office: www.ci.wilmington.de.us/departments/cultural.htm

Tina Betz, Director
Wilmington Film Office
Louis L. Redding City/County Building
800 N. French St., 9th Floor
Wilmington, DE 19801
Phone: (302) 576-2136

Incentives:

Delaware has no sales tax. Permit fees are low and generally negotiable. The state has no other incentives directly targeted toward filmmaking.

FLORIDA

Incentive information: www.filminflorida.com/incentives/ifi
Film office: www.filminflorida.com

Ally Hugg-Fields
Production Manager
Governor's Office of Film and Entertainment
Executive Office of the Governor
The Capitol
Tallahassee, FL 32399-0001
Phone: (877) FLA-FILM (toll-free), (850) 410-4765   Fax: (850) 410-4770
Email: Ally.Hugg@myflorida.com

Susan Simms, Los Angeles Liaison
Governor's Office of Film & Entertainment
5426 Simpson Ave.
North Hollywood, CA 91607
Phone: (818) 508-7772   Fax: (818) 508-7747
Email: filmflorida@earthlink.net

Incentives:
Florida Entertainment Industry Tax Exemption
Qualified motion picture, TV motion picture, TV series, commercial advertising, or music video production and sound recording companies engaged in Florida may be eligible for a sales and use tax exemption on the purchase or lease of certain items used exclusively as an integral part of the production activities in Florida. An application is available on the Florida Film Office website at www.filminflorida.com.

Qualified Target Industry Refund
Companies creating jobs in motion picture production in Florida, excluding location filming, are eligible for a Qualified Target Industry (QTI) Tax Refund. Pre-approved applicants who create jobs in Florida receive tax refunds of $3,000 per new job created and $6,000 in an Enterprise Zone or Rural County. For businesses paying 150% of the average annual wage, add $1,000 per job; for businesses paying 200% of the average annual salary, add $2,000 per job. For more information about this program, call Enterprise Florida at (850) 488-6300.

Rural & Urban Job Tax Credit Programs
Companies creating jobs in any of Florida's 17 designated rural counties and 13 designated urban areas can qualify for tax credits from $500 to $2,000 per qualified job. For more information, contact the Office of Tourism, Trade & Economic Development at (850) 487-2568.

Enterprise Zone
Business that create jobs within an enterprise zone may be eligible for additional tax credits, including a sales and use tax credit, tax refund for business machinery and equipment used in an enterprise zone, sales tax refund for building materials used in an enterprise zone, and a sales tax exemption for electrical energy used in an enterprise zone. For more information, contact the Office of Tourism, Trade & Economic Development at (850) 487-2568.

GEORGIA
Film office: www.filmgeorgia.org

Greg Torre, Director
Georgia Film, Video & Music Office
285 Peachtree Center Ave., Suite 1000
Atlanta, GA 30303
Phone: (404) 656-3591   Fax: (404) 656-3565
Email: film@georgia.org

Incentives:
Qualified film producers and qualified film production companies in George are exempt from sales and use tax on most below-the-line equipment rentals/purchases. Most below-the-line materials and service purchases are included in the exemption. Georgia state sales tax is 7%.

Qualified productions include: feature films, television movies and series, commercials, music videos, and documentaries that will be distributed to areas outside of the State of Georgia.

For more information or to obtain an Application for a Certificate of Exemption, visit www.filmgeorgia.org.

HAWAII
Incentive information: www.hawaiifilmoffice.com/incentives_credits.htm
Film office: www.hawaiifilmoffice.com

Hawaii Film Office
No. 1 Capitol District Building
250 South Hotel St., 5th Floor
Honolulu, HI 96813
Phone: (808) 586-2570   Fax: (808) 586-2572
Email: info@hawaiifilmoffice.com

Incentives:

Hawaii recently enacted some very impressive and generous tax incentives. Hawaii's high-tech investment tax credit provides a 100% return on cash investments in a qualified high-tech business (QHTB) on a front-loaded basis over 5 years (35% credit in the year of investment, 25% in the following year, 20% in the second year following, then 10% each in the third and fourth year following). Qualified research activities include performing arts products such as motion pictures. The credit is designed to give a 100% return for investments up to $2 million per year per QHTB. The credit applies against Hawaii income tax liability only. The credit can be taken by individuals and corporations paying Hawaii income tax, and by banks and insurance companies against their franchise and insurance premium tax.

Moreover, if money from outside Hawaii is invested, the tax benefits can be allocated to the Hawaiian investors so that they can obtain more than 100% return. So for example, if a Hawaii investor put up $500,000 and an Arkansas investor put up $500,000, the parties could agree to allocate all the tax credits to the Hawaii investor (since the Arkansas investor doesn't pay taxes in Hawaii, they are worthless to him anyway). So the Hawaii investors gets back 200% return over 5 years. In return, the Arkansas investor could be given a greater share of the back end, or preferred recoupment.

The production entity would be required to employ or own capital or property or maintain an office in Hawaii, to have more than 50% of its total business activities in performing arts products and to conduct more than 75% of those activities in Hawaii. In other words, 75% of the budget needs to be spent in Hawaii. I currently represent a Hawaiian company that can serve as the production entity that has received a comfort ruling from the Department of Taxation indicating that the company qualifies.

In order to qualify, companies need to stay in business in Hawaii for at least five years and should have some copyright ownership of the picture. There are many more details, but those are the basics. For additional information about Hawaii's tax incentives, go to www.state.hi.us/tax/hi_tech.html.

IDAHO

Incentive information: www.filmidaho.org/permits
Film office: www.filmidaho.org/

Idaho Film Bureau
700 W. State St.
Box 83720
Boise, ID 83720-0093
Phone: (800) 942-8338, (208) 334-2470   Fax: (208) 334-2631
Email: powens@idoc.state.id.us

Incentives:

Idaho offers an exemption from sales or hotel taxes on lodging stays of 30 or more days. The state offers no other incentive programs.

ILLINOIS

Film office: www.commerce.state.il.us/film

Illinois Film Office
100 W. Randolph St., 3rd Floor
Chicago, IL 60601
Phone: (312) 814-7179   TDD: (800) 419-0667

Springfield Office
620 E. Adams
Springfield, IL 62701
Phone: (217) 782-7500   TDD: (800) 785-6055

Incentives:
Illinois does not levy sales tax on 35mm film development for film productions. Hotel stays of 30 consecutive days or more are exempt from the 14.9% Illinois hotel-occupancy tax. After 30 days, all taxes are waived and the occupant is credited for the first month's tax.

INDIANA
Film commission: www.state.in.us/film
Indiana Film Commission
Indiana Department of Commerce
One North Capitol Ave., Suite 700
Indianapolis, IN 46204-2288
Phone: (317) 232-8829   Fax: (317) 233-6887
Email: filminfo@commerce.state.in.us

Incentives:
Indiana had no incentive information available at the time of printing.

IOWA
Film office: www.state.ia.us/film

Iowa Film Office
Phone: (515) 242-4726   Fax: (515) 242-4809
Email: filmiowa@ided.state.ia.us

Incentives:
Iowa has no incentive program.

KANSAS
Film office: www.filmkansas.com

Peter S. Jasso
Kansas Film Commission Manager
1000 S.W. Jackson St., Suite 100
Topeka, Kansas 66612-1354
Phone: (785) 296-2178   Fax: (785) 296-3490
Email: pjasso@kansascommerce.com

Incentives:
Louisiana does not levy hotel-occupancy tax for stays of 28 days or longer.

LOUISIANA
Incentive information: www.lafilm.org/incentives
Film office: www.lafilm.org

Incentives:
Sales and Use Tax Exclusion
Production companies based in Louisiana that have anticipated expenditures of $250,000 or more are excluded from the state's 4% sales and use tax. This exclusion is effective until January 1, 2007. To receive the exclusion, production companies must report the expenditures from a Louisiana checking account established in connection with the filming or production of one or more nationally distributed motion pictures, videos, television series, or commercials in the state of Louisiana within any consecutive 12-month period.

Labor Tax Credit
Motion picture production companies filming a nationally distributed motion picture in Louisiana are eligible for a labor tax credit if they create jobs for Louisiana residents in connection with filming a motion picture, video, television series, or commercial in state.

For projects with production costs in Louisiana of at least $300,000 but less than $1 million during the taxable year, the labor tax credit is equal to 10% of the total aggregate payroll for residents employed in the production.

For projects with production costs in Louisiana of at least $1 million during the taxable year, the credit is equal to 20% of the total aggregate payroll for residents employed in the production.

In both cases, total aggregate payroll does not include the salary of any employee whose salary is equal to or greater than $1 million.

The credit can be applied to any income tax or corporation franchise-tax liability applicable to the motion picture production company. If the motion picture production company is not subject to income or franchise tax, the credit flows through its partners or members.

Any unused credit may be carried forward no more than 10 years from the date the credit was earned.

Investor Tax Credit

Investors who are taxpayers domiciled and headquartered in Louisiana can claim an investor tax credit if they invest in a nationally distributed feature-length film, video, television program, or commercial made in Louisiana in whole or in part. The credit is earned at the time of investment.

If the total base investment is greater than $300,000 and less or equal to $1 million, each taxpayer can take a tax credit of 10% of the actual investment made by that taxpayer.

If the total base investment is greater than $1 million, each taxpayer shall be allowed a tax credit of 15% of the investment made by that taxpayer.

In the event that the entire credit cannot be used in the year earned, any remaining credit may be carried forward and applied against income tax liabilities for the subsequent 10 years.

MAINE

Incentives: www.filminmaine.org/faqtop.html
Film office: www.filminmaine.org

Maine Film Office
59 State House Station
Augusta, ME 04333
Phone: (207) 624-7631   Fax: (207) 287-8070
Email: filmme@earthlink.net

Incentives:

Sales Tax Exemption

Maine-based production companies and to out-of-state production companies working in Maine can apply for sales tax exemptions for equipment and machinery purchases and fuel and electricity costs.

Lodging Tax Reimbursement

Production companies staying in hotels for more than 28 consecutive days can apply for a lodging tax reimbursement.

Production companies must contact the Maine Revenue Service early in production to apply for these incentives. Contact the Maine Revenue Service at: Maine Revenue Services, Sales/Excise Tax Division, P.O. Box 1065, Augusta, ME 04332-1065;
Taxpayer assistance line: (207) 287-2336; e-mail address: sales_tax@state.me.us.

MARYLAND

Incentive information: www.mdfilm.state.md.us/salestax_frameset.html
Film office: www.mdfilm.state.md.us

Incentives:

Maryland offers an exemption from the 5% state sales tax for goods and services used in filmmaking. For most localities, hotel stays longer than 30 days are not charged local or state sales tax.

MASSACHUSETTS
The Massachusetts Film office has been closed due to lack of funding.

MICHIGAN
Film office: www.michigan.gov/hal/0,1607,7-160-17445_19275--,00.html

Michigan Film Office
702 W. Kalamazoo St.
Lansing, MI 48915
Phone: (800) 477-3456, (517) 373-0638   Fax: (517) 241-2930
Email: jlockwood@michigan.gov 5

Incentives:
Michigan offers a hotel tax rebate after a stay of 30 days or more.

MINNESOTA
Incentive information: www.mnfilm.org/board/exemption.asp
Film Office: www.mnfilm.org

Nicole Hinrichs-Bideau
Minnesota Film and TV Board
Phone: (612) 332-6493   Fax: (612) 332-3735
Email: nicole@mnfilm.org

Incentives:
Minnesota offers a 10% rebate on all Minnesota expenditures, free scouting,
free permits, no sales tax on commercials, no lodging tax on hotel stays of 30
days or more, and free production office space, depending on location.

MISSISSIPPI
Film office: www.visitmississippi.org/film

Mississippi Division of Tourism
Woolfolk State Office Building
501 West St.
Jackson, MS 39201

P.O. Box 849
Jackson, MS 39205

Phone: (601) 359-3297   Hot Line: (601) 359-2112   Fax: (601) 359-5048

Ward Emling, Manager
Phone: (601) 359-3422
Email: wemling@mississippi.org

Incentives:
Mississippi tax codes classify filmmaking as a manufacturing process. Raw
materials such as film and videotape are not taxed. Some equipment used in
production is taxed at 1% rather than 6%. In July 2003, the Mississippi
legislature will also consider additional production incentives, including job
tax credits and credits for film funding and investment.

MISSOURI
Incentive information: www.ded.mo.gov/business/filmcommission/html/
incentives.htm
Film commission: www.ded.mo.gov/business/filmcommission

Missouri Film Commission
301 W. High, Room 720
P.O. Box 118
Jefferson City, MO 65102
Phone: (573) 751-9050   Fax: (573) 522-1719
Email: mofilm@ded.state.mo.us

Incentives:
Qualified film production companies can receive a state income-tax credit of up to 50% of the company's expenditures in Missouri necessary for the making of a film, not to exceed $500,000 in tax credits per project. The tax credit is fully assignable, that is, the entity earning the credits may apply them against state income taxes or corporate franchise taxes, or they can be sold or transferred to another state taxpayer, who may then apply them to their Missouri income tax liability. The credits can be applied when earned or carried forward for up to five additional tax periods.

To qualify, the production company must spend $300,000 or more in the state on expenditures necessary for the production of the film. Qualifying expenses include costs for labor, services, materials, equipment rental, lodging, food, location fees, and property rental.

Note that Missouri will only grant $1 million in these tax credits per year. Companies must therefore apply as early in production as possible, and must apply before they have selected Missouri as the project's location.

MONTANA
Incentive information: montanafilm.com/faqs.htm#anchorFAQ4
Film office: montanafilm.com

Montana Film Office
301 S. Park Ave.
Helena, MT 59620
Phone: (800) 553-4563 (outside MT only), (406) 841-2876
Fax: (406) 841-2877
Info Hotline: (406) 444-3960
Email: montanafilm@visitmt.com

Incentives:
Montana has no sales tax. No room tax is charged for stays longer than 30 days. Out-of-state equipment used exclusively in the production of motion pictures, television, or commercials is exempt from property tax for 180 consecutive days. Out-of-state commercial vehicles used exclusively in the production of motion pictures, television, or commercials are exempt from licensing requirements for 180 consecutive days.

NEBRASKA
Film office: www.filmnebraska.org

Laurie Richards
Nebraska Film Officer
Nebraska Film Office
301 Centennial Mall South, 4th Floor
Lincoln, NE 68509-4666
Phone: (800) 426-6505, (402) 471-3680   Fax: (402) 471-3365
Email: laurier@filmnebraska.org

Incentives:
Nebraska has no lodging tax after a 30-day or longer stay at the same facility.

NEVADA
Film office: www.nevadafilm.com

Nevada Film Office, Las Vegas Office
555 E. Washington Ave., Suite 5400
Las Vegas, NV 89101
Phone: (877) NEV-FILM (877-638-3456), (702) 486-2711
Hotline: (702) 486-2727   Fax: (702) 486-2712
Email: lvnfo@bizopp.state.nv.us

Nevada Film Office, Reno/Tahoe Office

108 E. Proctor St.
Carson City, NV 89701-4240
Phone: (800) 336-1600, (775) 687-1814   Hotline: (775) 687-4901
Fax: (775) 687-4497   Email: ccnfo@bizopp.state.nv.us

NEW HAMPSHIRE

Incentive information: www.filmnh.org/laws
Film office: www.filmnh.org

The New Hampshire Film Office
172 Pembroke Rd.
P.O. Box 1856
Concord, NH 03302-1856
Phone: (800) 262-6600, (603) 271-2665   Fax: (603) 271-6870
Email: filmnh@dred.state.nh.us

Incentives:

New Hampshire does not levy sales tax, personal income tax, use tax,
property tax on machinery or equipment, or capital gains tax.

NEW JERSEY

Incentive information: Click on "Filming Regulations & Guidelines" on the
Commission home page.
Film Commission: www.njfilm.org

Joseph Friedman, Executive Director
New Jersey Motion Picture & Film Commission
153 Halsey St., 5th Floor
P.O. Box 47023
Newark, NJ 07101
Phone: (973) 648-6279   Fax: (973) 648-7350
Email: njfilm@njfilm.org

Incentives:

Productions that rent hotel rooms for 14 or more consecutive days during
production are eligible for a refund of room taxes.

New Jersey offers a Sales & Use Tax exemption for tangible property and services
purchased or rented for and directly used in the production of a motion picture or
video. Food and drink brought onto or made on the location or set for cast, crew
and employees is eligible for a sales tax rebate.

Companies must fill out an Exempt Use Certificate to be eligible for the sales
tax exemption.

NEW MEXICO

Incentive information: www.edd.state.nm.us/FILM/
RESOURCES/resource.htm
Film office: www.edd.state.nm.us/FILM

New Mexico Film Office
P.O. Box 20003
Santa Fe, NM 87504-5003
Phone: (800) 545-9871, (505) 827-9810   Fax: (505) 827-9799
Email: film@nmfilm.com

Incentives:

Gross Receipts Tax Deduction
Production companies filming in New Mexico can apply for an exemption
certificate. The tax deduction is given on many production costs at the point of
sale. For complete information on the point-of-purchase gross receipts deduction, contact the New Mexico Taxation and Revenue board and ask for Publication FYI 280: Sales to Qualified Film Production Companies.

15% Film Production Tax Credit
This is a fully refundable credit of 15% of eligible direct production costs against the filmmaker's New Mexico income tax.

To qualify for either incentive, production companies must register with the New Mexico Film Office. Qualifying companies may choose one incentive per expenditure; however, the state recommends that production companies shooting features, television programs, documentaries, shorts, and national advertisements shown in theatres should apply for both incentives as early in production as possible. Feature-length films must include an on-screen credit for the State of New Mexico.

No Location Fees for State-Owned Buildings
Filmmakers looking to shoot at any of almost 800 state-owned buildings can now shoot without paying location fees. In addition, the closed NM State Penitentiary property known as "Old Main"—a 1940s-era maximum-security prison facility with large open cellblocks, hospital wing, tunnels, and a vast array of office and open spaces—is also available for fee-free filming.

NEW YORK

Incentive information: www.nylovesfilm.com/tax.asp
Film office: www.nylovesfilm.com/index.asp

New York State Governor's Office for Motion Picture and Television Development
633 Third Ave., 33rd Floor
New York, NY 10017
Phone: (212) 803-2330   Fax: (212) 803-2339

Incentives:
The Motion Picture and Television office offers free access to their location library as well as assistance with location research and advice on securing permission to shoot at public facilities, including airports, railroads, highways, parks, bridges, and subways.

Sales Tax Exemption
Qualified motion picture, television, and commercial production companies can receive sales tax exemptions for most below-the-line costs, including services and consumables used to make the production.

This includes film editing, props, processing, assembling, and sets; purchases of machinery, equipment, parts, tools, and supplies used in production; the installation, repair, and maintenance of production equipment and the fuel and utility services used for production.

In addition, all production consumables and equipment rentals and purchases and their related services are also exempt from sales tax. These exemptions cover just about every aspect of film and video production and postproduction—from sets, props, wardrobe, and makeup to cameras, lighting, sound, special effects, editing, and mixing.

To qualify, production companies must become registered vendors by completing Form DTF-17 Application for Registration as a Sales Tax Vendor. The Governor's Office recommends submitting the form least 20 business days (but not more than 90 days) before you need the qualification. Production companies that qualify will be given a Certificate of Authority, which will provide you with a vendor identification number that must be used on all resale certificates and exempt-use certificates given to New York business providing services and consumables for the production.

For more information regarding New York's tax benefits for the film and video industry, call the New York State Department of Taxation and Finance at the following numbers and ask for Publication 28, "A Guide to Sales Tax for the Film Industry": New York State Business Information Center: (800) 972-1233; Outside the U.S. and Canada: (518) 485-6800; On the Web at: www.tax.state.ny.us.

NORTH CAROLINA

Incentive information: www.ncfilm.com/information/#tax
Film office: www.ncfilm.com

Bill Arnold, Director
North Carolina Film Office
301 N. Wilmington St.
Raleigh, NC 27601
Phone: (919) 733-9900   Fax: (919) 715-0151
Production Hotline: (800) 232-9227
Email: barnold@nccommerce.com

Incentives:

Tax and Fee Incentives
North Carolina offers fee-free use of state property and a 1% cap on sales and use tax. State sales tax for hotel room occupancy in excess of 90 consecutive days is refunded.

Filming Development Account
North Carolina is now offering grants through its Film Development Account. These grants are given to filmmakers who engage in production activities in-state with expenditures in-state of at least $1 million. The grant cannot be used for political or issue advertising and may not exceed 15% of the total spent in-state in one calendar year for goods and services. The grant will not exceed $200,000 per production.

All expenditure claims must be accompanied by a receipt or bill of sale and are subject to verification and approval by the NC Department of Commerce Finance Center, and reimbursements are subject to the availability of funds.

For more information about the Film Development Account, contact the North Carolina Film Office at either (310) 246-0076 (Los Angeles) or (919) 733-9900 (Raleigh, NC).

NORTH DAKOTA

Film commission: www.ndtourism.com/Resources

Mark Zimmerman, Director
North Dakota Film Commission
604 East Blvd., 2nd Floor
Bismarck, ND 58505
Phone: (800) 328-2871, (701) 328-2525   Fax: (701) 328-4878
E-mail: mzimmerman@state.nd.us

Incentives:

The Bank of North Dakota will consider co-financing motion pictures shot primarily in North Dakota if the production company has retained a domestic distributor or sales agent, has an experienced lead lender on board, has a completion bond in place, and has sold one territory large enough to validate the pre-sale estimates (this will be determined by the bank). The territory must be sold to a reputable and financially solvent distributor.

The bank can provide up to 50% of the film budget less any equity investment and any pre-sold territories. All revenue proceeds except sales commissions, financing costs, and collection-account fees shall be applied to debt-reduction. For more details, contact the Bank of North Dakota at (800) 472-2166 and ask about the Motion Picture Financing.

OHIO

Film commission: www.ohiofilm.com

Amir Eylon
Interim State Tourism Director,
Division of Travel and Tourism

Ohio Film Commission
Phone: (614) 466-8844
Email: aeylon@odod.state.oh.us

Incentives:
Ohio has no incentive program.

OKLAHOMA

Incentive information: www.oklahomafilm.org
Film office: www.oklahomafilm.org

Oklahoma Film Commission
Oklahoma City Office
15 N. Robinson, Suite 802
Oklahoma City, OK 73102
Phone: (800) 766-3456
In Oklahoma City: (405) 522-6760   Fax: (405) 522-0656

Incentives:
Oklahoma Film Enhancement Rebate Program
Oklahoma offers a 15% rebate on production money spent in state. Qualifying expenses include costs attributable to production, postproduction, and reproduction of long-form narrative film or television production. Expenditures must be documented. The rebate is refunded to the producers.

Sales Tax Rebate
As an alternative, production companies shooting in Oklahoma can apply for a refund of state and local sales taxes. The rebate is applicable to all goods and services used or consumed on almost any project shot in-state. The state's current sales tax is 4.5%. Local taxes, which vary from city to city, average between 1% and 4%.

OREGON

Film office: www.oregonfilm.org

Incentives:
Oregon has no sales tax.

The Portland/Multnomah County area has a parking-fee rebate program that can save productions up to $3500 on public parking area fees, depending on hotel-room usage. No hotel/motel tax on rooms held longer than 30 days.

TENNESSEE

Incentive information: www.state.tn.us/revenue/taxguides
Film office: www.state.tn.us/film

Tennessee Film & Music Commission
312 8th Avenue North
Tennessee Tower, 9th Floor
Nashville, TN 37243
Direct: (615) 741-FILM
Toll free: (877) 818-3456   Fax: (615) 741-5554   Hotline: (615) 532-2770
Email: tn.film@state.tn.us

Incentives:
Sales & Use Tax Refund:
Tennessee offers a refund on sales and use tax to production companies shooting in-state. Companies must first register with the Tennessee Film & Music Commission and the Tennessee Department of Revenue, and they must spend over $500,000 in connection with filming in Tennessee. Filming must be completed in less than 12 months and the rebate must be claimed no later than six months after the last day of production.

TEXAS

Incentive information: www.governor.state.tx.us/divisions/film/incentives
Film office: www.governor.state.tx.us/film

Incentives:

Sales Tax Exemption:

Texas offers production companies an exemption from sales tax on goods and services purchased, rented, or leased for the production's direct and exclusive use. This exemption applies to goods and services used in the production or postproduction of the film or video master. Texas state sales tax is 6.25%; local sales taxes range from 0.25% to 2%.

Productions eligible to qualify for this exemption include features, television projects, commercials, corporate films, infomercials, or other projects for which the producer or production company will be compensated, and which are intended for commercial distribution.

VERMONT

Film Commission: www.vermontfilm.com

Danis Regal, Executive Director
P.O. Box 129
10 Baldwin St.
Montpelier, VT 05601-0129
Hot Line: (802) 828-3680   Telephone: (802) 828-3618   Fax: (802) 828-2221
Email: vtfilm@state.vt.us

Incentives:

Vermont offers Sales & Use Tax Exemptions on the purchase or rental of goods and services used in the making of a motion picture. The goods and services must appear in the film or be used directly in making the print. State sales tax is 5%. Companies that book in advance and stay in a hotel for 31 days or more are exempt from hotel tax. For the time that non-resident performers are working in-state, income taxes are assessed at whichever rate is lower, i.e., if the performer is a resident of a state that does not charge income tax, then they will owe no Vermont income tax. If the performer is a resident of a state that assesses a higher income tax than Vermont, they will owe the lower Vermont income tax on their wages earned.

VIRGINIA

Incentive information: www.film.virginia.org/VirginiatheFilmOffice/
Incentives.htm
Film office: www.film.virginia.org

Virginia Film Office
901 E. Byrd St.
Richmond, VA 23219-4048
Phone: (800) 854-6233, (804) 371-8204   Fax: (804) 371-8177
Hotline: (800) 641-0810
Email: vafilm@virginia.org

Incentives:

Virginia offers Sales & Use Tax Exemptions that are offered at the point of sale (rather than as a rebate). Production items exempted include production facilities, cameras and related equipment, and editing, dubbing, and sound equipment. Tangible personal property and some production and crew services are also exempted. Companies that stay in a hotel for more than 90 consecutive days are eligible for a 3.5% lodging tax rebate. Filming in most state-owned buildings can be done free of charge.

WASHINGTON

Incentive information: www.oted.wa.gov/ed/filmoffice/incentives/index.html
Film office: www.filmwashington.com

Washington State Film Office
2001 6th Ave., Suite 2600
Seattle, WA 98121
Phone: (206) 256-6151   Fax: (206) 256-6154
Email: wafilm@cted.wa.gov

Incentives:
Tax breaks:
Washington offers a state sales-tax exemption on rental equipment and the purchase of services. There is no state income tax. Pro-duction companies can receive a refund on local, state, and special-use taxes on rental vehicles used in production. There is also a lodging tax exemption available for stays of 30 or more consecutive days. The production must contract the stay before arrival.

WASHINGTON, D.C.

Film office: www.film.dc.gov

Office of Motion Picture and Television Development
410 8th St. NW, 6th Floor
Washington, DC 20004
Phone: (202) 727-6608   Fax: (202) 727-3787

Incentives:
Washington D.C. has no incentive program.

WISCONSIN

Film office: www.filmwisconsin.org

Mary Idso
Film Office Coordinator
Wisconsin Film Office
201 W. Washington Ave., 2nd Floor
Madison, WI 53703
Phone: (800) 345-6947   Fax: (608) 266-3403
Email: midso@filmwisconsin.org

Incentives:
Wisconsin has no incentive program.

WYOMING

Incentive information: www.filmincasper.net/incentive.htm
Film office: www.wyomingfilm.org

Wyoming Film Office
214 W. 15th St.
Cheyenne, WY 82002-0240
Phone: (307) 777-3400 Toll-free: (800) 458-6657   Fax: (307) 777-2838
Email: info@wyomingfilm.org

Incentives:
The Wyoming Film Office and the Casper Area Film Commission have asked Wyoming businesses to offer production companies filming in Wyoming a 10% discount on production related services.

A list of statewide businesses participating in the program including hotels/ motels, restaurants, caterers, etc., can be found at www.filmincasper.net/ incentive.htm. To receive the discount, production companies must first request a Wyoming Production Incentive Program card from the film office.

INTERNATIONAL INCENTIVE PROGRAMS

General Information

Association of European Film Institutes:
www.filmeurope.co.uk
The Association of European Film Institutes is an umbrella body of film organizations that promote European moving-image culture and stimulate interest in European film.

Eurimages: www.coe.int/T/E/Cultural_Co-operation/Eurimages
Eurimages is the Council of Europe fund for the co-production, distribution, and exhibition of European cinematographic works. Eurimages aims to promote the European film industry by encouraging the production and distribution of films and fostering co-operation between professionals.

European Audiovisual Observatory: www.obs.coe.int
The European Audiovisuel Observatory website gives information about the audiovisual industry in 35 member states and the European Community.

European Broadcasting Union (EBU): www.ebu.ch
The European Broadcasting Union (EBU) is the largest professional association of national broadcasters in the world. It negotiates broadcasting rights for major sports events, operates the Eurovision and Euroradio networks, organizes program exchanges, stimulates and coordinates co-productions, and provides a full range of other operational, commercial, technical, legal and strategic services.

European Commission: www.europa.eu.int/comm
Comprehensive information about the work of the European Commission, which creates the European Union's policies for trade, industry, social, and economic initiatives, including media and filmmaking.

European Media Landscape: www.ejc.nl/jr/emland
This website provides information about the media in several countries in Europe. It gives an overview of the press, audio-visual media, main features of the media policies, professional organizations, recent media developments, and sources of more specific information.

Cinema d'Europa Media Salles: www.mediasalles.it
Media Salles is an initiative of the EU Media Programme and the Italian Government. The site explains various programs available to Italian filmmakers and production companies.

Nordicom: www.nordicom.gu.se
The website of the Nordic Information Centre for Media and Communication Research. The website lists resources, statistics, and trends in media covering the Scandinavian countries and Iceland.

Nordic Film & TV Fund (Scandinavia): www.nftf.net
Includes information about the Nordic Film & TV fund, which promotes the production of audio-visual projects in the Nordic countries by financing feature films, TV fiction, TV series, short films and creative documentaries. Projects considered must be suitable for theatrical release, television broadcasting, or other forms of distribution within the Nordic countries.

Peacefulfish: www.peacefulfish.com
A general film production website with links and information about film financing programs around the world.

AUSTRIA

Austrian Broadcasting Regulatory Body: www.rtr.at

Austrian Film Commission: www.afc.at

Austrian Film Institute: www.filminstitut.at

AUSTRALIA

Tax Offset: Australia offers a tax offset for big-budget films (above 15 million Australian dollars) shot in Australia. This benefit is equivalent to 12.5% of a film's qualifying Australian production expenditure. The offset amount is applied against Australian Federal tax liabilities accrued in the production of the film, with any excess refunded. This program is not for low-budget independent films, and since the benefit is in the form of a tax credit, it does not provide actual cash funds to make the movie. Unless a bank or other lender is willing to lend against this tax offset, the producer has to find another way to provide the production funds.

10BA: This program aims to encourage private investment in culturally relevant, high-quality Australian film and television productions by providing an accelerated tax deduction of 100% in the year the investment is made. To be eligible, the motion picture needs to be certified as a "qualifying Australian film." This means that the picture must be substantially made in Australia, be an official co-production, or have significant Australian content. Projects certified under this section can also apply for investment by the Australian Film Finance Corporation.

10B: This program is more liberal than 10BA in that it accepts more formats, including series, multimedia, and educational programs. It requires first ownership of the copyright to the production, and offers a tax deduction over two financial years. 10B films are not eligible for Australian Film Finance Corporation financing.

For additional information about 10BA and 10B taxation incentive schemes contact: Film and New Media, Department of Communications, Information Technology and the Arts, GPO Box 2154, Canberra ACT 2601. Phone: 02 6271 1066, Fax: 02 6271 1688, email: film.info@dcita.gov.au, website: www.dcita.gov.au

Film Finance Corporation: The Film Finance Corporation Australia Ltd. (FFC) has 50 million Australian dollars from the government for financial year 2002/2003 to support a variety of Australian films, TV movies, miniseries, and documentaries. The FFC invests in projects that are co-financed by private investors and/or other partners such as a distributor. For feature films, the FFC will generally invest no more than 50%-60% of the budget. It is important to the FFC that the producer demonstrates that there will be a market for the project when completed. Consequently, as a prerequisite to providing financing, the FFC expects the producer to enter into one or more arm's-length transactions with third parties, such as a television license or guarantees, advances, or pre-sales from distributors.

Most government incentives are available to films that are not Australian films if they are made pursuant to an official co-production treaty. Australia has entered into such treaties with the United Kingdom, Canada, Ireland, Italy, Israel, France, and New Zealand. Co-production program guidelines are available at: www.afc.gov.au/filminginaustralia/copros/fiapage_2.aspx

In addition, producers may be eligible for various incentives offered by state governments. For example, Queensland offers a payroll tax rebate, a cast and crew salary rebate (8%-10% of weekly wage), an internship scheme (pays for 80% of wages), and a traffic and fire services rebate. Website: www.pftc.com.au/shootInQLD/incentives.asp

One should note that the immigration laws in Australia are exacting and the producer may experience difficulty in obtaining permission to bring in an actor from abroad.

BELGIUM

Audiovisual Services of the French-Speaking Community: www.cfwb.be/av

Conseil Supérieur de l'Audiovisuel de la Communauté Française: www.csa.cfwb.be

CANADA

Treaties: Canada has entered into co-production treaties that are in effect for 58 countries, but not for the United States. The treaties set minimum standards for financial and creative participation, and they are administered by Telefilm Canada. Qualifying co-productions are eligible for all government incentives and benefits accorded Canadian films. A U.S.-controlled entity will not qualify as Canadian for purposes of the treaties. However, subsidiaries of U.S. companies that are incorporated in other countries might qualify under the terms a co-production treaty with the other country. Moreover, a U.S. rights-holder might license rights to a Canadian company for production with distribution handled by the U.S. company.

The Canadian Film or Video Production Tax Credits: The Canadian Audio-Visual Certification Office (CAVCO) and the Canadian Customs and Revenue Agency (CCRA) administer this refundable tax credit. The credit is only for Canadian films, and to qualify either the director or screenwriter and one of the two highest-paid actors must be Canadian. Moreover, the production must earn at least six points based on key personnel being Canadian. The credit amounts to 25% of expenditures for services provided by Canadians.

The Production Services Tax Credit: This is a federal refundable tax credit to promote production in Canada. The applying corporation can be a production services company that has contracted with the copyright owner. The credit is 11% of the amounts paid to Canadian residents for services rendered in Canada.

Provincial Government Incentives: Canadian provinces provide additional incentives. For example, British Columbia offers a variety of incentives, including a production-services tax credit of 11% of qualifying wages paid to British Columbia residents (www.bcfilm.bc.ca). Information about other in-centives can be obtained from the appropriate agency: Alberta (www.cd.gov.ab.ca/affta), Saskatchewan (www.saskfilm.com), Manitoba (www.mbfilmsound.mb.ca), Ontario (www.omdc.on.ca), Quebec (www.investquebec.com and www.sodec.gouv.qc.ca for dubbing tax credit), New Brunswick (www.nbfilm.com), Nova Scotia (www.film.ns.ca), Prince Edward Island (www.gov.pe.ca and www.techpei.com), Newfoundland and Labrador (www.newfilm.nf.net), and Yukon (www.reelyukon.com).

DENMARK

Danish Film Institute: www.dfi.dk
Radio and Television Board: www.mediesekretariat.dk

FINLAND

Finnish Film Foundation: www.ses.fi
Finnish Telecommunication Regulatory Authority: www.ficora.fi/englanti

FRANCE

Centre National de la Cinematographie: www.cnc.fr
Francois Hurard
Film Production Director
12 rue de Lubeck
75784 Paris
Cedex 16 France
Phone: 0033 1 44 34 36 26
Fax: 00 33 1 44 34 36 97

Cofiloisirs: www.banque-obc.fr/visiteurs/cofiloisirs.htm

Coficiné: Email: contact@coficine.fr

Conseil Supérieur de l'Audiovisuel (CSA): www.csa.fr

Fondation GAN: www.fondation-gan.com

IFCIC: www.ifcic.fr

Médiamétrie: www.mediametrie.fr

Soficas: www.senat.fr/rap/r98-011/r98-01115.html

Listing of types of aid (regional, shorts, foundations): www.analysescript.com

GERMANY

Incentive information: www.bawi.de
Herr Begovici Bundesamt für Wirtschaft
Postfach 51 71 65726
Eschborn, Germany
Phone: 0049 6196 404 401 or 405
Fax: 0049 6196 404 422 or 0049 6196 94 226 or 0049 6196 06196 404 212

General information: www.general-cinema.de/links

Funds rating agency: www.gub-analyse.de/html2/anbieter/medien.htm

Media Fund Tax legislation: www.bundesfinanzministerium.de/fachveroeff

Medienfonds Consulting: www.mc-berlin.de

Arbeitsgemeinschaft der Landesmedienanstalten: www.alm.de

Filmförderungsanstalt (FFA): www.ffa.de

Spitzenorganzation der Filmwirtschaft e.V. (SPIO): www.spio.de

Filmboard Berlin Bradenburg: www.filmboard.de

Infobase on German Film Sector/Film funds: www.screenlink.de/infobase

Filmbüro NW: www.filmbuero-nw.de

Film Fernseh Fonds Bayern: www.fff-bayern.de

Film Förderung Hamburg: www.ffhh.de

Filmbüro Niedersachsen: www.filmbuero-nds.de

Filmstiftung Nordrhein-Westfalen: www.filmstiftung.de

Filmverband Sachsen: www.filmverband-sachsen.de

Mecklenburg-Vorpommern Film: www.landesfilmzentrum.de

Medien & Film Gesellschaft Baden Würtenberg: www.mfg.de/film

Mitteldeutsche Medienförderung: www.mdm-foerderung.de

German Funds
Apollo Media Filmmanagement: www.apollomedia.de

Alcas GmbH: www.alcas.de

CFB Commerz Fonds Beteiligung: www.cfb-fonds.de

Cinerenta Geselleschaft für International Filmproduktion mbH: www.cinerenta.com

DCM Deinböck Capital-Management AG: www.dcm-ag.de

Hollywood Partners TV-und Film-Productions GmbH: www.Hollywood.de

KC-Holding: www.kc-holding.de

MBP Medienbeteiligungs-u. Produktionsgesellschaft mbH & Co. KG: Email:
Kessel.mbp@t-online.de

Mediastream AG: www.mediastream.de

Victory Verwaltungs-GmbH: www.victory-media.de

VIDEAL Gesselschaft zur Herstellung von audiovisuellen Produkten mbH &
Co: www.videal.de

GREECE
Greek Film Center (GFC): www.gfc.gr

HUNGARY
Motion Picture Foundation: www.mma.hu

ICELAND
Incentive Program: www.film-in-iceland.org

IRELAND
Film Institute of Ireland: www.fii.ie

Irish Business and Employers Confederation: www.ibec.ie

Irish Film Board: www.filmboard.ie

Irish Film Board Incentive information: www.filmboard.ie/incentives.php

Irish Revenue Office: www.revenue.ie/services/film.htm
www.revenue.ie/service/sect35.htm

Minister for Arts, Culture and the Gaeltacht:
www.ealga.ie

Tax relief for investment: www.boylandodd.com/film.html

Ireland offers an "artists exemption" to people relocating to Ireland. Under this
program, individuals who become residents are entitled (upon request) to tax-
free income derived from publication, production, or sale of books, screen-
plays, plays, and musical compositions deemed original and creative, with
cultural or artistic merit.

Irelands EU approved 10% tax rate has proved an attractive stimulus to foreign
investment in Ireland for many years. It applies to manufacturing companies
(including film production companies), international finance services companies in the Custom House Docks Area of Dublin (including film finance
companies), and companies that trade from Shannon Free Zone (including
film distribution and licensing companies).

10% rate applies to income after deduction of trading expenses.

No withholding tax on dividends paid by Irish companies.
Certain double-taxation agreements permit foreign owners to receive the after-
tax profits without any further tax payable by them in their home country or
allows them to defer further taxation.

Where a double-taxation agreement applies, it provides that any dividends,
interest, or royalties paid to an Irish company suffers minimal, if any, withholding tax (see below under Double Taxation Agreements).

The tax rate payable by companies on Irish profits is 12.5% for 2003 onward.

Ireland has entered into comprehensive double-taxation agreements with
Australia, Austria, Belgium, Bulgaria, Canada, China, Cyprus, Czech Republic,
Denmark, Estonia, Finland, France, Germany, Hungary, India, Israel, Italy,
Japan, Korea (Rep. of), Latvia, Lithuania, Luxembourg, Malaysia, Mexico,
Netherlands, New Zealand, Norway, Pakistan, Poland, Portugal, Romania,

Russia, South Africa, Spain, Sweden, Switzerland, United Kingdom, United States of America, Zambia.

Co-Production Treaties
Ireland has entered into co-production treaties with Canada and Australia. In addition, the country has ratified the European Convention on Cinematography.

The aims of this Convention are to promote the development of European multilateral cinematographic co-production, to safeguard creation and freedom of expression, and to defend the cultural diversity of the various European countries.

In order to obtain co-production status, the work must involve at least three co-producers, established in three different Parties to the Convention. The participation of one or more co-producers who are not established in such Parties is possible, provided that their total contribution does not exceed 30% of the total cost of the production. The co-produced work must also meet the definition of a European cinematographic work set forth in Appendix II to the Convention.

Once these conditions have been fulfilled, the Convention assimilates all co-productions that have been given the prior approval of the competent authorities of the Parties, with national films; i.e., they are entitled to the benefits granted to the latter. The Convention also covers the following: the minimum and maximum proportions of contributions from each co-producer; the right of each co-producer to co-ownership of the original, the picture, and the sound; the general balance of investments and compulsory artistic and technical participation; the measures to be taken by the Parties to facilitate the production and export of the cinematographic work; and the right of each Party to demand a final version of the cinematographic work in one of the languages of that Party.

ITALY

Autorita per le Garanzie delle Communicazioni (AGCOM): www.agcom.it

Associazione Nazionale Industrie Cinematogrische ed Affini: http//www.anica.it

Associazione Nazionale Esercenti Cinema: www.cinetel.org

Film Commission: www.filminginitaly.com
Dr Francesco Ventura Il
Dirigente Ministero per I Beni e le Attivita' Culturali Ufficio II Ripartizione 1
Attivita Cinematagrafiche
Via deall Ferraratella in Laterano n. 51
Roma Italy
Phone: 00 39 06 773 2424
Fax: 00 69 06 773 2468

LUXEMBOURG

Film Fund Luxembourg: www.filmfund.lu

Service des médias et de l'audiovisuel: www.etat.lu/SMA

MEXICO

Film Commission: www.imcine.gob.mx
IMCINE
C.P. Pablo Fernandez Flores
Coordinador General
Insurgentes Sur 674
Colonia Del Valle

Codigo Postal 03100
Delegacion Benito Juarez
Phone: 55 23 11 20, Extension 53 89
Email: coordina@imcine.gob.mx

NETHERLANDS

Commissariat voor de Media: www.cvdm.nl

Dutch Film Fund: www.filmfund.nl

Film Investors Netherlands bv: www.find.nl

Holland Film: www.hollandfilm.nl

Ministry of Finance: www.minfin.nl

Rotterdam Film Fund: www.rff.rotterdam.nl

NEW ZEALAND

Incentive information: www.filmnz.com/filmnz/Content/Production/
Development/FilmFinance/Finance.html

Film Commission www.nzfilm.co.nz
Mladen Ivancic
Deputy Chief Executive
PO Box 11-546
Wellington, New Zealand
Phone: 00 64 4 382 7680
Fax: 00 64 4 384 9719

Private investors in New Zealand films may wish to take advantage of special tax incentives available in the Income Tax Act 1994.

To qualify for these tax incentives, the film in question must first be certified as a New Zealand Film. The Film Commission is authorized to certify a film or television program as a New Zealand Film provided it contains significant New Zealand content as set out in Section 18 of the New Zealand Film Commission Act 1978, which says:

(1) In carrying out its functions, the Commission shall not make financial assistance available to any person in respect of the making, promotion, distribution, or exhibition of a film unless it is satisfied that the film has or is to have a significant New Zealand content.

(2) For the purposes of determining whether or not a film has or is to have a significant New Zealand content, the Commission shall have regard to the following matters:

(a) The subject of the film.

(b) The locations at which the film was or is to be made.

(c) The nationalities and places of residence of:

(i) The authors, scriptwriters, composers, producers, directors, actors, technicians, editors, and other persons who took part or are to take part in the making of the film; and

(ii) The persons who own or are to own the shares or capital of any company, partnership, or joint venture that is concerned with the making of the film; and

(iii) The persons who have or are to have the copyright in the film.

(d) The sources from which the money that was used or is to be used to make the film was or is to be derived.

(e) The ownership and whereabouts of the equipment and technical facilities that were or are to be used to make the film.

(f) Any other matters that in the opinion of the Commission are relevant to the purposes of this Act.

Certification allows a film to qualify for a one-year tax write-off in the year in which the film reaches double-head fine-cut under the New Zealand Income Tax Act.

NORWAY

Ministry of Cultural Affairs: www.odin.dep.no/kd
Nina Okland
Head of Division
Royal Norwegian Ministry of Cultural Affairs
PO Box 8030, Dep. N-0030
Oslo, Norway
Phone: 0047 22 24 90 90   Fax: 0047 22 24 95 50 or 0047 22 24 95 52

Norwegian Film Fund: www.filmfondet.no

Norwegian Film Institute: www.nfi.no

Nordic Film & TV Fund: www.nftf.net

PORTUGAL

Alta Autoridade para a Communicaçao Social (AACS): www.aacs.pt

Instituto do Cinema, Audiovisuel e Multimedia: www.icam.pt

Inspecçao Gerai des Actividades Culturais: www.igac.pt

SPAIN

Instituto de la Cinematografia y de las Artes Audiovisuales (ICAA): www.mcu.es/cine

Insitut de Cinema Catala: Email: icc@logiccontrol.es

Regional
Basque Country: www1.euskadi.net/helbideak/estru_gv/indice_c.htm

Generalitat de Catalunja: www.gencat.es

Generalitat Valencia: www.gva.es/consell/cult-c.htm

Junta de Andalucia: www.junta-andalucia.es/cultura/contenido.htm

Xunta de Galicia: www.xunta.es/conselle/cultura/organig.htm

Ibermedia: www.programaibermedia.com

SWITZERLAND

List of national and cantonal subsidizing organizations: www.filmnet.ch/subv.htm

SWEDEN

Swedish Broadcasting Commission: www.grn.se

Swedish Film Institute: www.sfi.se

Regional: Film I Väst: www.filmivast.se/eng/guide.htm

UNITED KINGDOM

The U.K. provides incentives for filmmakers in the form of sale-leaseback transactions. A U.K. taxpayer can qualify for a 100% capital allowance in the year in which production expenditures are incurred for British films. To qualify, the film must be made by a company that is registered and managed in the U.K., the European Union, or certain countries that have signed an association agreement. Moreover, 70% of the production cost must be spent in the U.K. These deals are structured so that the U.K. taxpayer purchases a qualified British film from the seller, which is often the production company, and then the U.K. taxpayer leases it back to the seller, who then arranges for its distribution. The seller is required to deposit with a bank most of the purchase price as security for the rental payments due under the lease, which may extend for up to 15 years. For details visit www.culture.gov.uk/interfilm.htm.

Broadcasting Standards Commission (BSC): www.bsc.org.uk

British Council: www.britfilms.com

British Film Commission: www.britfilm.co.uk

British Film Institute: www.bfi.org.uk

British Film Office (Los Angeles): www.britfilmusa.com

Department for Culture, Media, and Sport: www.culture.gov.uk

The Film Centre (lists U.K. funding agencies): www.filmcentre.co.uk/faqs_fund.htm

Film Council: www.filmcouncil.org

Independent Television Commission (ITC): www.itc.org.uk

Media Agency for Wales: www.sgrin.co.uk

Radio Authority: www.radioauthority.org.uk

Scottish Screen: www.scottishscreen.com

UK government (DCMS): www.culture.gov.uk/creative

Northern Ireland Film development fund: www.nifc.co.uk

Ingenious Media: www.ingeniousmedia.co.uk

GLOSSARY OF TERMS

Above-the-Line Costs Portion of the budget that covers major creative participants (writer, director, actors and producer) including script and story development costs.

Adaptations Derivative works. When a motion picture is based on a book, the movie has been adapted from the book.

Adjusted Gross Participation Gross participation minus certain costs, such as cost of advertising and duplication. Also called "Rolling Gross." If many deductions are allowed, the participant is essentially getting a "net profit" deal.

Administrator Person appointed by a court to manage the assets of a deceased person.

Advance Up-front payment that counts against monies that may be payable at some time in the future. Non-recoupable advances are payments that are not refundable even if future monies are never due.

Affirm To ratify or approve.

AFMA Trade organization for film distributors. Used to be abbreviation for American Film Marketing Association, but this organization now just calls itself AFMA.

Aforesaid Previously said.

Amend Change, modify.

Answer Print The first composite (sound and picture) motion-picture print from the laboratory with editing, score, and mixing completed. Usually color values will need to be corrected before a release print is made.

Art Theater Shows specialized art films, generally in exclusive engagements, rather than mass-marketed studio films.

Aspect Ratio (A.R.) The proportion of picture width to height.

Assign Transfer.

Assignee Person receiving property by assignment.

Assignor Person giving or transferring property to another.

Assigns Those to whom property has or may be assigned.

Attorney-in-Fact Person authorized to act for another.

Auteur A French term; the auteur theory holds that the director is the true creator or author of a film, bringing together script, actors, cinematographer, editor, and molding everything into a work of cinematic art with a cohesive vision. Anyone who has worked on a movie knows what complete nonsense this theory is. Filmmaking is a collaborative endeavor and the director is only one of the contributors.

Author Creator, originator. Under U.S. copyright law, the author may be the employer of the person who actually creates the work. *See* Work-for-Hire.

Back End Profit participation in a film after distribution and/or production costs have been recouped.

Balance Stripe A magnetic stripe on the film, which is on the opposite edge from the magnetic sound track.

Below-the-Line Costs The technical expenses and labor, including set construction, crew, camera equipment, film stock, developing, and printing.

Blind Bidding Requiring theater owners to bid on a movie without seeing it. Several states and localities require open trade screenings for each new release. Guarantees and advances may also be banned.

Blow-Up Optical process of enlarging a film, usually from 16mm to 35mm.

Box Office Gross Total revenues taken in at a movie theater box office before any expenses or percentages are deducted.

Box Office Receipts What the theater owner takes in from ticket sales to customers at the box office. A portion of this revenue is remitted to the studio/distributor in the form of rental payments.

Break To open a film in several theaters simultaneously, either in and around a single city or in a group of cities, or on a national basis.

Breakout To expand bookings after an initial period of exclusive or limited engagement.

Cause of Action The facts that give a person the right to judicial relief.

Cel A transparent sheet of cellulose acetate used as an overlay for drawing or lettering. Used in animation and title work.

Color Correction Changing tonal values of colored objects or images by the use of light filters, either with a camera or a printer.

Color Temperature The color in degrees Kelvin (K) of a light source. The higher the color temperature, the bluer the light; the lower the temperature, the redder the light.

Completion Bond A form of insurance that guarantees completion of a film in the event that the producer exceeds the budget and is unable to secure additional funding. Completion bonds are sometimes required by banks and investors to secure loans and investments in a production. Should a bond be invoked, the completion guarantor will assume control over the production and be in a recoupment position superior to all investors. Do you really want an insurance company finishing your film?

Consideration The reason or inducement for a party to contract with another—usually money, but it can be anything of value: the right, interest, or benefit to one party, or the loss or forbearance of another. A necessary element for a contract to be binding.

Contrast The density range of a negative or print. The brightness range of lighting in a scene.

Convey To transfer or deliver to another.

Covenant An agreement or promise to do something or not to do something.

Cross-Collateralization Practice by which distributors offset financial losses in one medium or market against profits derived from others. For example, the rentals obtained from France are combined with those from Italy, and after the expenses for both are deducted, the remainder, if any, is profit. Filmmakers don't like to have the markets for their films cross-collateralized because it may reduce the amount of money they are likely to see.

Crossover Film Film that is initially targeted to a narrow specialty market but achieves acceptance in a wider market.

Dailies (Rushes) Usually an untimed one-light print, made without regard to color balance, from which the action is checked and the best takes selected.

Day and Date The simultaneous opening of a film in two or more movie theaters in one or more cities.

Day Player An actor who works a day at a time on a film. In other words, actors with bit parts.

Deal Memo A letter or short contract.

Decedent A deceased person.

Defamation A false statement that injures another's reputation in the community.

Default Failure to perform.

Deferred Payment Writers, directors, actors, and others may take only part of their salary up-front in order to reduce the budget of the picture. The rest of their fee is paid from box-office and other revenues that may, or may not, accrue later.

Depth of Field The distance range between the nearest and farthest objects that appear in sharp focus.

Development The process by which an initial idea is turned into a finished screenplay. Includes optioning the rights to an underlying literary property and commissioning writer(s) to create a treatment, first draft, second draft, rewrite, and polish.

Direct Advertising Direct outreach to consumers such as mailing flyers. Usually targeted to a specific interest group.

Direct Broadcast Satellite (DBS) A satellite broadcast system designed with sufficient power so that inexpensive home satellite dishes can be used for reception.

Display Advertising Advertising that features artwork or title treatment specific to a given film, in newspaper and magazine advertising.

Dissolve An optical or camera effect in which one scene gradually fades out at the same time that a second scene fades in.

Distributor A company that markets a motion picture, placing it in theaters, and advertising and promoting it. The major studios nowadays are mostly in the business of financing and distributing films, leaving production to smaller independent companies.

Distribution Expenses Includes taxes, guild payments, trade association dues, conversion/transmission costs, collection costs, checking costs, advertising and publicity costs, re-editing costs, prints, foreign version costs, transportation and shipping costs, copyright costs, copyright infringement costs, insurance, royalties, and claims and lawsuits.

Distribution Territories There are 33 principal distribution centers for pictures in the United States.

Domestic Rights Usually defined as rights within U.S. and English-speaking Canada only.

Double Distribution Fees Where a distributor uses a sub-distributor to sell to a territory. If both distributors are allowed to deduct their standard fees, the filmmaker is less likely to see any money.

Double-System Sound The recording of sound on tape and picture on film so that they can be synchronized during editing.

Downbeat Ending A story that ends unhappily or in a depressing manner.

Droit Moral French term for Moral Rights. A doctrine of artistic integrity that prevents others from altering the work of artists, or taking the artist's name off of the work, without the artist's permission. For example, the doctrine might prevent the buyer of a painting from changing it, even though the physical item and the copyright to it have been transferred to the buyer.

Dubbing The addition of sound (either music or dialogue) to a visual presentation through a recording process to create a sound track that can be transferred to and synchronized with the visual presentation.

Dupe A copy negative, or duplicate negative.

Edge Numbers Sequential numbers printed along the edge of a strip of film to designate the footage.

Exclusive Opening A type of release whereby a film is opened in a single theater in a major city, giving the distributor the option to hold the film for a long exclusive run or move it into additional theaters based on the film's performance.

Execute To complete; to sign; to perform.

Executor A person appointed to carry out the requests in a will.

Feature Film Full-length, fictional films (not documentaries nor shorts), generally for theatrical release.

Film Noir Dark, violent, urban, downbeat films, many of which were made in the forties and fifties.

Film Rental What the theater owner pays the distributor for the right to show the movie. As a rough rule of thumb, this usually amounts to about half of the box office gross.

Final Cut The last stage in the editing process. The right to final cut is the right to determine the ultimate artistic control over the picture. Usually the studio or the financier of a picture retains final cut.

First-Dollar Gross The most favorable form of gross participation for the participant. Only a few deductions—such as checking fees, taxes, and trade association dues—are deductible.

First Money From the producer's point of view, the first revenue received from the distribution of a movie. Not to be confused with profits, first monies are generally allocated to investors until recoupment, but may be allocated in part or in whole to deferred salaries owed to talent or deferred fees owed the film laboratory.

First Run The first engagement of a new film.

Floors In distributor/exhibitor agreements, the minimum percentage of box office receipts the distributor is entitled to, regardless of the theater's operating expenses. Generally decline week by week over the course of an engagement. Generally range from 70% to 25%.

Force Majeure Superior or irresistible force. A Force Majeure clause in a contract may suspend certain obligations in the event that the contract cannot be performed because of forces beyond the control of the parties, such as a fire, strike, earthquake, war, or Act of God.

Foreign Sales Licensing a film in various territories and media outside the U.S. and Canada. Although Canada is a foreign country, American distributors typically acquire Canadian rights when they buy U.S. domestic rights.

Four-Walling Renting a theater and its staff for a flat fee, buying your own advertising, and receiving all the revenue. The exhibitor is paid his flat fee regardless of performance and receives no split of box office receipts.

FPM Feet per minute, expressing the speed of film moving through a mechanism.

FPS Frames per second, indicating the number of images exposed per second.

Front Office The top executives, the people who control the money.

General Partners Management side of a limited partnership (the position usually occupied by the film's producers), which structures a motion picture investment and raises money from investors who become limited partners. General partners control all business decisions regarding the partnership.

Grant To give or permit. To bestow or confer.

Grantor The person who makes a grant. The transferor of property.

Grassroots Campaign using flyers, posters, stickers, and building word-of-mouth with special screenings for local community groups.

Gross After Break-Even The participant shares in the gross after the break-even point has been reached. The break-even point can be a set amount or determined by a formula.

Gross Box-Office Total revenue taken in at theater box office for ticket sales.

Gross Participation A piece of gross receipts without any deductions for distribution fees or expenses or production costs. However, deductions for checking and collection costs, residuals, and taxes are usually deductible. A "piece of the gross" is the most advantageous type of participation from the filmmaker or writer's point of view. In an audit, it is the most easily verified form of participation.

Gross Receipts Studio/distributor revenues derived from all media, including film rentals, television sales, merchandising, and ancillary sales.

Heirs The persons who inherit property if there is no will.

Hot Anyone whose last picture was a big hit, won an Academy Award, or is being lionized by the media. A transitional state.

House Nut Weekly operating expenses of movie theater.

Hyphenates Persons who fulfill two or more major roles, such as producer-director, writer-director, or actor-director.

In Perpetuity Forever.

Incapacity Inability. Want of legal, physical, or intellectual capacity. A minor or a person committed to a mental institution may be legally incapable of contracting with another.

Indemnify Reimburse. To restore someone's loss by payment, repair, or replacement.

Interlock The first synchronous presentation of the workprint and the soundtrack (on separate films) by means of mechanical or electrical drive between the projector and the sound reproducer.

Internegative A color negative made from a color positive.

Interpositives A positive duplicate of a film used for further printing.

Inure To take effect; to result.

Invasion of Privacy A tort that encompasses a variety of wrongful behavior such as an unjustified appropriation of another's name, image, or likeness; the publicizing of intimate details of another's life without justification; or intrusions into another's privacy by eavesdropping or surveillance in an area where a person has a reasonable expectation of privacy.

Irrevocable That which cannot be revoked or recalled.

Key Art Artwork used in posters and ads for a movie.

Letterbox A process of film-to-video transfer that maintains the original film aspect ratio by matting the top and the bottom of the screen with black bars. Standard TVs have an aspect ratio of 1.33 (4/3), while contemporary feature films have such aspect ratios as 1.66, 1.83, 1.85, 2.33, and 2.35. The more conventional transfer process is called Pan & Scan.

Libel The written form of defamation. Compare to slander, the spoken form of defamation.

Licensee Person who is given a license or permission to do something.

Licensor The person who gives or grants a license.

Limited Partnership Instrument of investment commonly used to finance movies. General partners initiate and control the partnership; limited partners are the investors and have no control of the running of the partnership business and no legal or financial liabilities beyond the amount they have invested.

Litigation A lawsuit. Proceedings in a court of law.

M&E Track Music and Effects Track.

Magnetic Track Audio recorded on a film or tape that has been coated with a magnetic recording medium.

Master The final edited and complete film or videotape from which subsequent copies are made.

Merchandising Rights Right to license, manufacture, and distribute merchandise based on characters, names, or events in a picture.

Mini-Multiple Type of release that falls between an exclusive engagement and a wide release, consisting of quality theaters in strategic geographic locations, generally a prelude to a wider break.

Multi-Tiered Audience An audience of different types of people who find the film attractive for different reasons, and who must be reached by different publicity, promotion, or ads.

Negative Cost Actual cost of producing a film, including the manufacture of a completed negative (does not include costs of prints or advertising). It may be defined to include overhead expenses, interest, and other expenses that may inflate the amount way beyond what was actually spent to make the film.

Negative Pickup A distributor guarantees to pay a specified amount for distribution rights upon delivery of a completed film negative by a specific date. If the picture is not delivered on time and in accordance with the terms of the agreement, the distributor has no obligation to distribute it. A negative pickup guarantee can be used as collateral for a bank loan to obtain production funds.

Net Profit What is left, if anything, after all allowable deductions are taken. This usually amounts to zero. Typically expressed in terms of 100% of net profits, although payable out of the producer's share.

Novelization A book adapted from a motion picture.

NTSC National Television System Committee. The standard for North America, Japan, and several other countries, which is 525 lines, 60 fields/30 frames per second. Compare to PAL.

Obligation A duty imposed by law, courtesy, or contract.

Off-Hollywood American independent films made outside the studio system.

Officer Person holding office of trust or authority in a corporation or institution.

On Spec Working for nothing on the hope and speculation that something will come of it.

Optical Soundtrack A soundtrack in which the sound record takes the form of density variations in a photographic image, also called a photographic soundtrack.

Original A screenplay that has not been adapted from an article, book, play, old movie, etc.

Original Material Not derived nor adapted from another work.

Overexposure A condition in which too much light reaches the film, producing a dense negative or a washed-out reversal.

PAL Phase Alternation Line. The standard adopted by European and other countries, which is 625 lines, 50 fields/25 frames per second. Compare to NTSC.

Pan A horizontal movement of the camera.

Pan & Scan Used to transfer a film to video for use on standard television because of the different image aspect ratio (the ratio of the width versus the height of the image). The transfer camera focuses on a portion of the total film image. Compare with *Letterbox.*

Pari Passu Equitably, without preference.

Platforming A method of release whereby a film is opened in a single theater or small group of theaters in a major territory and later expands to a greater number of theaters. and process. Compare with *Regional Release, Rollout.*

Player Actor.

Playoff Distribution of a film after key openings.

Positive Film Film used primarily for making master positives or release prints.

Power Coupled with an Interest A right to do some act, together with an interest in the subject matter.

Print A positive picture usually produced from a negative.

Pro Rata Proportionately.

Processing A procedure during which exposed photographic film or paper is developed, fixed, and washed to produce either a negative image or a positive image.

Quitclaim To release or relinquish a claim. To execute a deed of quitclaim.

Raw Stock Motion picture film that has not been exposed or processed.

Regional Release As opposed to a simultaneous national release, a pattern of distribution whereby a film is opened in one or more regions at a time.

Release Print A composite print made for general distribution and exhibition after the final answer print has been approved.

Remake A new production of a previously produced film.

Remise To remit or give up.

Rescind Rescission. To abrogate, annul, or cancel a contract.

Right of Privacy   The right to be left alone, and to be protected against a variety of intrusive behavior such as unjustified appropriation of one's name, image or likeness; the publicizing of intimate details of one's life without justification; unlawful eavesdropping or surveillance.

Right of Publicity   The right to control the commercial value and use of one's name, likeness, and image.

Roll-Out   Distribution of film around the country subsequent to either key city openings or an opening in one city, usually New York.

Rough Cut   A preliminary assemblage of footage.

Run   Length of time a feature plays in theaters or a territory.

Sanction   To assent, concur, or ratify. To reprimand.

Scale   The minimum salary permitted by the guilds.

Sequel   A book or film that tells a related story that occurs later than the original. A continuation of an earlier story, usually with the same characters.

Shooting Script   A later version of the screenplay in which each separate shot is numbered and camera directions are indicated.

Sleeper   An unexpected hit. A film that audiences fall in love with and make a success.

Slicks   Standardized ad mechanicals, printed on glossy paper, which include various sizes of display ads for a given film, designed for the insertion of local theater information as needed.

Sound Track   The portion of a film reserved for the sound.

Specialized Distribution   As opposed to commercial distribution, distribution to a limited target audience, in a smaller number of theaters, with a limited advertising budget and reliance upon publicity, reviews, and word-of-mouth to build an audience for the picture.

Stills   Photographs taken during production for use later in advertising and/ or publicity. Stills should be in a horizontal format, and should list such information as film title, producer/director, and cast below the photo.

Stock   General term for motion picture film, especially before exposure. Film stock.

Story Analyst or Reader   A person employed by a studio or producer to read submitted scripts and properties, synopsize, and evaluate them. Often young literature or film-school graduates who don't know a great deal about storywriting or filmmaking—but then again their bosses sometimes know even less.

Story Conference   A meeting at which the writer receives suggestions about how to improve his/her script.

Stripe   A narrow band of magnetic coating or developing solution applied to a motion picture film.

Subdistributor   In theatrical releases, distributors who handle a specific geographic territory. They are subcontracted by the main distributor, who coordinates the distribution campaign and marketing of all subdistributors.

Successors Persons entitled to property of a decedent by will or as an heir.

Successor-in-Interest One who follows another in ownership or control of property.

Survivor One who survives or outlives another.

Synchronization The positioning of a sound track so that it is in harmony with, and timed to, the image portion of the film.

Syndication Distribution of motion pictures to independent commercial television stations on a regional basis.

Talent The word used to describe those involved in the artistic aspects of filmmaking (*i.e.*, writers, actors, directors) as opposed to the business people.

Target Market The defined audience segment a distributor seeks to reach with its advertising and promotion campaign, such as teens, women over 30, yuppies, etc.

Television Distribution Fee Typically 10%-25% for U.S. network broadcast sales, 30%-40% for domestic syndication, and 45%-50% for foreign distribution.

Television Spin-Off A television series or miniseries based on characters or other elements in a film.

Test-Marketing Pre-releasing a film in one or more small, representative markets before committing to an advertising campaign. The effectiveness of the marketing plan can thereby be assessed and modified as needed before the general release.

Theatrical Distribution Fees Generally between 30% and 40% of gross film rentals.

Trades The daily and weekly periodicals of the industry, such as *Variety* and *The Hollywood Reporter.*

Translation The reproduction of a book, movie, or other work into another language.

Treatment A prose account of the storyline of a film. Usually between 20 and 50 pages. Comes after outline and before first-draft screenplay.

Warranty A promise. An assurance by one party as to the existence of a fact upon which the other party may rely.

Wide Release The release of a film in numerous theaters (800-2,000).

Window Period of time in which a film is available in a given medium. Some windows may be open-ended, such as theatrical and home video, or limited, such as pay television or syndication.

Work-for-Hire (or Work-Made-for-Hire) Under the Copyright Act, this is either 1) a work prepared by an employee within the scope of employment; or 2) a specially ordered or commissioned work of a certain type (*e.g.*, a motion picture, a contribution to a collective work), if the parties expressly agree so in a writing signed by both before work begins.

Workprint A picture or soundtrack print, usually a positive, intended for use in editing only so as not to expose the original elements to any wear and tear.

INDEX

301

ABOUT THE AUTHOR

Mark Litwak is a veteran entertainment attorney with offices in Beverly Hills, California. His practice includes work in the areas of copyright, trademark, contract, multimedia law, intellectual property, and book publishing. Litwak also serves as a Producer's Rep, assisting filmmakers in the financing, marketing, and distribution of their films.

Litwak is the author of five books including: *Reel Power, The Struggle for Influence and Success in the New Hollywood; Courtroom Crusaders; Dealmaking in the Film and Television Industry* (winner of the 1995 Krazna-Kranz Moving Image Book Award); *Contracts for the Film and Television Industry;* and *Litwak's Multimedia Producer's Handbook.* He the author of the popular CD-ROM program Movie Magic Contracts.

Litwak has been a lawyer for 26 years. He has taught entertainment and copyright law at UWLA, UCLA, and Loyola Law School, and has lectured for the American, California, and Texas bar associations. A frequent speaker, he has presented seminars across the United States and in England, Australia, South Africa, and Canada.

As a Producer's Rep, Litwak has arranged distribution for numerous independent films. He has packaged movie projects and served as executive producer on such recently completed feature films as *The Proposal, Out Of Line*, and *Pressure.*

Litwak has been interviewed on more than 100 television and radio shows, including ABC, The Larry King Show, National Public Radio's *All Things Considered*, and CNN Network. Feature articles have been written about him in *California Law Business, Australian Lawyer*, and *L.A. Weekly.* He is the creator of the website Entertainment Law Resources: www.marklitwak.com

ORDER FORM

Ship To: _____

(Name) _____

(Company) _____

(Street Address) _____

(City, State & Zip) _____

(Telephone Number) _____

(E-mail) _____

Credit Card Number _____

Expiration Date _____

3 digit security code (on signature strip) _____

Billing Address ZIP Code _____

❏ MasterCard   ❏ Visa _____

System Requirements for Automated Contracts:

Windows 3.1, 95/98, NT 4.0, or higher, MAC OS 8.5 or higher and one of the following: JavaScript capable browser including Netscape Navigator 3.05, 4.0 or Internet Explorer 4.01, or greater.

Contracts are available on CD-ROM or 3.5 inch High-Density disks.

Orders are shipped via UPS Ground. Prices are subject to change without notice.

All sales are final. Allow 2-4 weeks for delivery. For faster service, include your Federal Express account number. Visa & MasterCard accepted.

QTY.	DESCRIPTION	UNIT PRICE	TOTAL
	Automated Contracts for the Film and TV Industry CD-ROM	$199.95	
	Multimedia Contracts on Disk Choose format: ❏ MS Word ❏ WordPerfect	$99.00	
	Dealmaking in the Film/TV Industry on Disk Choose format: ❏ MS Word ❏ WordPerfect	$99.00	
	*Sales Tax: Los Angeles County residents add $8\frac{1}{4}$%, California residents add $7\frac{1}{4}$%	Subtotal	
		Tax*	
	**Add $8.50 for first CD-ROM, $2.00 for each additional disk. Shipping fees vary for orders outside the Unites States.	Shipping (UPS)**	
		Total	

Mail Order to:

**Hampstead Enterprises, Inc.
c/o Mark Litwak & Associates
433 N. Camden Dr., Suite 1010
Beverly Hills, CA 90210-4414**

**You may also order by fax: (310) 859-0806
Or order online: www.marklitwak.com**